HALLELUJAH

memoirs of a singing priest

First published in 2019 by

 **columba**BOOKS

23 Merrion Square North
Dublin 2, Ireland
www.columbabooks.com

Second Printing

ISBN: 978-1-78218-368-6

Set in Adobe Garamond Pro 12/16
Cover and book design by Alba Esteban | Columba Books
Cover Image by Alexis Sierra
Printed by ScandBook, Sweden

HALLELUJAH

memoirs of a
singing priest

FATHER
Ray Kelly

columba
BOOKS

Contents

CHAPTER 1

··

Early Years

My earliest memory is when I was brought to the door of my mother's bedroom to peep in at the new baby girl. Mary Regina was born on the 31st of May 1956. I was no longer the baby of the family. I had held that title since I was born over three years earlier on 25th April 1953. It was a title that I loved and enjoyed the perks of for three years and 36 days. I reaped all the benefits of being the youngest. Mammy's boy in every way. I knew I was loved, curls and all. Trouble? I was never in trouble! I was always right in Mammy's eyes. The only disadvantage was that I was dressed in all the hand-me-down clothes from my older brother Joe who was one year and seven months older than me. I had heard later in life that there was a miscarriage between Regina and I. Mary Regina, or Regina as she was known by her family, was the only child of Joe and Mona Kelly born in the new midwife's residence. My older sister Rosemarie, my older brother Joe and I were born in the house of our grandparents, Joe and Teresa Gavigan. They were my mother's parents and lived up in the main village of Tyrrellspass, just opposite the beautiful village green.

Tyrrellspass was one of the little villages that you would have to drive through on the main road from Dublin to Galway. It was a picturesque village of shops, pubs, a post office, the local Garda station, two garages and a chemist shop.

The Catholic Church of St Stephen was at the end of the village just opposite the castle. It was beside the site where the Battle of Tyrrellspass took place in 1597, where between 300 and 400 Irish, led by Richard Tyrrell, defeated the English army. It is reported that out of 1,000 English troops only one survived. However, more prominent than St Stephen's Church and a real feature of the village, is the Church of Ireland Church of St Sinian's, built around the year 1810. The main primary school was opposite the village green, just a few houses up from where I was born in my grandparent's house. My mother, Mona, and all her five sisters after her were born in this house too. Indeed, I often heard my mother telling us the story of how her parents came to live there. Her father Joe Gavigan, or Bamba to his grandchildren, was a native of Ring, a small rural farming area outside Tyrrellspass. It seems it was always his ambition to live in the village. He married a lady much older than him who lived in this house with her elderly mother. After a few years of marriage, the lady he married died, and soon after that her elderly mother passed away too; so he got his wish and settled in the village, eventually marrying Teresa Carey, a native of Toar, another farming area outside Tyrrellspass. For many years their home was used as a doctor's surgery and the sitting room of the house was given over for this purpose. It was also used as a boarding house to accommodate the doctor and other guests.

When my mother and father married in 1948, they lived in that house for about four years, and it was the birth place of my two older siblings and myself. Soon after I was born, the family moved to a rented house fondly known by the family as Judges. This old style house, which was not much more than a run-down shed, was damp and cold. At the time, a new house was being built for us on a sand-pit on the Mullingar Road. Because my mother was the district midwife with Westmeath County Council a new residence was being provided. I guess I was no more than 18 months old when we moved into the new house.

My father, Joe, was a native of Cumminstown, Kilbeggan, Co. Westmeath. He was the youngest of five children. He received his primary education with the Mercy Sisters in Kilbeggan. He was taught how to play a few musical instruments while there; he loved most of all to play the button accordion, which he continued to do all his life. His father, Michael, died when he was only a few months old, so he had never experienced a father figure in his life. His mother, Rose Anne, took on the running of the farm and the rearing of the five young children. She died a few months before I was born, but I was told she was a very tough and hard woman who learned how to deal with even the most ruthless neighbours around, particularly in the area of buying and selling livestock. My father often said that his mother was honest and upfront about everything – I guess she had to be in those times. I know this was a trait my father inherited from her. He was a sheep and cattle dealer, so buying and selling at the local fairs in the various parts of Ireland was what he did. He often shared with us the story of buying 20 ewes at the fair in Loughrea, Co. Galway and arriving home with 21 in the lorry! I remember him often telling us how he was envied by many of the local farmers because he married a woman with a salary.

He would tell us stories of hearing the banshee in the area of Cumminstown where he lived. The word banshee comes from the Irish bean sí (pronounced ban-shee) which, when translated, means woman of the fairy mounds. The banshee is supposedly a female spirit and is regarded as an omen of death. She roams the countryside and can be heard making wailing or shrieking sounds when she predicts a death in the area. While he admitted he had never seen the banshee, he described her as a woman with long streaming hair, wearing a grey cloak over a green dress, with very deep red eyes from continual weeping. If a person heard this wailing woman it was a sure sign of a death in the family, and on a few occasions when my father's aunt or uncle died he heard the banshee's cries.

At my father's childhood-home in Cumminstown lived his brother Michael and his wife May and their six children. We were very close as a family; as children growing up in Tyrrellspass we loved to get out to the countryside and run around the fields with our cousins. When summertime came we always spent a week or two on holidays there and then the cousins would come to our home in Tyrrellspass for a return holiday.

My father's other sister Minnie and her husband Jack lived in The Meelihans, a country area a few miles outside Tullamore. They had no children. So on Sundays as a family we would either visit Cumminstown or The Meelihans. Minnie and Jack lived just across the fields from the main railway line between Dublin and Galway and Dublin and Westport. We loved nothing more than to get up close to the line and watch the trains passing by. My father would often put two pennies, one on top of the other, on the line to see if they would be stuck together when the train crossed over them. On a few occasions it happened, but more often than not the wheels of the train flung the pennies off to kingdom come.

My mother was baptised Mary Josephine, but got the name Mona from one of her sisters who could not pronounce her name. She was the oldest of six girls and her education did not go beyond the Inter Cert with the Sisters of Mercy in Rochfordbridge school. She learned how to play the piano while at school there. She loved Irish dancing too – indeed all her five sisters did as well and won various competitions at the local feis. She often talked about her first job working in a shop in Moate about 15 miles away from Tyrrellspass. It was a shop that sold a little bit of everything and was owned by the Rhattigan sisters. She was accommodated there in a small room and got home for one day every week.

However, like all young girls of her era, she had her dreams. She wanted to become a nurse and train specifically in the area of midwifery. She applied to Holles Street maternity hospital in Dublin and was accepted on a two-year training course. Her father, Joe, was reluctant to let her go to Dublin. I guess he was concerned for her safety and a young naïve country girl going up to the big city of Dublin. However, my mother was determined and got her way. Indeed, she often spoke of her time there and loved to tell us as children of her first experiences of bringing babies to houses. In fact, I remember well her telling us of her very first delivery that was under the supervision of the Master of Holles Street maternity hospital, where twin boys were born to a 20-year-old unmarried girl. When as children we would want something, either toys or clothes, she would often remind us how lucky we were compared to many other children who had a lot less than we had. She would tell us of the many times she had to attend the delivery of babies in the tenement houses in

Dublin, and the poverty she witnessed among children and parents there.

One story that I always remember was about a fourth-class house, graded according to its size. The house was unfit for human habitation. It was occupied by five families, consisting of about 20 people, three sets of parents and 14 children. All three rooms were occupied – a room for each family. It had one bathroom for all 20 people. When the baby was due, the room would usually be occupied by the expectant mother, the father and the other two mothers who resided there. The poverty was so extreme that the only hot towels available were rags pulled from the window ledges and gaps used to keep the draught and cold out. I know this experience of poverty stayed with her for many years, and as I say, Mammy often liked to remind us of such poverty when we wanted more toys.

My mother and father were married on 16th February 1948, and, after the first miscarriage, Rosemarie was born on 15th October 1950. She was the apple of my father's eye – he adored her. She was born with white hair, supposedly inherited from my mother's aunt Mary Anne Carey, a sister of my grandmother and a single woman who lived in Killane, Edenderry, Co. Offaly. My brother Joseph was born 11 months later on 26th September 1951. My mother often spoke of the severe haemorrhaging she experienced after his birth, and how she was rushed to Mullingar hospital and not expected to survive. As a midwife she knew she was critical and on leaving for the hospital she suggested to my father Joe that if she died he was to give Joseph over to his sister and her husband. I guess she thought this was the best option thinking that my father would not be able to look after two babies. Well, as you know she survived, or I would not be sharing this story with you now. And on 25th April 1953, a year and seven months after my brother Joseph, I came into the world. There were no complications this time. When my mother went into labour with me, she got Master Clarke, the head school teacher who lived next door to her parents, to drive out to Cumminstown to find my father and tell him. He arrived back just in time to see Nurse Brian, the midwife, help my mother deliver me. I was a fine, healthy, chubby ball of fat with blonde curly hair weighing in at 7 lb 13 oz.

My first real separation from my mother came before I started primary school, when I was just about four years of age. My brother Joseph and I were born with a squint in one of our eyes, which meant that our eyes did not align properly; one eye turned inward while the other eye focused on one spot.

I remember both of us wearing a patch across the good eye in order to strengthen the weaker one. I know my condition was a lot more noticeable than my brother Joseph's. My mother used to talk about having the same problem when she was a child, so I guess Joseph and I inherited our lazy eye from our mother. My mother had set up arrangements for us to have corrective eye surgery. She didn't tell my father about the date or time of the appointments. It was on a Wednesday, the day he would have been at the market in Dublin selling his lorry load of sheep off the North Circular Road on Prussia Street. We set off at about nine o'clock in the morning. Granny Gavigan accompanied us. As we drove along the road to Dublin, my mother recognised my father's blue lorry returning home in the distance. She quickly took off her own glasses for fear of being recognised by him as she hadn't told him of what was happening. I don't know about my brother Joseph, but I honestly didn't know where I was going. As we got to the steps of the Mater Hospital, I looked up and saw this huge stone building and I knew something was not right. I could smell the hospital smells, and I held on to my mother's hand for dear life. I remember clearly being left there with my brother totally confused as to what was happening. I cried uncontrollably as Mammy and Granny walked out and took a last look as they closed the door. It wasn't long after that that I was put in my pyjamas and in a cot. Joseph was in a bed beside me. I know I cried and cried. I didn't understand – how could I? Eventually, because of my persistent crying, the nurse lowered the bars of the cot and placed me in the bed beside my brother Joseph. At least I was not on my own anymore.

Afterward, my mother would tell me that when she and her mother got home, my father was there searching for myself and Joseph everywhere. When she explained where we were my father was angry, but eventually calmed down. I often wondered why my mother chose to keep our scheduled surgery to herself, but she explained afterwards that if she had told him, he would have fought tooth and nail not to let it happen.

I have no recollection of being put asleep for the surgery. I remember being in a bed beside Joseph with a bandage across both my eyes. With a bit of effort, I was able to push the bandage down a bit in order to see around me. I could see Joseph in the bed next to me and was happy enough knowing he was there. During those seven days in the Mater hospital the only visitors I can remember calling to see me were Jimmy Gaye, a neighbour from Tyrrellspass, and Chris Flynn, a first cousin of my mother. Chris lived in Palmerstown, Co. Dublin so I guess my mother asked her to go to visit us. She brought us in a lovely big bag of Kimberly biscuits, and Joseph used to throw some across to me in my bed and hope I would catch them. More often than not I didn't because of the bandage across my eyes. Every time I see a Kimberly biscuit now that memory comes back to me so clearly.

Eventually the day came for us to have the bandages removed and to go home. Mammy and Aunt Kitty were coming to Dublin to collect us and when I saw them my excitement was euphoric. I ran into Mammy's arms and held her tight, and as she went to Joseph to hug him Aunt Kitty hugged me. It was the happiest day of my life. All I wanted now was to see Daddy and my sisters. Even today, when I think of those hugs I tear up. Later, Joseph and I returned on a day visit to the Mater Hospital to see how successful our surgery was. Joseph's surgery was a complete success and he would not need to wear glasses. However, my surgery was not successful and I would continue to have the squint or crooked eye for many years until my 40s, when I would have corrective surgery. Unlike early years, when it was nescessary to spend seven days in hospital, I could now have the surgery as one overnight procedure. It was a complete success, however I still need to wear glasses. I remember thinking that after wearing them for over 40 years I would feel naked without them.

I started primary school at the age of four and a half in September 1957. I remember well my first day or, should I say, my first hour. Nicholas Gaye and his family lived across the road from our house in Daltons House on the Mullingar Road. Nicholas was in third class and assigned with the job of escorting me up the road, past the devil's stone on the wall of St Sinian's Church graveyard. I don't know how it got the name, but it was a black stone right in the middle of the high stone wall. Past the stone wall was St Sinian's Church and then we would cross the huge green into the school. The green with an old pump in the centre is a beautiful attractive feature of the village, and was the main feature of the village when it won the Tidy Towns Competition in 1969.

I don't know how my mother felt about letting me go to school, but I was not happy. It was my very first experience of school as there were no pre-schools at that time. I was being torn away from my mother: the most secure place I had ever known. Perhaps the experience of being separated from her for a whole week while in hospital was foremost in my mind. By the time I got to the school I was uncontrollable. The tears flowed so much that I was more a disruption to the school than anything, and Miss Kellehan did not like any noisy, screaming kids. Within an hour my mother came to the school to collect me. I was safe again. I had won the battle, but not the war. The next day was calmer, I think my mother promised me a reward of a new toy and the excitement of that was my primary focus. I seemed to settle after that and by the weekend my mother had bought me a cuddly stuffed toy of a lovely black lamb. It was perfect; I brought him to school to show off for about a week or so and brought him to bed every night.

The school was fairly basic – four classrooms. The boys' classes were downstairs and the girls' classrooms were upstairs. There were no indoor toilets then, but what you might call dry outdoor toilets with wooden seats and basically a hole in the ground. If there was no toilet paper then newspaper was the next best option. Miss Kellehan was our teacher for my first few years. She came from Mullingar and drove the ten miles to Tyrrellspass every day. She was a middle-aged lady, probably a lot younger than I realised, but she definitely was not married and had no children. As I was always left-handed, she would force me sometimes to write with my right hand. However all she ever got from me that way was scribble, and all I got from her was a slap across the ear. I know this went on for some time before I had the courage to tell my mother. Within a few days I was left alone. As I found out afterwards my mother had paid a visit to Miss Kellehan and politely told her to leave me alone. Miss Kellehan did not like noise either and with the girls' classroom above ours there was always the trample of feet. When it got very bad Miss Kellehan would get a brush and pound the top of the brush off the ceiling returning the noise; it always worked – for a short while anyway. Unlike my brother Joseph who loved football, I had two left feet when it came to taking part, and more often than not I was put standing between the goalposts as the goalie. As I was one of the few boys who wore glasses, a common nickname for me was "four eyes". I know I was very sensitive to such name calling, but it seemed to be part of the culture at that time. Still, I felt very uncomfortable at school being called names and pressurized into being a goalie.

My mother got permission for me to sometimes go to my granny's house during my lunch times. It was only three houses away from the school on the same side of the street, so there was no crossing of the road. I loved my granny's house. My granny and her husband Joe, or Bamba as we called him, lived there along with their daughter Kitty and her husband

Gerald Lenihan. Kitty and Ger had no children of their own though, so I know when I was there I was the golden boy. I loved my dinners there, especially the Friday dinner of colcannon with a big nob of butter in the middle and fried eggs. Even after school I would often go to my granny's house and enjoy the comforts. Sometimes I would help Granny make butter with the churns or help her pick the cooking apples off trees for storage in straw. She usually had enough of a supply to distribute to all her daughters, especially the four that lived away in Edenderry. One of my other chores when there was to collect the eggs in the hen shed. Granny would then wash them, and, if she had a good supply, I would be sent with them up to Moore's shop where they would be traded in for some of the items on the shopping list, like tea, sugar, bread, whatever was the most urgent need of the household. My uncle Ger had a workshop down the yard behind the house and was a very highly skilled carpenter and known all over Ireland for making wardrobes and kitchen units. Sometimes I would spend hours in his workshop watching him putting together timber and admiring the finished products. He was truly a genius at his work.

The fair day in Tyrrellspass was always exciting for me as a child growing up in the village. It was held on the first Friday of every month. Indeed, the life of many of the farmers revolved around having their stock ready for each fair. I would be excited about seeing all of the animals and farmers arriving on my way to school. In fact, some would have arrived during the night or early morning and have already taken up their position on the street. We always got a half-day from school on fair day. I couldn't wait for the school to close;

once closed I would drop my school bag at my Granny's and I was free to mingle around the village and watch the selling and buying of sheep, calves, heifers, bullocks, bulls, pigs and bonhams. Fowl, chickens, geese and turkeys were on sale in the donkey and pony carts confined inside the creels. There were vegetable stalls selling all kinds of home-grown vegetables. My Granny and Bamba would often have vegetables for sale as well as day-old or very young chicks. Once they had everything sold, my grandfather was under strict orders from Granny to come home. He did, but not before he had at least two bottles of stout. My father always had sheep for sale there too. I was always fascinated by the way the sheep would be tied with hay ropes around their necks forming a complete circle. Other times they would be confined in sheep pens brought and set up by the farmer himself. The smells of the sheep and their continual bleating is always a memory that will stay with me. The cattle were easier to control without wandering off or having to be tied in. Sometimes the farmer's sons would watch over them while the farmer wandered around, sometimes haggling. I loved to watch the farmers haggle over prices before a deal was made. They would have their sticks in their hand and would poke the cattle to examine them before money was mentioned. Eventually a deal was made with slapping palms, agreeing the price and the terms. The deal was more or less done. They would then go into one of the nearest pubs, Gonoud's, or Fagan's or one of the pub-grocery shops like Byrne's or Claffey's, which were decorated with straw on the floor to keep them as clean as possible from the sheep shit and cow dung on the farmers' wellingtons. The wad of notes was exchanged for the livestock. A few bottles of stout were consumed. The deal was done. By then the wives would have come to town, maybe in the pony and traps, a few bills were settled, the tea, sugar, butter, bacon, bread and other essentials were bought. The shopping done. The big clean up began on Saturday morning as the smells got worse before they got better. When the shops were swept out and the footpaths hosed, the village was back to itself. By Sunday morning as people walked to Mass, you would never have known that the fair day had taken place.

As a child growing up I wanted for nothing. I remember our home was one of the first in the village to get a television. It was a black and white 20-inch screen. I remember the excitement of Walter Glynne Senior building a big 60-foot aerial at the side of our house. It was balanced with a number of wires or stays so as to make sure it would stay up in windy conditions. The only channels we had were BBC One, Two and UTV. The first ever Irish TV channel, Teilifís Éireann, would open about six months after we got the television. I know we were the envy of many people in the village with our television, and if there was a soccer match on we would have plenty of visitors. My favourite programme was on BBC One, *Top of The Pops*. I loved the dancers on the show *Pans People* and waited with excitement each week to see what song would be number one. Any song that made top of the charts would be played last. The Rolling Stones and "Jumpin Jack Flash", the Bee Gees and "I've Gotta Get a Message to You", Mary Hopkin's "Those Were The Days" and The Beatles and "Hey Jude". Oh I could go on and on.

The Bog Boreen, now called Power's Way, was a little country single lane road that ran alongside our house. It ran for about a half mile until you came to a gateway which led right into a large bog. My grandfather, Joe Gavigan, was one among many others who owned about nine acres of the bog. I loved going there and watching him cutting his turf with a slean. It would then be loaded up in a barrow and spread out to dry for a few weeks. The next part was the footing, where it was placed upright for further drying. It involved placing five or six sods of turf upright and leaning against each other. This is where my grandfather brought me and my brother Joe and my father along. It wasn't a skilled job, all I needed was a good back and plenty of patience. Finally, the turf was brought home and stored in sheds and we were guaranteed warmth for another cold winter. Now of course much of this turf cutting is not allowed because of the bogs being protected by EEC rules and regulations.

There was only one resident on the Bog Boreen. His name was Dick Power and he was an old man, living alone in an old stone house. Once a week, he would be seen walking up past our house on his way to the post office to collect his pension and do his weekly shopping. He dressed poorly and smelled more of bog and turf than anything else. On the way home he would call into our house for a cup of tea and a sandwich. Indeed, if my mother was serving up the dinner he was always welcome to a spud and whatever was going. Sometimes my father would take me and my brother and sisters for a walk down to see Dick. He was always welcoming and always had a bag of sugar barley or liquorice allsorts sweets to offer us. He had a huge open fire. Over the fire were the fireplace hangers used for hanging the kettle and other cooking pots. The mantelpiece and the wall around the fire were completely black from smoke.

I loved when he started the procedure to make a cup of tea for my father. He stored his Lyons tea, butter, sugar, milk, Marietta biscuits, bread and other edible essentials in a box with a lid suspended on a beam over the kitchen table. After boiling the kettle, he would untie the twine from the side of the table and gently lower the box onto the table to take out whatever was needed to entertain his guests. After we had partaken of his hospitality and before we left, he would put all the items back into the box, close the lid, pull the twine until the box was suspended again and tie the twine to the side of the table. Sometimes he would ask me to pull the twine to raise the box to its original position. I never had the courage to ask him why he needed to keep all his food suspended like that, but daddy told me afterwards that it was his way of protecting it from mice and rats. I guess it certainly did that.

Power's Way provided access to a few fields before the gate leading into the bog and Dick's house. These fields were where the hay was made. I used to look forward to the summertime when the hay was being made; indeed I often used to help my grandfather. First the grass was cut and left for a week or so to dry out. Often during the week, the cut grass would have to be turned to ensure proper drying before being raked up and made into cocks of hay. The raking was usually my job, as it was less strenuous. Then there was the making of the hay ropes used to tie the cocks down so the wind would not blow them away. I loved this part too. It really was an art in itself. The final part was bringing home the cocks of hay on the bogy. A rope was tied around the cock of hay and from two arms of the bogy, and the gradual up and down movement of the arms rolled the cock onto the bogy. I loved this part and always got my place sitting up on the bogy. When we got back to my grandfather's yard the cock of hay was rolled off the bogy and with a fork was loaded into the hay shed.

Christmas was always such a happy, memorable time in our home - my favourite time of the year. On the eighth of December every year, Mammy and Daddy would climb into the attic and blow the dust off the box of Christmas decorations. All hands were on deck for the decorating of the Christmas tree with Daddy replacing any of the blown bulbs of the Christmas tree lights. Once our letters were written to Santa Claus, we knew he would deliver. Our names were placed on four kitchen chairs so that Santa Claus left the appropriate gift in the right place. Christmas Eve was always an early night to bed for us. I was always afraid to get up during that night for the toilet for fear of meeting Santa in the hallway. I remember so well my brother Joseph and I were fighting in our bed and we were warned that Santa would not deliver if we didn't behave. Daddy told us Santa was going around checking on bold children. Within an hour he came into our bedroom; and I remember singing Jingle Bells in the fastest, most frightened voice for him while shaking at the same time. Bold or not, the toys always arrived. It was always so exciting to wake up early on Christmas morning and check to see what Santa had brought, whether it was a train set, a pony and cart, a Meccano-set or a Lego-set. However, at six in the morning, once we knew Santa had done his job, and drank his bottle of porter and eaten a bit of Christmas cake, we got ready before breakfast for 7am Mass. I know I kept one eye on the baby Jesus in the crib, eager to return home to the gift Santa had brought me. Meanwhile the choir sang all the old favourites such as "Silent Night" and "O Come All Ye Faithful". If the snow started falling as I left church, it was perfect and indeed it often did.

The Lego set was to be my last official Santa Claus present. About two months before that Christmas, mammy gave me money along with a bill from Glynn's Garage to go up the village and pay the bill. I went in and met Olive Glynn in the office and duly paid the bill for her. As I was leaving Olive quietly said to me "Will you tell your mammy I got all of the toys she ordered except the guitar, but I may be able to order that from another catalogue?" I must have looked confused and bewildered because Olive asked, "Do you know what I'm talking about?" I said "No." And then I could see Olive's face turning red as she mumbled to herself almost under her breath but loud enough for me to hear, "Oh my God what have I done!" I returned home, and met Mammy in the kitchen, still confused about the message I was to pass on; I gave her the marked paid invoice, which she duly put through a wire string with all of the other invoices. "Oh Mammy," I said, "Olive told me to tell you she got all of the toys you ordered except the guitar, but she may be able to get that from another catalogue." Mammy looked at me for what seemed like an eternity but was probably a matter of seconds. "Where is Regina?" she asked. "She's across the road in Gaye's playing with Dettie," I said. Mammy closed the back door and sat me down beside her and told me, "Ye know you are old enough now to know that your daddy and I buy all of the toys that come from Santa every Christmas. Regina is not old enough to know that yet, and you are not to tell her, but you are old enough.

I order them from Olive Glynn from the toy catalogue every year." I was ten years old.

Mammy and Daddy loved nothing more than to play music, especially if visitors called to the house. Daddy would take out the accordion and play a few waltzes or quicksteps, and mammy would accompany him on the piano. My brother Joseph learned the accordion from daddy and picked up the guitar himself. My sisters learned the piano at Mercy Secondary School in Rochfordbridge with Sr Joseph. I was the only one of the family who didn't learn to play a musical instrument. In fact, my father often teased me when someone would ask "What instrument does Raymond play?", he would say "Oh Raymond plays the gramophone". My grandparents, Joe and Teresa, had given me their gramophone a few years before that, with some old 78 records. I remember there were loads of Gallowglass Céilí Band ones, and a few I loved were Delia Murphy's, especially "If I were a Blackbird" and "The Spinning Wheel". So I didn't play any instrument, but boy could I sing and, with the rest of my siblings, we were put out there by Mammy and Daddy to do our party pieces. I remember I used to love to be asked, but I would pretend to be shy. As I got a bit older I was a bit shy, but still I loved to perform, and the song I was always asked to sing was "The White Rose of Athens". "Till the white rose blooms again, you must leave me lonely, lonely, so goodbye my love till then, till the white rose blooms again…"

The day after Christmas, St Stephen's Day, was the day when we hunted the wren. Historically, a wren was captured and thought to bring good luck for the new year. Over time, the tradition became associated with mumming. These mummies would dress up in costumes sometimes made of straw and would often sing or dance and entertain. As a family, we would dress up in costumes to disguise ourselves. Mammy and my sisters would dress up as boys, while Daddy, my brother Joseph and I dressed up as girls. I know I was always dressed up as a very big busted woman. We would then set off in the car and entertain in all the local pubs around the village of Tyrrellspass and the neighbouring villages of Rochfordbridge and Kilbeggan. While Daddy played the accordion and Joseph played the guitar, my sisters would go around collecting with a hat while Mammy and I would sing; or we would take out all the "pint of Guinness" men at the bar for a waltz and believe me I often got more squeezes than I ever wanted. We often collected over £100 and would give that to a charity. By evening time we always finished up with our cousins in Cumminstown or Edenderry where we were always well fed and were asleep in the car long before we got home.

We were very happy growing up. Mammy and Daddy made it that way in the home for us. If there was a coolness between them and they were not speaking to each other for a day or two, it was usually over Daddy drinking too much. That usually only happened if he was after buying or selling cattle or sheep. He was mainly a sheep dealer and would attend the various marts around the country. He had his farmer clients too who would order their regular supply of ewes every year. He then would provide the ram and once the ewes were pregnant between 20 to 21 weeks the lambs would be born. By late spring my daddy would go back to the farmers and buy the lambs. He then would bring the lambs up to the marts in Dublin or to Cosgrave butchers in Ranelagh.

During school holidays we would often go with Daddy to Dublin for the trip; and we looked forward to coming home by the Phoenix Restaurant on the quays for our regular sausage and chips.

If Daddy was not home at a respectable time, I always knew there was going to be a confrontation between Mammy and Daddy. He would arrive in and head straight to bed. However, Mammy always wanted answers and sometimes did not have the patience to wait for the answers until the next morning. Within a few hours, or at the most a day, the silence between them would have passed. I always dreaded those silences and was glad to see them end.

CHAPTER 2

....

The Midwife's Son

The subject of babies and pregnancy was always a hot topic in our house, though as a young boy I really didn't understand it very much. All I knew was Mammy would be called out day or night to someone's house, and a baby would arrive there within hours or a day or two of her call out.

Kitty Cox was a young girl of about 15 or 16, from a small rural village called Ballinagore. Mammy and Daddy employed her for a few years to help with the children and housework. She was lovely, and I loved Kitty. She was gentle and kind to all of us, but I sometimes got the feeling that she was a bit afraid of Mammy. Maybe Mammy was a bit too authoritarian towards her. She did all the work expected of her even though she was only a teenager herself. I guess to me she seemed a lot older. If Mammy was on a delivery, Kitty would prepare the meals for us and help with the household work, like washing the dishes, doing the laundry, helping us with our homework and so on.

My Aunty Kitty was also on call sometimes. Though, as I've said, she had no children of her own, of all her 25 nieces and nephews on my mother's side of the family, I always felt we were definitely her favourites. I know she was a favourite aunt among all of her nieces and nephews and indeed a favourite sister too to all her sisters. They would often call on her to come to Edenderry where three of her sisters lived. If there was a new baby born in any of the households, Aunty Kitty was called upon to stay a few days and help out the family. I always felt especially close to my Aunty Kitty, because nearly every day after school I would go to my grandparents' house where she and her husband Ger and my grandparents lived. I always felt special there. I would help my grandfather milk the cows and then drive them down the road back to the field. I would then watch or even help as Granny set about to make the butter. After the milking was done, the milk was left to settle in a cool place in my grandparents' kitchen. Eventually the cream would rise to the top and be skimmed off and put into the churn. It would be my job to help with the churning. I would turn the handle while the paddles inside the churn beat constantly off the cream. If my arms got tired Granny or Kitty would take over for a while. Eventually, as the turning of the handle got harder and harder to do, I knew the butter was forming.

If it was autumn I would help Granny pick the apples off the trees. Kitty made all the Christmas cakes and pudding for many of her sisters too including my mother sometimes. I loved watching her do that, mixing in all the fruit, eggs, flour and spices. I would help her stir and stir, and maybe when she wasn't looking I would stick my finger into the mix and get it into my mouth before she noticed. When I told Aunty Kitty that I knew where Santa Claus' presents came from she burst into a fit of laughter. I can still see and hear her laugh. I asked her why was she laughing and she said, "And do you know your mammy always hides all of your Christmas toys here upstairs in the spare room?" I was shocked! All the times I had been in this house over the years not knowing our gifts were hiding upstairs. Aunt Kitty then went on to say, "And all the times you have been in that spare room and you would never find them. When you were all in bed on Christmas Eve Ger and I would bring them all down to your house." The penny dropped. That explained why while in bed on Christmas Eve, I would always hear their voices in the kitchen before I would go to sleep.

When Mammy would get home after delivering a baby to a family she would often share with us whether the baby was a boy or a girl, the colour of its hair if it had any, how big the baby was and the weight of the baby in pounds even though I had no concept of the weight or size of the baby. She would share with us the excitement of the new baby's brothers and sisters, if there were any, on seeing their new brother or sister for the first time. My younger sister Regina and I used to love to hear all about it. When Mammy had to do follow up nursing care for the mother and the new baby, we would often go in the car with her; and when the time was right she would come out to the car to get us and bring us in to see the new baby. I loved to see how tiny it was and the smallness of its fingers and toes.

What was common with all of Mammy's visits and indeed call outs for the first time was her brown medical bag or case. Mammy always kept the medical bag locked. Somehow Regina and I knew it was an essential part of Mammy bringing a baby to every household. If the medical bag was gone from the hallway, we knew Mammy was not at home. She left it in the hallway in case she would have to go to a call out very quickly. Indeed, we often asked her when she was going to bring a baby to our house, however we never really got an answer to that question. When the bag was sitting in the hallway, and if Mammy had gone to the shops or up the village to see her mother and father, Regina and I would often spend time sitting on each side of the locked bag just listening. There was never any conversation between us, but each of us knew we were there for the same reason. We were there hoping to hear the sound of a baby in the bag. You see, we could not understand how Mammy could bring babies to so many other houses in the locality, but would not bring one to our house. Sometimes, I would find myself alone sitting at the medical bag for the same reason. One day when I was about ten years old, Regina came up to the hall to tell me there was no point in sitting listening to the bag for a baby, as there was no baby there. When eventually I had the wisdom to ask her how she knew, she told me exactly how babies were made and where they came from. After been enlightened by Regina, I now had a totally different view of what happened and found myself asking Mammy a lot more questions about her work.

My brother Joseph and I shared a bedroom at the front of our house. My uncle Ger, Aunty Kitty's husband, had built on an extra bedroom along with an extension to our back kitchen. When it was completed Mammy and Daddy decided to move into the new bedroom and gave me and Joseph their bedroom. When the tap came to the window it was soft and gentle at first. It could be mistaken for a bird tapping its beak searching for food or water. It was followed by a much louder series of taps accompanied by a voice of shouting "nurse, nurse, nurse". If the tapping didn't wake me, certainly the man's voice did. It was sharp, rapid and panicky. I struggled to get out of bed and ran in panic into Mammy and Daddy's bedroom. I poked Daddy enough for him wake up and told him someone was tapping at my window. He quickly came to my bedroom and pulled back the curtain for a peek. Despite the heavy frost on the window pane, he knew it was Johnny McGuinness. I quickly made out the features of a man in his late 30s with a grey and black stubble on his face. Daddy forced open the window only slightly to keep the cold out, but enough to hear Johnny McGuinness. I could clearly hear him whisper to Daddy, "Is the nurse there, Nelly has gone into labour. I think the baby is coming soon." Daddy told me to go back to bed, but I was thirsty, so I went to the kitchen to get a drink of water and passed the bedroom door and saw Daddy waking Mammy. He gently touched her arm and woke her with a soft whisper, "Mona, Mona". I know it had happened many, many times before, but not always at six o'clock in the morning.

I suppose I should not have been surprised at this call out for Mammy. About a week before that as I was coming out of school, passing through the village in convoy were Johnny, Nelly and their family, along with Johnny's two brothers, their wives and children and Nelly's sister and her husband. They were heading for the Blackwood Road just beside the entrance to the New Forest Estate. The entire convoy chose this spot convenient to Tyrrellspass where we lived. I knew it could only mean one thing, one of the families were going to get a new baby. When I got home from school I told Mammy about the travellers passing through the village, and she said to me, "They must be going to get a new baby."

Sure enough, Nelly, along with her sister Margaret and some of their children, arrived at our house. They came to book Mammy for the arrival of the new baby. Nelly and

Margaret would come in to our house have a cup of tea or a bowl of soup, and I was always asked by Mammy to go out and play with Nelly and Margaret's children while she got all the details from Nelly about the pregnancy and the expected arrival date of the new baby. Mammy would always have saved up a black sack of old toys and second-hand clothes belonging to us Kelly children which we were now grown out of to give to Nelly and Margaret. Before they would leave I always got a chance to look into Nelly and Margaret's baskets. I loved to see the selection of items they had like pot scrubs, carbolic soap, face cloths, hand towels, hair brushes, combs, shoe and bootlaces and holy pictures. With such a selection of items in their baskets they were always well received by the houses around Tyrrellspass. Mammy would always buy some items from them, particularly some carbolic soap, and she always gave them some tea grains and sugar, possibly a bit of ham and bread, and of course a few pennies for the kids.

It was always great to see Nelly and her extended family. I remember the last time they camped on the Blackwood Road when Nelly's sister Margaret had her son. If Daddy was going out with sheep anywhere and he had to pass the Blackwood Road, Mammy would always pack a bit of food and have collected a few bits of clothing for the McGuinness family camped there. I used to love to go with him because I would get to meet all the McGuinness family. Nelly and Johnny had six girls, and Johnny's brothers had five children between them and then Nelly's sister Margaret had three. The 14 children ranged in age from 11 down to Margaret's six-month-old Peter. Mammy brought baby Peter to the family too. I loved the smell of the burning fire and crackling of the sticks gathered from along the narrow road. I would usually kick a bit of football along with the children or show them some of the toys we brought out to them. Nelly and Johnny's two oldest girls, Theresa and Ellen, told me they knew that their mammy was going to get a new baby because she was getting fat and had been sick and vomiting. They hoped the baby would be a boy because unlike their cousins they had no brother. While I played and chatted with the girls, daddy would often stay chatting with all of the family for maybe a half hour or more. Nelly and Johnny's bender tent was the first in a row of six along with their horse-drawn caravan. The extended family were camped behind.

I didn't go back to bed as Daddy asked. I put on the kettle and made some tea for Mammy. She cut a few slices of her brown bread and buttered them. The brown bread was Mammy's specialty. Sometimes she would make her brown bread at three or four in the morning after she would have returned from bringing a baby to a family. While Mammy was enjoying her cup of tea and brown bread and was ready to have her first Craven A cigarette of the day, Daddy walked up the village just a five-minute walk away and threw a few small stones at my Aunty Kitty's window; she would oblige us day or night when called upon to stay with us while Mammy was gone to deliver a new baby. I sat with Mammy and poured myself a cup of tea when Daddy came rushing in and said, "Kitty is on the way, Mona. I can't let you go out on the road in that weather. There's at least three inches of snow on the ground, the roads are treacherous with ice and snow is still falling heavily." When I heard Daddy say that my first thought was, will there be school today at all? He then went out to start up the lorry and de-frost the windows. Once before Daddy had to use his sheep lorry to bring Mammy to a family where a baby was coming when Mammy's old Ford car wouldn't start. My Aunty Kitty arrived to our house just as Mammy was checking her medical bag to make sure everything was there.

It was now coming up to seven o'clock in the morning. I was wide awake and had no intention of going back to bed. I would normally be getting up for school in another hour anyway. I chatted with my Aunty Kitty and told her of the early morning call over a cup of tea. She started making the porridge as I heard Daddy and Mammy drive out in the lorry. The journey to the Blackwood Road was no more than seven minutes, but because the roads were frozen over with ice it would take them a bit longer to get there. I would look forward to asking Mammy loads of questions of what happened when she returned later in the day, and I knew she would share with me as much as she could. Meanwhile, the eight o'clock news came on the radio and announced that all schools were closed for today because of the snow and I couldn't hide my smile from Aunty Kitty.

After hearing such great news, I ran up to the bedroom to wake-up my brother Joseph to tell him of a no school day. My sisters Rosemarie and Regina were up already and equally excited about there being no school. Aunty Kitty had the porridge and cornflakes ready and we could start the day. The plan was to make the biggest snowman possible. We dressed ourselves in warm jumpers, woolly hats, scarves and waterproof gloves, woolly socks and wellingtons and we went to work. There was about five inches of snow on the ground and while it had eased off from snowing, I knew more would be falling before the end of the day. The snow was moist and packable - perfect for the ideal snowman. We used the front lawn for the site under a large tree, which would provide shelter from the glaring sun and was surrounded by lots of snow and visible to passers-by. After all, we wanted everyone to see and admire our handy work. Since my brother Joseph was the strongest of us he was in charge of the base of the snowman and started by rolling it along the snow on the ground and patting it tight to make it secure. My sisters were making the middle section and when Joseph had the base ready and in place, the four of us lifted the middle section onto the base. I was in charge of the head and as I was rolling it to a proper size and patting it, my sisters were tiding up the base and middle section. We lifted the head on and now only had to add the decorating bits. Rosemarie went in to Aunty Kitty and got the carrot for the nose and two large buttons for the eyes. Together we made a mouth from small stones. Joseph got two sticks for the arms and gently pushed them into the middle section of the snowman. We got one of Daddy's old hats and a scarf, and there he was - the finest snowman ever seen. Just as we were almost finished, Daddy drove into the yard. Mammy was tiding up after helping Nelly deliver her baby, and Daddy would go back in an hour to collect her.

Mammy got home about two o'clock in the afternoon. I knew she was tired. Usually after an early call like that and having to work under such extreme conditions she would go to bed and rest. As she said herself "sometimes I would sleep, more times I would just lie awake and rest for an hour or two." So to facilitate Mammy's rest, the four of us would go up to our granny's house with Aunty Kitty just to leave the home as quiet as possible. When we arrived back home by five o'clock our snowman was standing as sturdy as ever and the cold evening was gaining force with heavy frost descending. Mammy was up and it was nearly time for dinner. By six o'clock we were all hungry and ready to eat.

I loved to hear the stories of what Mammy did on her call outs. She always shared with us to a level we would understand. She knew that what she told us at the dinner table would stay there. Daddy had told us he would be bringing Mammy up to the camp site later in the evening just to check on Nelly and the new baby. When he drove her there in the early hours he drove the lorry up in front of Nelly's tent to shine the lights of the lorry into it. Johnny's brothers had the two fires blazing when they arrived with lots of pots full of boiling water. Daddy kept warm by keeping the engine of the lorry running and Johnny sat in beside him. Johnny shared with Daddy about the different places they had been since the birth of little Suzie now two years and two months old. Before Suzie was born, the family had been on their annual trip to Knock, Co. Mayo at the shrine of Our Lady. They had a great devotion to Mary and the shrine of Knock. Many of the travellers attended Knock during the Novena from the 15th August to the 22nd. They had many superstitions, for example, they would never start a journey from one town to the next on a Friday, and particularly a Friday that fell on 13th because Jesus' crucifixion took place on a Friday. When they would buy a new horse at the horse fair in Ballinasloe to pull the caravan they would whisper the creed into the horse's left ear on a Wednesday and into the right ear on a Friday.

After Daddy had told us of his chats with Johnny, Mammy told us that Nelly felt very secure and relaxed having her there. As a midwife she had a one hundred percent success rate in her deliveries. If there was going to be any complications she would know well in advance and have the local doctor on hand and if necessary, an ambulance for hospitalisation. I loved when she would always remind us and say, "Giving birth is an everyday miracle, something beautiful and incredible that is as common as us having a meal. It never ceases to be a wonderful, magical miracle. That miracle happened for Nelly and Johnny today." Nelly told my mammy, "Nurse Kelly, ye know I was in the town yesterday evening, myself and Johnny, and I had four bottles of porter." "Four bottles of Guinness porter," my mother replied "well do you know Nelly a few Guinness have been known to bring on labour. If you have this one quick Nelly, I think this is definitely going to be a case of Guinness induction." Within an hour of that conversation Mammy told us, Nelly gave birth to her first son. I could tell that as Mammy told us this story she spoke with excitement. Excitement for another successful delivery, but also for Johnny and Nelly having their long awaited first son.

From previous stories of Mammy's work we knew what came next. She tied the umbilical cord of the little fellow and wrapped him in a warm blanket and placed him in his mother's arms. Daddy told us he never saw a man so excited as he saw Johnny when Nelly's sister came rushing out of the tent shouting "Johnny, Johnny, come quick you have a son, after all the girls you have a son." Daddy said "Johnny leapt from my truck leaving the door wide open to the cold." Johnny squeezed into the tent, and Mammy said he beamed at his little red-headed son. Then she said tears filled his eyes as he stretched out his arms to hold his son for the first time. I love happy ever after stories and indeed Mammy loved telling them to us. "Well Johnny," Nelly said, "what will we call him? Johnny Junior, J J, John? What do you think?"

Mammy and Nelly's sister Margaret came out of the tent, and sat around the blazing fire as the rest of the family joined them leaving the happy parents to savour the moment. Indeed it would not be long until this little one was going to meet his six sisters for the first time. They passed around the cigarettes and drank tea. Afterwards, Mammy said she went into the tent to tidy up her bag. "Well Nelly," she said, "have you and Johnny picked a name for him yet?" "No, not yet, Nurse." Mammy said, "Ye know Nelly those few bottles of Guinness really helped to induce your labour. I am convinced of that. Thanks to Arthur Guinness, this little man wanted to see the world." "Arthur, that was Johnny's father's name. Arthur, that's it nurse, that's it, that's what we will call him: Arthur Johnny McGuinness, or AJ for short," said Nelly. Arthur Johnny McGuinness, or AJ, was born at six minutes past two o'clock - a full 9 lb 11 oz.

CHAPTER 3

....

Secondary School Years

I was 12 years old when I started going to our local secondary school. As there was no secondary school in Tyrrellspass, the nearest one was St Joseph's Secondary School or Mercy Convent School in Rochfordbridge, which was three and a half miles east of Tyrrellspass. My parents could have chosen to send me to the Mercy Secondary School in Kilbeggan about five miles west of Tyrrellapass, however the Bridge, as we called it, was nearer and it was also the school my mother attended herself for a few years. My sister Rose and my brother Joseph were already there, one and two years ahead of me, so I guess it was a no brainer.

Before I started attending school, there was the long summer holidays, and I looked forward to our annual week at Ryan's Caravan Park in Laytown, Co. Meath. It was always a week full of fun, sport and games. I loved the long beach and swimming in the sea. I remember one time when we were driving along the beach, our Ford Anglia car CLI 818 got stuck in the soft sand. We all got out of the car and pushed as Mammy steered. However, as we pushed the car seemed to be getting deeper and deeper in the sand. The tide was fast approaching too and there seemed to be no way out. Within an hour the car would begin to fill up with water. I think it was the first time I'd seen panic on my father's face. Daddy sent my sister Rosemarie back to the village, which was a good mile away, to get help and possibly someone with a tractor to pull us out. After what seemed like an hour or more, but was probably only about ten minutes, a man and his wife were walking past along the beach. He came over to us and suggested to Daddy to reverse back on the tracks in the sand. Mammy was still at the wheel and put the car into reverse and with a heavy push the car moved backwards onto its tracks and we were free. I could see the relief on Mammy and Daddy's faces as they thanked the man before he caught up with his wife to continue the walk. We loaded up into the car and drove back towards the town and caught up with my sister Rosemarie. It was time for a well-earned ice cream to cool down.

During that week in Laytown on holidays we were invited to tea at the Mercy Sisters holiday home along the beach. Different convents of the Mercy Sisters would take it in turn to spend a week there. During our visit the Mercy Sisters from our school in Rochfordbridge would be there. We would have a lovely evening of tea, buns and cakes followed by music and singing. Mammy would accompany herself on the piano with a few songs. The number one hit for her was always "Dee-ol-ee-ay" or "The Old Refrain": "I often think of home dee-ol-ee-ay, when I am all alone and far away. I sing an old refrain dee-ol-ee-ay, for it recalls to me of bygone days..." Daddy and my brother Joseph would play the button accordion and I would always have a song or two up my sleeve, "The White Rose of Athens" or "Sailor" being my favourites. The sisters themselves would sing and play as well.

During those summer holidays, the weather always seemed warm and sunny. Daddy always gave us money to spend every day at the local amusements in the town. I loved the swinging boats, the bumping cars and the chairoplanes. As I soared into the air and drove like a mad man, the sound of Scott McKenzie filled my head with his hippy anthem "San Francisco". All I wanted was to let my hair grow, wear a bandana, a pair of platform shoes and bell-bottom jeans and I was in heaven.

Two weeks later the dream of long hair and a bandana were long gone as my father prepared me for my first day in secondary school with one of his special neat almost crew cut haircuts. As for the bell-bottom jeans, well they were replaced by my grey school uniform and short pants. I guess I was small for my age, so the short pants seemed to be normal wear. There were five boys in my class and I was the only one in short pants. I know for definite I felt very uncomfortable being the only boy in my class wearing short pants among five boys and 25 girls. I don't remember objecting to my mother, but perhaps I didn't have the language to object. I knew it was only for my first year there in the school and perhaps knowing that was the reason I didn't complain about it. St Joseph's Secondary School was primarily a boarding school for girls for many years. However, there were day pupil girls there also. Our class of five boys was only the third year that had boys in the school. So in our school of about 200 pupils, about 80 were boarding girls, about 100 were day pupil girls and about 20 day pupil boys.

I know I never felt comfortable or happy in secondary school. I never over achieved, but I passed most of my exams fairly ok. My favourite subjects were maths and science, which I seemed to get the highest marks in for my Christmas and Summer exams. I know I used to get in the 90th percentage for my math exams and was always in the top three or four in my class in that subject. I used to love it so much when Sister Carmel would announce that in our classroom, however I was not so high up in other subjects, especially in languages.

I used to love our choir practice with Sister Dolores and Sister Regina. I could still sing falsetto as it was comfortable and familiar to me. In fact, because I could sing so comfortably in the falsetto range I can't actually remember my voice breaking as a normal 12 or 13 year old teenager. As a result, I never realised I had quite a good tenor voice or head voice until my late twenties when I joined the seminary. Colonel Con O'Sullivan, who taught us speech, drama, and homiletics, helped me realise the beautiful tenor voice that I have; and then I was able to combine the two voices: falsetto and head voice. There is so much more to tell about Colonel O'Sullivan and my seminary days, but we'll come back to this later.

Back to my days in secondary school. During my first two years in secondary school, 1966/1967, there was no such a thing as school bus transportation. So I would set off on my bicycle with my brother Joseph and a few other lads from the village of Tyrrellspass on the three-and-a-half mile cycle to school. There was no such thing as bicycle helmets at that time either, in fact, they hadn't been invented. However, my mother Mona invented her own protection and insisted that during the winter months we would wear her knitted black balaclavas. I guess the idea was to keep the cold out and the heat in, and mother knew best. I know I was never one for getting in trouble in secondary school, like being caught out smoking or even courting any of the girls during our school breaks around the grounds of the school. My brother Joseph fell in love early enough with a boarding girl in my class. Olive Gray was the girl and she sat right behind me in the classroom. Indeed, I often acted as the postman between them, passing notes from one day to the next. I also used to find my school bag filled with at least a half a dozen Valentine cards addressed to my brother Joseph. There was not even one addressed to me. However, when I would get home from school there was always one card waiting for me on the kitchen table. I never knew what girl sent it to me and I never questioned the fact that there was no stamp on the envelope, which meant it was dropped in the letterbox.

Some years later, I happened to be searching for something in my mother's bedroom and came across two unused Valentine cards still in a brown paper bag. I asked my mother about them and she smiled and said, "Now you know who sent you your annual Valentine's Day card". I laughed, gave her a big hug and said, "Thanks Ma".

My brother Joseph and Olive were married a few years after finishing school in December 1971 and 47 years later have nine grandchildren and seven children of their own; two of the little girls died early on: Alywynne at 13 months born with spina bifida and hydrocephalus, and Naoimi at three months as a result of heart problems.

When I started secondary school, I attended it on a Saturday morning for a half day. It would be totally unheard of today, but up to the mid 60s it was the norm. The Saturday morning classes were usually a double geography or science and a double art. It wasn't until a year after I started in secondary school in 1966 that free education was introduced by the then minister for education, Donogh O'Malley. Corporal punishment was very common in secondary schools too and our school was not immune to it either. As I said, I pretty much went unnoticed through my secondary school years. However, I did on one occasion receive the cane from the Reverend Mother. One Friday morning a small amount of muck carried in from a shoe or a football boot from the football field was discovered on the wall beside a classroom. Reverend Mother was very angry and was determined to find the culprit. It being a small piece of muck from the football field, she assumed it was definitely one of the 25 boys in the school. However, not one of us owned up to it. I am not even sure whoever put it there knew that they did, nevertheless Reverend Mother lined up all 25 of us; and one by one we got a slapping from her cane. By the time she was through it seemed her anger had turned to exhaustion. She might have thought that was the end of the matter, but it wasn't. Before the school day had finished word started spreading among the senior boys right down to the first year boys that what she did was unjust. So to show our dissatisfaction we organised that instead of attending classes on Saturday morning we would stage a strike. Placards and all from 9am we marched up and down the road with our banners "STRIKE ON HERE". We were being noticed, many of the classes were disrupted, some were cheering at us out the windows. A few cars stopped to ask what was going on. The nuns were coming out begging us to stop acting the clowns and come back into class. We knew it wouldn't last, but we were hoping someone from the local newspapers, like the *Westmeath Examiner*, would turn up. Alas they never did. By 11am, one or two of the first year boys on strike felt guilty enough to break rank, and within half an hour we were back in our classrooms. Needless to say we got no apology from Reverend Mother, but we had made our point.

The Summer of '69 came and holiday time from school. Tyrrellspass started entering the national Tidy Towns Competition in 1967 and had won the County Award that year. The purpose of the competition was to encourage communities to improve their local environment and make their area a better place to live, work and visit. From early summer every man, woman and child would be out with a wire-brush scrubbing and cleaning, pulling weeds, picking litter morning and evening, cutting grass and painting anything that might look a bit unsightly or in need of a coat of paint. Our community had done well in the first two years of the competition and we were in the top few towns and villages to take the overall award in 1969. When the results were announced in early September and Tyrrellspass was declared the winner, the entire village was ecstatic. The news was greeted with great joy all over Co. Westmeath. It was absolutely wonderful news for our village. So much effort had gone into achieving the result and immense credit was due to all the dedicated volunteers who worked tirelessly to keep Tyrrellspass looking its best. The bunting went up and was draped across the street, and every household put out their GAA flags and any other flag they could find. The celebrations began in earnest and tourists from all over Ireland and beyond were seen pulling up in the village and chatting to the locals. That was the summer of '69 and while the village has never won the overall award since then, it has been up there looking its best and winning the County Award year after year since that time and indeed many other awards as well.

As I approached my last year in secondary school, I still had no idea what I wanted to do. I knew I would have loved to become a doctor, but I knew my results and ability would never reach that standard. I thought I would love to be a nurse as well, but during those years nursing was never an option for young men, so that seemed to be knocked on the head as well. I never really thought about priesthood or religious life until a religious order from the Missionary of the Sacred Heart priests visited our school to share their life and work with the fifth and sixth year boys. I remember listening so intently to what they had to say; I know at the time it aroused a certain interest and excitement for me. They left information leaflets and flyers for us to fill up if we needed more information. However, I never bothered thinking about it after that and didn't even complete the flyer for more information.

I guess it must have been about three months after that visit when Mother Carmel called me out of class to say there was a priest who wanted to meet me. I explained to her that I didn't know what it was about, but I went down to meet the priest. He greeted me politely and thanked me for completing the flyer and requesting more information about their work. I felt really embarrassed and blushed in nervous tension. I told him I hadn't completed the flyer and that obviously some of the other guys at his talk had put my name instead of their own. He laughed and said it happens all the time. However, I did tell him that I had found his talk very interesting. We chatted for another while as he shared more of his life and work. We concluded our meeting with a prayer and he left his personal details as vocational director of the order to contact him if and when I was ready to talk more, or go further by attending a live-in at their seminary for a few days. I know I put it at the back of my mind after that as my focus was on my Leaving Cert exam coming up in about four months' time. My sister Rosemarie had just got engaged too and was planning her wedding for 20th March 1971. For some reason I got it in my head that if I was in a seminary I would not be able to attend my sister's wedding, so that was even more reason to put the thought of priesthood further down the line as it were. Little did I know or even think that ten years later I would be contemplating priesthood again with the same feeling of excitement as I felt during that priest's talk at the school. Only then I seemed to have no excuses, but I would try and create some.

CHAPTER 4

....

First Jobs and
Pope John Paul II

I sat my Leaving Certificate in June of 1970. Being quite honest, I wasn't expecting great results as I always felt I lacked the confidence to be academically a high achiever. At least, that is what I was led to believe from my mother and from the teachers at St Joseph's Secondary School in the Bridge. I suppose when people tell you that on a frequent basis, you eventually learn to believe that is the case. At that time the Leaving Certificate was based on honours or pass, and to get into university the required standard was at least four honours. In my case, even if I got the four honours my parents could never afford to send me to university.

Nevertheless, I did pass all my subjects and achieved very well in maths and science, my two favourite subjects. With the help of my mother, I applied for various jobs at the Bank of Ireland and Ulster Bank. I remember travelling up to Belfast to sit an aptitude test and interview for the Ulster Bank position. It was at the height of the Troubles in Northern Ireland and my mother and Wally Arthur, a neighbour across the road from our home, and her mother-in-law Mrs Catherine Arthur travelled on the train with me. We were booked into a B&B by a relative of Mrs Arthur. From the train station we made our way to our B&B which was near Queen's University where I was to sit the aptitude test and interview. During that 24 hours I never remember my mother being so frightened as we saw so many British soldiers all around armed with sniper rifles, machine guns and Glock 17s. I knew she wanted to get out of Belfast as quickly as possible. We returned home the next evening and within a few weeks I got a letter beginning with, "I regret to inform you…". I was called for interview at various insurance company posts. Interviews were never really my thing. I just did not have the confidence in my ability at the age of 17. I travelled to Athlone to sit a civil service exam for the position of Clerical Officer. My mother always scouted the newspapers to see what was being advertised.

At the end of June 1970 when my exams were completed, I got a part-time job working in a shop in Rochfordbridge. My mother was attending the owner of the shop Angela Daly and her husband Joe, who happened to be a second cousin to my father, as she was about to have a new baby, and that is how the contact was made. I enjoyed it immensely behind the counter and serving petrol and diesel. As I always regarded myself as being shy and introverted, working there was my first experience of, for want of better words, "coming out of myself a bit" and feeling a little more confident in myself. Meeting people on a friendly basis was what I was beginning to enjoy, and definitely my few months as a shop boy sowed the seed for that. I guess my enormous salary of £4.00 per week was an added bonus having a few bob in my pocket. While I was there working, Angela delivered her baby with the help of my mother. Needless to say the arrival of another Daly boy created great conversation in the shop when customers would come in.

Our neighbours across the Mullingar Road were Larry and Wally Arthur. Wally was a first cousin of my mother. Wally's husband Larry worked in Bord Na Mona at the Derrygreenagh Works just outside of Rochfordbridge. My brother Joseph was already working there training as a fitter. Larry told me of a summer job in the Bonus Office working with a man called Tom Barry. So after nine months working in Daly's shop I finished up and in May 1971 I started working at the Bord Na Mona Derrygreenagh Office for about a four-month period over the summer months with the possibility of something more permanent coming up. Tom was a very nice man and showed me all the ropes regarding the work. As summer was the busy season for working with this semi-state company there was plenty of overtime available, which I was happy to take on. My starting salary was about £16.50 per week and double pay and treble pay for weekends. I felt I would be a millionaire by the time I was 20 if I held on to this job. But of course, it was only a summer job and therefore I knew it wouldn't last. I have to say, I also struggled a bit with the work in the office. Out on the bogs the workers were milling, ridging and harvesting the peat. They would then submit to us in the office the amount of work they would get done every day on each section of the bog. We, in the Bonus Office, would then chart it on a big wall chart in the office. We entered it up on our charts with brown, green and orange colours; as I was partially coloured blind I always struggled to enter the correct colours on the chart. My colour blindness is something that I knew I had from a very early age. I knew black from white, red from yellow, but when it went into the various greens, browns, and pinks I really struggled. I learned that colour blindness was a gene that male children often inherited from their mother who would be a carrier, but not colour blind herself. I have gone through some embarrassing moments with people; especially my sisters, nieces and nephews who knew of my condition and would sometimes ask me what colour certain objects were in order to embarrass me and set me up. I guess it was a form of getting a laugh by making fun of me. I honestly don't think they wanted to hurt me, but they did.

When the seasonal work at Derrygreenagh was over, I was kept on on a temporary basis and boy was I delighted. Meanwhile, the results of my civil service exam came through, and I got a letter from the civil service commission. They regretted to inform me that my rank of 656th out of a couple of thousand sitting the exam was not high enough to offer me a position, however they went on to say that the panel would remain open for one year. I was not disappointed because I was earning good money at Bord Na Mona; perhaps down the road there was a chance of being offered a more permanent position. In July of that summer I received a letter from the civil service commission offering me a position as a clerical officer. As I was still only employed on a temporary basis in Bord Na Mona, I decided to accept the position in the civil service and completed the various forms and the medical test required. Once I accepted to take up the offer of working in the civil service, the same old feelings of anxiety and fear surfaced. It was not unlike the feelings I had when starting primary school, secondary school and even the temporary employments at Daly's and at Bord Na Mona. "Would I be able for the work?", "Would I make a fool of myself?", and taking up the civil service job had an added anxiety, "How would I cope being away from home?" My mother was a strong influence in me accepting the civil service job as she always believed that having a civil service job was a secure job with the guarantee of a good pension when I would retire. On 25th September 1971 I reported to the Department of Defence Headquarters at Parkgate St, Dublin. I was quickly informed that this location would not be my place of work and that my three days at this location were for introductory information on the workings of the Department of Defence. For almost the next 11 years my location of work would be at Colaiste Caoimhin (Kevin's College), Glasnevin, on the north side of Dublin.

Colaiste Caoimhin was the headquarters for a lot of the administration of the Department as well as various payment sections for the army. I was assigned to the payments section of FCÁ (Fórsa Cosanta Áitiúil): a reserve unit set up by the Department. Of course at this time there was no such thing as computerised payments and everything was recorded on large ledgers and payments were issued accordingly. I got B&B accommodation in Inchicore with Gretta and Dermott Larkin and their family. Gretta was a native of near my home and her nephew Joey Malone stayed in the house also. I would take a 15 minute walk every morning to Rialto and then the 19A bus right across the city to the north side in Glasnevin and my place of work. I was quickly introduced to others who were starting work for the first time. I was introduced to my Staff Officer boss, Eddie Lawlor, and all the other staff in the FCÁ section. I would undergo a training period for a few weeks before being assigned my own selection of work.

Indeed, I remember taking to the work very easily as most of it had to do with accounts and figures, so I felt quite at home. It was a five-day week job, Monday to Friday, 9.15am to 5.30pm. On Friday I could finish work at 5 and head for Busáras to get the bus home to Tyrrellspass.

It was so good to get home for the weekend and share the experience of my new job with my family. Early on Monday mornings my father would be heading to Dublin with a load of sheep for the market or for Cosgrove Butchers in Ranelagh at about 5am, and Joey Malone and I would travel with him. I know for a while I always returned with a heavy heart, but once I got into work I seemed to feel less anxious as I chatted my work mates and caught up on their weekends. My first car was a mini minor SLI95. Having the car gave me huge independence, especially for travelling home at weekends. Of course it made me very popular with a lot of my working colleagues as well. As I settled more and more into Dublin city life, I would sometimes stay over to socialize with working colleagues on a Friday night and drive home on a Saturday.

Friday night was always one of the better nights to go out in Dublin. The Irene Country Club was one of the most popular spots where there was a live band playing and loads of country people like myself. Mind you I was very shy to the scene for a long time. I would choose to dance with some of my female work mates because I knew they would not say no to me, so my confidence would not be shattered. My mother had taught me how to waltz many years before while we would be hunting the wren on St Stephen's Day. I had also learned to jive and quick-step, and I knew the girls loved to dance with a guy who could dance pretty well; my popularity grew as well as my confidence. But sometimes my confidence was shattered too, especially if a girl refused me a dance. I always seemed to take it on board that I was ugly. I guess having the squint and wearing glasses didn't exactly give me confidence either. So there was always a tug of war going on in my head as I learned to believe in myself, trust in myself and assure myself that I was ok. If Friday night was for dancing than usually Thursday night was a night out in some of the local pubs, especially where there was music or karaoke. Needless to say I was always easily persuaded to get up and sing a few songs. As I was singing with an alto voice some of my favourites were "The White Rose of Athens", or some of Demis Roussos' songs like "My Friend the Wind", "Goodbye My Love, Goodbye" or "Forever and Ever". I loved to sing some of the Bee Gees songs too. In some of the pubs like The Drake Inn in Finglas there would be regular talent competitions and indeed I would often enter and compete in the various rounds. I would always have a large following of work colleagues with me; as audience voting was often the way to decide the winners, I always did pretty well. But I was learning to believe I was pretty good too.

I was enjoying the experience of attending the College of Music in Chatham at Chatham Row where I would attend on a weekly basis for vocal coaching. My first vocal coach was a man named Leo Maguire. Leo had a very distinguished voice. He was a prolific composer of over 100 songs including his most famous hit "The Whistling Gypsy". He was the host of RTÉ Radio's Walton's Programme, which was aired for almost 30 years. His catch phrase was, "Do drop in if you happen to be passing 2-5 North Frederick Street Dublin 2, and if you feel like singing do sing an Irish Song." I loved the relaxed way Leo and I worked. I wasn't going to be taking any vocal exams so there was no pressure. After about two years with Leo, I moved on to another vocal coach Kathleen Uhlemann whom I stayed with for three more years.

The summer of 1972 was my first taste of bereavement. My grandfather Bamba died on 16th July. He was my mother's dad and she had phoned me on the Wednesday prior to his death to tell me that he had a stroke and it didn't look good. I guess at the age of 92 his long life had caught up with him. His daughter Lily Abbott from Edenderry, my mother's second youngest sister, was fighting cancer too and her treatments didn't seem to be working. I arrived home the day after my mother's phone call and was so happy to be there with Bamba. I had grown up with him in my life for all my years and we were very close. He was a character. He loved to tell stories of growing up in Ring outside Tyrrellspass and of his desire to live in the village. He loved his Woodbine cigarettes, and his wife Teresa, who was 11 years younger than he was, always kept a close eye on the number of cigarettes he was smoking. Of course what she didn't know was that he would ramble down to our home on the Mullingar Road and always take a few Craven A cigarettes from my mother, especially when she would not be looking. Now in his last days all he wanted was a pull or two from a cigarette and needless to say we obliged. As I sat with him, I would hold a cigarette for him and let him have a pull of it. He hadn't a lot of strength, but a few pulls was all he wanted. About a half hour before he died on the Sunday, he took three pulls as I held the cigarette to his mouth. He was ready to go and we were ready to let him go. Less than five months later on 4th December, his daughter Lily, my mother's sister and my godmother, gave up her fight too. As I reflect on those few months, I certainly was very unaware of the grief my mother must have been experiencing. Losing her father and sister in the space of six months. Indeed, many years later I would know the pain of loss like everyone else when I would be without my parents and my younger sister.

After my first year of accommodation with the Larkin Family, I grew in independence and I knew it would only be a matter of time before I would move out of the B&B accommodation and look for an apartment nearer my work. Indeed, it would be the first of many addresses in Dublin over my nearly 11 years. From an apartment in Glasnevin to a bed-sit at Mountjoy Square, sharing with my cousin Pat Finnegan. Some of Pat's friends were renting a house in Murtagh St off the North Circular Road and they were looking for two guys to share it with them. Pat eventually married his long term girlfriend Elizabeth Gahan and they moved to a rented house in Tallaght. I moved with them for a short time, however this was a long way across the city for my work and eventually I moved out and got a lovely apartment at Kincora Ave, Clontarf. The apartment was in a private house owned by Jane Rodgers. She lived there with her cousin Fr Tom - a retired priest. We had a great relationship. Sometimes I would be invited to join them for dinner, or if Fr Tom was celebrating Mass with Jane, I would be invited to join them. Of course the location was very convenient for my work being just a minute drive up Collins Ave. During those first few years in DOD I would have moved to different sections, from the FCÁ section where I began, to the officers' pay section and the soldiers' pay section.

In 1978 I was promoted to a Staff Officer grade and took on a new role with the department. I was visiting army barracks around the country and inspecting their inventory of various things from army ammunition to day to day materials. It was a job that I liked but knew I wouldn't want to be on the road as much as was required. Needless to say with all of the travelling I needed to change my car and upgraded to a Datsun. However, I was living out of a suitcase a lot of the time, and while financially it was worthwhile, living out of a suitcase and staying in B&Bs can be very lonely. Eventually I made a request to go back to a post at the office of Colaiste Caoimhin.

A vacancy arose for a staff officer position in the soldiers' pay section. I was delighted to be posted there because I was back working with a lot of my friends again whom I missed when on the road travelling. I was also working in the same section as my girlfriend Catherine. We were going out only for a short while, so our relationship was not serious. Obviously working in the same office and going out together meant we saw a lot more of each other.

I had been living in rented accommodation now for over seven years, so I started looking into the idea of buying my own house. I knew on my salary I would be limited with the amount of loan I would get from a building society, so I started looking into houses for sale around my price level. I also wanted to be near enough for my work, possibly even walking distance. Eventually, I found a small two-bedroom house in Cabra. I remember I bought the house for about £14,995. I was borrowing about £11,500 and the interest rate from the building society was huge, 14.5% at one stage rising to over 16%. Comparing it to the interest rates now it was sheer madness but then the price of houses was a lot lower. I knew I would easily manage and taking in a lodger for my spare room helped.

This was also the year Pope John Paul II was to visit Ireland. I remember so well the huge sense of excitement of being in the Phoenix Park for the open air Mass on September 29th 1979. Everyone seemed so patient and happy. I walked along with my family for miles on that Saturday morning to be part of the million or more people gathered for the visit. It was such a huge event and the beginning of an extraordinary weekend. It propelled the entire country in a unity of purpose and spirit. My family and I entered the park through the Chapelizod Gates and were directed from there to our roped corrall. As the Pope's Aer Lingus plane swooped low over the park on route from Rome to Dublin Airport, there was a roar of cheers, which I'm sure could be heard for miles. About an hour later his helicopter hovered over the crowds before touching down; I remember being in awe at the number of cardinals, bishops and priests all in their vestments ready to concelebrate mass with Pope John Paul. When he ascended up onto the altar and began the Mass with the Irish blessing, "In ainm an Athar agus an Mhic agus an Spioraid Naoimh," the crowd erupted. The following Sunday, Pope John Paul had an open-air youth mass at Ballybrit racecourse in Galway. I was not able to attend, however I watched it all on TV and can still hear the thousands singing out hymns like "Freely, freely, you shall receive" and "How lovely on the mountains are the feet of him who brings good news, good news". There is no doubt that on that day his words to the young people of Ireland, "Young people of Ireland I love you", touched the hearts of so many young people in Ireland; they certainly did with me.

CHAPTER 5

....

Visiting Rome

I grew up in a typical Irish Catholic family and religion played a big part in our lives. My parents believed very much in passing on the faith to their children. There was the regular Sunday Mass, and confessions once a month on a Saturday. As a family we attended Benediction and the various novenas and sodalities on a regular basis, as well as the Mission every few years. During the month of May, we made a lovely May altar to Our Lady, as well as decorating a May bush outside our front hall door. The bush was often a hawthorn bush set up to celebrate an occasion like the beginning of summer. It also gave some families the feeling of protection by Mary, the Mother of God, against unseen forces. The decorations usually consisted of ribbons, cloth streamers, sometimes even a bit of tinsel and maybe a few painted eggshells. There was the annual Corpus Christi procession through the village. The arrival of Ash Wednesday meant receiving the ashes on our foreheads at Mass and the beginning of the six weeks of Lent. That meant that we gave up sweets, and if we were given any during that period they were saved up to be devoured on Easter Sunday. Sometimes we got a dispensation to eat some on St Patrick's Day. During the season of Lent my father got us all up for eight o'clock mass followed by breakfast and off to school. The recitation of the rosary most evenings before bed was also a common occurrence. Indeed, if any of us, particularly my brother Joseph or me, were "acting the mick" like poking or punching each other, or laughing during the rosary or indeed during Mass in the Church, the punishment was as often as not to kneel down for ten minutes in front of the Sacred Heart Picture as it stared back at us; its eyes seem to follow us if we moved ever so slightly from our positions. I remember very clearly that when the punishment was dished out to me I always took it with a heavy heart like a "put-down".

Starting a new life in Dublin meant that I was able to unconsciously unshackle myself from a lot of my childhood Catholic practices. Nevertheless I still attended Mass on the weekend when at home with my parents. I would also attend Mass on holy days in Dublin, usually an 8am holy day Mass at the pyramid church, also known as Our Lady of Dolours in Glasnevin, just across the road from where I worked.

After Pope John Paul's visit in September of 1979, I decided the following season of Lent, which began on Ash Wednesday 20th February, 1980, to do an extra bit of penance as I was taught when I was a boy. Since there was a regular daily 8am Mass on in the pyramid church, I would arise that little bit earlier and attend before I would cross the road for work. It was a lovely quiet time of prayer and silence which I began to enjoy. I would meet the same people nearly every morning and during the Mass offer them the sign of peace, and usually have a short chat on the way in or out. When the season of Lent was over, I decided to continue attending the 8am Mass at the pyramid church. I just fell in love with the quiet time. However, another thought entered my head during my quiet time in church. The thought was that maybe I could be up there on the altar where the priest was and celebrate the mass with the people. It was a thought that didn't last very long, and being honest I was glad when the thought had passed.

In the meantime, I picked up a flyer from the notice board of the Church. The flyer was from the Catholic Youth Council; they were organising a week long return visit to Rome of 1,000 young people as a repayment of the historic visit of Pope John Paul II to Ireland to thank the Pope for coming to Ireland. I brought the flyer into my work place and showed it around to some of my friends. There was huge interest from my friends, so we made contact with the Catholic Youth Council and attended various meetings in planning for the trip. There was a lot of planning to get 1,000 young Irish people over to Rome. We were going to see the Pope first of all at St Peter's Square. We would meet the Pope then for an 8am morning Mass at his summer residence at Castlegandolfo; the following evening there would be a garden party where we would stage a concert at Castlegandolfo for His Holiness. Auditions were held for those who would like to perform and I remember auditioning. At the audition I sang a version of the song "Danny Boy". About a week later I got word that, time permitting, I would be one of the acts to perform for Pope John Paul II. I couldn't contain myself with excitement. I had about three rehearsals before our departure for Rome. Before we departed, all 1,000 of us young people were put into groups of 50. We would then be picked up by our appropriate bus at the Leonardo de Vinci airport in Rome. This would be our group for the entire week.

Saturday 23rd August 1980, the day of our departure came, arriving in Rome in the early hours of Sunday morning and straight to our hotel that was our home for the next nine days. The first few days were sightseeing around Rome. Piazza San Giovanni was our first tour visiting the Holy Stairs, Baptistry, Basilica and Cloister. Then we had a beautiful Sunday evening Mass in St John Latern's.

On our way back to the hotel we stopped off for dinner at the Ristorante Scoglio di Frisio. A group of 12 of us sat down and studied the menu. As we did not understand a lot of the food listed in Italian, we decided to play it safe and order spaghetti bolognese all around. The waiter got his count wrong and brought out 11 plates of spaghetti bolognese. When I pointed this out to him, he produced an empty plate and decided to take a little off everyone's plate to make up the shortfall. All we could do was laugh our heads off.

The following day was a lot of sightseeing again at Castel Sant'Angelo, Piazza del Popolo, Borghese Gardens, Spanish Steps, St Mary Major, the Irish College, the Colosseum and Circus Maximus, followed by an afternoon on the beach and a few hours at the Luna Park Carnival Centre. On Tuesday we celebrated Mass at Monte Cassino followed by an afternoon on the beach again. On Wednesday, the excitement was building. We began our day with Mass in the underground Church of the Catacombs of S. Domitilla; in the afternoon we departed for St Peter's Square with a sightseeing tour first and then assembled in St Peter's Square for the general open-air audience with His Holiness, Pope John Paul II. Pope John Paul welcomed all the people naming their country, and when he said Irlanda, he specifically welcomed the 1,000 strong young people from Ireland. Well the cheers could be heard certainly all over Italy and Ireland, if not the world. My heart lifted.

On Thursday morning we set off at 6.30am for our Mass with Pope John Paul at Castelgandolfo. It was the most beautiful experience of my life as the Holy Father prayed with us - it was unforgettable. The enthusiasm of 1,000 young people and many adults was electric as we sang out many of the hymns that were heard in Galway almost a year before "Freely, freely, you have received", "He's got the whole world in his hands", "Totus Tuus" and many more; the Pope was enjoying every moment of it. We then had a group photograph taken with the Holy Father. I was profoundly moved by his vigorous presence and his deep and obvious spirituality. He had a charisma that animated everyone. His faith in God, his devotion to Mary and his love of people especially the youth, never ceased to impress me. After that experience, I am not sure if there would be anything to top it, but there would be. Before that, however, we had a beautiful tour of the city of Rome by night stopping at the Trevi Fountain, Piazza Colonna, Via Veneto and the Pantheon.

On Friday morning we had a special guided tour of the Vatican Gardens followed by a visit to the Sistine Chapel. At half four in the afternoon we departed for Castelgandolfo for our garden party and concert. This was the evening of evenings as 1,000 emotional Irish youngsters assembled onto the grounds of this splendid hilltop summer residence over-looking Rome. I was in awe as I sat starry-eyed at this highly moving and awesome occasion in the Mediterranean pine-lined gardens of the world's most powerful religious leader. The excitement built up as I waited patiently in the garden, which was dotted with young pilgrims waving white and yellow papal flags as well as the Archbishop of Dublin Most

Rev. Dermot Ryan, Bishop Forrestal and the Catholic Youth Council director Fr John Fitzpatrick, Fr John Magee (later Bishop of Cloyne), as well as the Lord Mayor of Dublin Fergal O'Brien and his wife and many more. The garden, which was cut off from the remainder of the 20 acre castle grounds and palace by a high laurel hedge, was ringed by the Pope's security men and armed police. Soon I joined in the shouts of joy which rang out for the Pontiff as he quietly emerged from the graceful splendour of his castle to the grounds where we were gathered for the party. He slowly walked down the floodlit pathway surrounded by cheering Irish guests. He sat down with Archbishop Ryan and Bishop Forrestal on either side, and was introduced to the various dignitaries and organisers of this Youth pilgrimage from the Catholic Youth Council.

When the formalities ended the papal gardens rang out with "In Dublin's Fair City" and "The Wild Rover". Pope John Paul smiled broadly and quietly joined in on the occasion by reading the words of the songs from a book he had been presented with earlier. That was followed by a group of young Irish Dancers dressed in a multitude of colours that danced to a group of traditional musicians playing the harp, the violin, the tin whistle and the bodhran. At this stage my heart was pumping as I knew I would be performing after two sisters from Navan. Then I walked forward, bowed in reverence before the Pope and stepped up to the microphone as the introduction music of the song "Danny Boy" began. Strangely, once I started singing I felt a calmness come over me as I sang out the words *"Oh Danny Boy, the pipes, the pipes are calling…"*. As I reached the high notes I noticed the Holy Father saying the words in a gentle silence and I smiled. My three minutes of song ended to a rapturous applause. Then as the other performers did, I approached Pope John Paul and knelt before him as he took my hand and presented me with rosary beads. I stood up and bowed in reverence. My moment with the Holy Father had ended, but it would stay etched in my memory forever. I returned back to the area where the other performers were located, and the tears just flowed as I realized the enormity of what had happened.

When the concert was over, Pope John Paul spoke to us in good but faltering English. There was a huge roar from the crowd when he recalled his visit to Ireland almost a year before and described it as being a wonderful experience. He said a special part of it was the Holy Mass in Galway which was attended by mainly young people. Referring to the fact that many of the Catholic Youth Council group had to save hard for their trip to Rome he said, "What you had to sacrifice to come here was much greater than what I had to sacrifice going to Ireland… I thank you for your singing and dancing. It was a special privilege to be part of it. To you I am embracing all people of Ireland, especially young people." Apologising for not giving a long speech and pointing out that even Popes need sleep, he blessed the pilgrims saying, "God bless Ireland".

We returned to our hotel and reached there before 1am. But I couldn't sleep, neither could the other pilgrims staying at the hotel. We sat up until about 4am as gradually we filtered off to bed. I was wrecked, I was emotionally drained, but I was on cloud nine. The next day we began winding down after such a highly emotionally charged few days. We had Mass in St Mary Major Basilica and then shopping in the afternoon. Then on Sunday we had a tour of the Colosseum and Mass at St John Lateran Cathedral.

I felt so honoured and privileged to meet a man who not only served his community with great distinction but also worked hard for a better world for everyone. John Paul was a man of peace and a great bridge-builder. He brought the Catholic community closer to the world and the world closer to his own community. He was a man who did his best to promote understanding and respect between all world religions and faiths. I have always been inspired and touched by his strength and ability to stay strong to Church teaching and his ability to forgive. Especially around the time of the attempted assassination on his life. During the years of his leadership so much good has occurred for a deeper understanding between Catholics and all other religions and faiths. I think he will be especially remembered for his commitment to the dignity of every human person and respect for all human life from conception to natural death. In his book, *Go In Peace: A Gift of Enduring Love*, John Paul wrote, *"Christ's passion is orientated towards Resurrection. Human beings are thus associated with the mystery of the Cross in order to share joyfully in the mystery of the resurrection"*. So he is telling us that suffering has a value, and that we are created for eternal life. Certainly, meeting John Paul touched my heart, and little did I know at the time that my visit to Rome and meeting His Holiness Pope John Paul would change my life forever.

My 89 year old grandmother was a very special lady in my life. As a child I spent a lot of my youth and years after with her. She was always number one on my visiting list when I would arrive home from Dublin on weekends. Every

Halloween was always the time for me to help Granny, and climb up the apple trees for her and pick all the apples off the trees. This Halloween after my visit to Rome would be no different. Granny always wanted the apples picked off the tree that way she could store them up in a tea chest with straw; they would be preserved that way in order to be distributed to all her daughters throughout the year. If they had fallen from the tree to the ground the chances are that the skin might be broken, so preserving these would result in them rotting very quickly. On the bank holiday Monday after our apple picking Granny had a stroke. The family gathered around and I did not return to work. I wanted to be by her side. All her family called, including most of her 25 grandchildren too. Everyone wanted to know what she might have been up to that might have brought on the stroke. In fact, sharing the apple picking story almost made me feel guilty as if I shouldn't have allowed her to be out helping me.. Aside from that her age was against her too. She let go of her 89 years of life on Saturday 1st November 1980.

CHAPTER 6

....

The Call

I arrived into work at DOD on Tuesday morning after my trip to Rome, tired certainly but on cloud nine. I felt totally just overwhelmed at what had happened to me in the last nine days. I wasn't the only one – so were my friends that had come with me, Eddie, Rita, Mairead, TP, and Oliver. We just could not stop talking about our experience. We made so many new friends: Greg who was returning to the seminary a week after the trip, Nora and Dina were on the phone to me later that day too. It was like we wanted to continue talking about our trip and relive all the various days and experiences. The enormity of what had happened to all of us was only gradually sinking in. It was a once in a lifetime experience for all of us, and we did not want to let it go. There was no doubt about it that I felt the Lord had touched my life and urged me to continue to seek him in earnest prayer. With such heart-to-heart communication with me and the other 999 young people, Pope John Paul had created a friendship with all of us, which obviously is the prerequisite to all evangelisation. Of course as I write that now, at that time, I would never have for one minute understood what it all meant. Later I would. Over the next few weeks as the day to day work in defence continued, there were the evenings to party, meet some of the new friends from our trips at the pub over a few beers and reminisce about all that had happened. It was infectious.

I went home to Tyrrellspass and my family on the weekend, and brought home all my gifts and souvenirs for family and neighbours. After Mass on Sunday, Fr Tom Farrell, the local priest, came over to me to inquire about the trip. I filled him in on my experience, and then he asked me if would I like to share the details of the trip with the people at Mass. I remember thinking, "I could never have the courage to get up on the altar and do that". He obviously read my face and reluctance, but wouldn't take no for an answer. So during the following week I put to paper my experience of meeting Pope John Paul and what it had meant to me and all the other young people. Then at the weekend masses I spoke for about 15 minutes, indeed I could have gone on for an hour. I got a huge round of applause and was very proud of myself. Indeed, loads of people came over to me after Mass to congratulate me. I was on a high.

About a month after the trip, the Catholic Youth Council organised reunions for all 1,000 young people over a few weeks; each bus group of 50 met separately. We already had exchanged addresses and phone numbers before we broke up at Rome, and again we relived the trip all over as if it just happened the day before. There was even talk among our group that Pope John Paul was making a trip to the UK in about 18-months time; the suggestion was rampant among us that we would organise a trip to one of his masses.

Meanwhile, I was back attending my 8am Mass at the pyramid church and enjoying my quiet time. After about a week of having this quiet time at 8am in the mornings, it started again; that voice in my head, "Ray, you know you could be up there doing what that priest is doing". Soon the Mass was over and I was back at my desk at work. I thought no more about it. The next morning at Mass that little voice again, "Ray, you know you could be up there doing what that priest is doing". In fact, that was the same line for over two weeks. Then it disappeared, completely. I smiled inwardly and knew that was that. It definitely was all in my imagination and it was gone now. I reckoned it came back over the last few weeks because of my experience of meeting Pope John Paul. I felt confident and happy once I had moved on from the Rome trip that the little voice would move on too. However, it didn't. It must have been a month before that voice came back again. But during that month I was missing that voice, I felt disappointed that it was gone. I realised that I had heard that voice in my head and that I had listened to it so intently and had even at moments got excited about what I was hearing. However, I was completely thrown again, not by a voice in my head, but by an image before my eyes. This time it wasn't in the pyramid church across the road. I happened to be at a funeral Mass of the father of a working colleague. As I was about to receive Holy Communion, for a second I saw myself giving myself Holy Communion dressed as a priest. The image in my head distracted me, and as I walked back to my seat, I just kept on walking out the door of the church and back to my car. I was angry. I was annoyed. What in the name of God was going on? Why was I thinking like that? It didn't make sense. I was 27 years of age; it was over ten years since I was a student; I had my own car and was in the process of changing it for a new one; I had my own house with a mortgage; I was not giving up all that - no way. What would my mother say if I gave up my good pensionable job? So the tug-of-war went on in my head for months. When that little voice in my head gave me a break, I felt relieved, it was like respite. But I was also missing it, I was missing the feeling of excitement it gave me. As soon as I settled with the thought that it was only my imagination, there it was again, "Ray, you know you could be up there doing what that priest is doing". I was getting very angry and frustrated. What was I going to do? Who could I talk to about this? What would my friends say? Could I, should I, share it with anyone? What would my mother and father say? What would my brother and sisters say? So many questions plagued my head, and I was getting no answers as I hadn't the courage to bring the subject up to anyone for fear of being laughed at. So I set about creating as many distractions as I could in the hope of putting this tug-of-war in my head to bed for once and for all. I went ahead and changed my Datsun car for a new Mazda hatchback. I planned a few house parties. I even stopped going to my 8am morning Mass and quiet time because it wasn't quiet time anymore, since that was the place where that voice in my head started. I was fighting this distraction anyway I could. And it worked for a while.

Michael Holly, a work colleague, lived with me in my house. He was one of my best friends and I was delighted that he moved into the house with me soon after I bought it to help me pay the mortgage. Michael, soon after starting to work in Defence, had requested a transfer to nearer his home in Ballylongford, Co. Kerry. But I know he had pretty much given up on getting that transfer now after all those years and I know he loved to live in Dublin. One afternoon at work, Michael came over to me at my desk and informed me that to his surprise it looked like his transfer has come through and he was moving to the Department of Social Welfare in Listowel, Co. Kerry. He didn't look overly enthusiastic about the move so as he left me I said in passing to him that I might be moving on myself. He looked at me and I said I'd fill him in later. Even when he left my desk, I questioned myself as to what am I going to tell Michael. "I might be moving on myself." My God, had I said too much? When we got home, he asked me what I meant by moving on. "Don't laugh at me please," I said, "but for the last year or so I have been having these thoughts about becoming a priest." Silence; total silence. "Say something Michael," I said, "say something." All I heard back was, "Jesus Ray, Jesus Ray, Jesus Ray," but in those three "Jesus Rays" I felt like a huge weight had been lifted from my brain. I said, "Let's go out for something to eat and then get drunk." "Good idea," he said, "good idea." We didn't talk any more about our big moves until we were ordering our food. Then I asked Michael about his move. I think he was still in shock about hearing that his transfer had come through. He had completely forgotten about the request for a transfer that he had made many years before. I knew he loved Dublin - the social life in particular. But as he said, he was an only son, his parents were getting on in years and maybe it was time to help out in the running of the farm. Then I shared with him about my inner struggle over the last 18 months. "Have you said anything to Catherine yet?" he asked. "No" I said. Michael knew my relationship with Catherine hadn't moved on hugely, but we were still friends, good friends. We would go out for a drink, go to see a film but nothing more than that. But Michael was right that my next move would be to talk to Catherine.

While Catherine worked in the same office as I did, she loved her Irish dancing and was about to qualify as an Irish dancing teacher. Catherine knew me better than I thought; when I told her she was relieved because for a long while she felt something was not right, and even had thoughts that I was suffering from some kind of illness. So I guess for me to share what was going on for me was quite a relief to her. Of course that was probably the reason that our relationship had not moved on either.

Before I could share my decision with anyone else, I knew I would have to make contact with a priest and tell him what I was going through. I had thought about being a priest in Ireland and working in Dublin or my home Diocese of Meath, but for some reason it just didn't appeal to me. So I made contact with a missionary order of priests at their headquarters in Dublin. I think that was because about ten years previously a priest from that order had visited me at my school in Rochfordbridge. I arranged to meet the vocations director at the Missionaries of the Sacred Heart (MSC) headquarters and Seminary in Dublin. I spent a full Saturday in his company and we chatted about everything, family, friends, work, interests, hobbies and my standard of education. He made me feel so relaxed and at ease. He assured me that everything I had gone through seemed very like a calling to priesthood. I really felt good about hearing that and it made what I had been going through seem so normal. We promised to keep in touch. In the meantime Michael had packed his bag and moved home to Ballylongford and his new working life in the Dept. of Social Welfare in Listowel. We were on the phone every other day and kept each other posted about all the happenings in our lives.

While it was getting a little easier to accept the possible forthcoming changes in my life, the next part was probably one of the hardest bits. I had to go home and tell my parents and family what I was thinking and planning. Like Catherine, my mother and father knew there was something not right about me for a long time. They thought I was very quiet and unhappy about something. They knew if I was ill they would be the first to know, so it wasn't that, but they knew something wasn't right. So when I broke the news over dinner on Saturday the first thing my mother said was, "And what about your good pensionable job?" I assured her that I had made inquiries about that and was reliably informed that because I was leaving my job to pursue a vocation, in the event of it not working out, my job would be there for up to 12 years. I have to tell you that knowing this gave me a lot of peace and comfort in moving ahead. My father said very little but he gave me a big hug and said, "Your Mammy and I love you and are here to support you and help you along to whatever brings you happiness." I knew Mammy had more questions and they came quick and fast. "What about your house and car? What are you going to do with them?" I hadn't fully got the answers for her, but I knew I could let the house and the rent could pay my mortgage, or I could sell it and hopefully get enough to keep me in pocket money while in the seminary. As regards to the car, well I knew I would have no problem selling that.

After Michael Holly had moved home to work, I was fortunate to get another tenant. Donal Hackett was a very friendly young man and training to be a nurse. He was a native of Thurles in Co. Tipperary. Like myself he was big into music and having a good social life. We got on famously together and it wasn't long before my house was a regular spot for weekend parties with either my working colleagues, or his, or indeed both. Like myself, Donal came from a very loyal, faithful Catholic background. Indeed, he had two uncles who were priests and whom I had met on a few occasions. Interestingly, Donal had been a seminary student himself for four years and when I shared with him my intentions he was very excited for me. Of course there was a big difference in our age as we entered the seminary; he was just 17 years of age when he joined the Diocesan Seminary in Thurles; I would be 29 when I would join up.

Meanwhile the vocations director from the MSC order made contact with me and invited me to a "Come and See" weekend at their seminary. I went along with ten other young men who were considering a vocation. The old feelings of nervousness and negativity surfaced again before the weekend. But there was also a certain confidence and assurance that I would be ok. It was a feeling that everything seemed to be coming together right and fitting into place. The three days I spent in the seminary were truly wonderful. I chatted with the other prospective seminarians like myself. Many of their journeys so far were very similar to mine. They ranged in age from 17 to 35 years, so I knew straight away that age was not a barrier. In fact it was pointed out to me that the formation team of priests always found that the more mature a prospective student was, the stronger possibility of a real vocation to priesthood. I found out that I would attend UCD and achieve a degree of my choice within my ability. I also discovered that my formation period before ordination would last six possibly seven years. Since the MSC priests worked mainly in Africa, I would more than likely be appointed to one of their missions in an African country.

After my three days at the "Come and See" weekend, I was on cloud nine. I felt so positive about what I was doing. It was like the feeling I had after I came back from Rome; I wanted to share my new found experience. However, Catherine, Michael and my parents were the only ones I shared with as they were up to date with events. I told my friend Eddie Fitzgerald later that day too. While I was home at the weekend, my mother told me she had told her first cousin Fr Joe Pettit about what I was considering. Fr Joe was a Missionary priest too and was a member of St Patrick's Missionary Society, or the Kiltegan Fathers. He was home on holidays from Nigeria where he had worked for over 30 years. He came for dinner on Sunday and I told him of my few days at the "Come and See" with the MSC order. He suggested that maybe before I make a final decision on where I go to study that I should "shop around", and that I contact the vocations director with the Kiltegan Fathers. The following week I was speaking to Fr Donald Mc Donagh. I filled him in on my journey so far. He informed me of a forthcoming "live in" during Holy Week at the seminary in Kiltegan and he invited me to come along. I agreed.

The village of Kiltegan is situated in the western part of Co. Wicklow. It is situated about an hour and a half drive from Dublin. I had never been to that part of Wicklow before. It is a small village similar to my home village of Tyrrellspass, and like Tyrrellspass, Kiltegan won the overall Tidy Towns Competition in 1973. Humewood Castle is one of the distinguished features of the village. St Patrick's Missionary Society Offices and Seminary is located about two miles outside the village. The Kiltegan Fathers' origins stem from an appeal by Bishop Joseph Shanahan who was a member of the Holy Ghost order. In 1920 he made an appeal to the seminary students in Maynooth College for missionaries to Nigeria where he was a Bishop. He had only about 23 priests working for him in his vast diocese in Nigeria, and his plan was to get some of the students from Maynooth to give the first five years of their priesthood in Nigeria. Fr PJ Whitney from the Diocese of Ardagh and Clonmacnoise went with Bishop Shanahan to Nigeria and grew to believe that what was needed was a more permanent priesthood for Nigeria. So, in March 1930 St Patrick's Missionary Society was born on a trial basis with Fr Whitney as Superior. A headquarters was established at Kiltegan, Co. Wicklow where a tea-merchant, John Hughes, had given over an old house and 20 acres of land for that purpose.

Needless to say the entire place had grown hugely over the 50 plus years. As I drove through the gates up the half mile long avenue, I was completely in awe of the beautiful green fields with cattle grazing everywhere. The sparse woodlands almost encircled me. As I drove around the lake, the Spiritual Year buildings were the first I saw, followed by the Society offices and then driving on up the hill to the massive hotel-size building that was the students' accommodation. I already loved the entire setting. I parked the car and was greeted by a number of priests, students and prospective students. I knew this was where I wanted to be. I immediately fell in love with the surroundings. I also felt that after living and working in Dublin for nearly 11 years it would be better for me, when making such a huge change in my life, that I leave the hustle and bustle of Dublin behind. I felt by doing that it would give me a better opportunity of discerning whether this new life was really for me. I met Fr Mc Donagh and many other of the formation team of priests and lecturers. I met many of the students, some were Deacons and just two months away from ordination, others were one, two and three years and so on. The Holy Week ceremonies were absolutely beautiful - very prayerful and uplifting. I don't think I ever felt as close to God as I did during those days. I met many of the guys that would start off their seminary life with me, though I didn't know it then, no more than they knew it of me.

Every hour of these few days I felt more and more assured that I was on the right road. It would be a long and indeed winding seven years of preparation. I would be past my 36th birthday when I would be ordained a priest. It seemed a life-time away. I promised myself that I would embrace each day and week, and after my first year I would review my situation and decide whether to carry on or not. My first year would be a spiritual year - a year of prayer and discernment. It would be a year of spiritual direction, music, fun, laughter and tears as God drew me closer and closer to Him, and I grew closer and closer to God. As I bade farewell on Easter Sunday to all my new friends, I went home to Tyrrellspass to Mammy and Daddy. They could see the change in my countenance. I shared with them my whole weekend and asked them if they were happy for me. We gave each other hugs and I knew I was home, safe and surrounded by love.

The Summer of '82 was going to be the summer of all summers. When I returned to DOD on the Tuesday after

Easter, I approached my boss in my section and informed her of my decision. She was 100% behind me and put me in the right direction straight away regarding who to write to and contact. I met the Welfare Officer and she outlined what would happen and the procedure to follow. Everything was falling into place so conveniently and I was so happy. I had a lot of annual leave saved up and would have to use it up before I left the civil service in September. Meanwhile, many of us who had been on the Rome trip were now signed up to travel to Edinburgh on 31st May for the Papal Visit to UK and the Mass at the Murryfield Rugby Stadium. Oliver, my friend who had moved to Sligo, was coming and he phoned me at work to hear the final details. He asked me if there was any other news. "Yes," I said, "a bit." "What?" he said. "I'm leaving the civil service to go study to become a priest." "So am I," he said. "And you never told me?" I said. "You never told me either!" he said. We both laughed our heads off. But I wondered if Oliver heard the same voice and words as I did. "Oliver, you know you could be up there doing what that priest is doing." Or did he see himself giving Holy Communion to himself dressed as a priest? In time Oliver would share with me what he has been going through over the last 18 months as, indeed, I would with him.

Meanwhile word spread like wildfire about Ray Kelly going off to study to become a priest, and the parties started. Between the parties there was our trip to Edinburgh to celebrate Mass with Pope John Paul. As the disciples of Jesus said on Mount Tabor, "It is wonderful for us to be here," and indeed it was. Our weekend was full of fun, laughter and the Mass was beautiful; it was nothing like our personal encounter with Pope John Paul while in Rome, nevertheless still beautiful. My mother, sister Regina and I spent five days at Our Lady's Shrine at Lourdes during that summer too. I found it a calming few days to be there with two of the most important people in my life, and while I didn't know it at the time, they were struggling hard with my decision. My friend Michael Holly was coming up to stay with me for a few days because we were going to Torremolinos for two weeks. Needless to say there was a party at my house after all, loads of Michael's friends wanted to meet him and socialize with him.

On the day before we departed, I decided we should go to a fortune-teller. However, Michael changed his mind and I went in alone. I held out my hands and said nothing. She looked into my hands and then my eyes and said, "You were in Lourdes recently. Your eyes are full of kindness and goodness. Did you ever think of becoming a priest?" I smiled. "Don't worry there is a buyer out there for your house, it won't take long and everything will work out for you." There were few other things that were off the mark, but still I was gobsmacked. It was my first and last time ever to go to a fortuneteller.

Michael and I had a great holiday, and we worked on the tan for the two weeks. When I got home I got my house valued to get an idea of what to ask for. I advertised it for three evenings on the Evening Press on Monday, Tuesday and Wednesday. There was no auctioneer involved. There were several viewings and by Friday evening I had secured £1,000 deposit and slept with the money under my pillow for three nights. A local man at home in Tyrrellspass bought my car. I was ready to go. On the 5th September 1982 I retired from my good pensionable job in the civil service with the

Department of Defence after almost 11 years. All had been done. I was ready to go. There was about two weeks of parties and goodbyes, but Tuesday 21st of September was coming and I would be there.

CHAPTER 7

....

Spiritual Year

Even having decided to make such a huge change in my life, the decision was not without its doubts. Sure everything fell into place as regards my leaving of the civil service, or to quote my mother "leaving your good pensionable job", selling my house and car. Nevertheless the closer I got to D-day those negative feelings gathered like a ton of bricks. The week coming up to the 21st September, I kept as busy as possible. I visited all my aunts and uncles, my neighbours at home in Tyrrellspass, and especially my brother and sisters and their children. I was always very close to all my 15 nieces and nephews and made sure I was always part of their lives. In fact, saying goodbye to them was probably the hardest of all. There were still a few local parties at home too in the local pubs of Charlie Dillon's, Gonoud's and Mossy Fagan's.

The morning of Tuesday 21st came and my stomach was in knots. My mother cooked me a big Irish breakfast and, while it looked lovely, all I could do was pick at it. I think my mother and father were feeling uneasy too but not showing it. The car was packed with all my bags and my new bicycle. I had to bring bed clothes and a duvet as well. My brother-in-law Seamus drove the car and as we drove out the avenue of our house, I just looked back and thought I may not see the old home place for almost three months. This would be the longest period I had ever been away from home. The drive to

Kiltegan would take about two hours and Mammy was full of talk and questions. My father did most of the chatting to her. I only heard her voice in the distance. My head was full of doubts. What was I doing? Am I crazy at 29 years of age to be doing this? What brought me to this? Why was I putting such pressure on myself? I was driving into the unknown. What came over me to punish myself like this? Is it any wonder there was a lump in my stomach?

As we drove over the cattle grid at the entrance to the college, the rattle of the tyres against the loose grid took me out of my questioning and feeling sorry for myself. Then the feeling I had when I crossed that grid last April came back to me as I saw the beauty of the place that would be my home for the next nine months. Calmness and peace of mind hit me and excitement filled my being. The first building we came to was the Spiritual Year area which would be my home for nine months. I slowed up and was directed by some of the students to park nearby. We got out of the car and after initial introductions we were directed into a dining room for tea and refreshments. I was gradually introduced to many of the new students like myself. I met Fr Sean Barry who would be my Spiritual Director for the year and Fr Micheal Noone who would be our Dean. Then Fr Sean Deegan came over to us. Fr Sean was from Clonfad, Tyrrellspass about two miles down the road from our home. In fact, my mother always boasted that she brought Sean into the world all those years ago. Following a tour of the college and getting my bedroom for the first time, we got help to carry in all my luggage and Mammy started to make up the bed for me. I knew she wanted to, so I let Mammy be Mammy for me. It was soon time for my parents to leave; few words were said except, "Ring me tomorrow and don't forget to write every day". We hugged as the tears flowed. In those tears I understood for the first time that this was not all about me. I never questioned the effect of my changed lifestyle on my parents. However, even if I did all I would get is, "If this is what you want, whatever makes you happy Ray". I also knew that whatever age I was, 29, 19, nine or even nine months, they are my parents and would always worry and fret over me. I am pausing now for a while because the memory of that time is taking me back almost 37 years ago and the tears that were flowing then are flowing once again. Tears of love, tears of letting go, but now most of all they are my tears of grief.

I had never lived in a community setting like this before. I knew it would take a bit of getting used to. Having been so independent away from home for so many years, I was now entering the world of religious community life. The first two weeks were really a getting to know each other time. Some of the guys had come straight out of secondary school, others had just finished their degree at third level and the rest of us were previously employed. Since I had more than 11 years of employment behind me, I was the "daddy" of the group being the oldest at 29. The youngest of our group had just turned 18. The first real pull at my heart strings for home came five days after I arrived. My mother had phoned to pass on the message that my sister had a baby boy. I knew Rose was about to deliver before I began my life in Kiltegan. When I got word indirectly I just felt so lonely. I have always been close by when all my nieces and nephews were born, and within a day or two I would have met my new niece or nephew. Now my newest nephew, Jude Coyle, was born and I wouldn't get to meet him until Christmas.

At Kiltegan certain parts of the day were structured. So there was early morning bell at 7.00am, morning prayer at 7.30am, followed by a half hour of meditation and morning mass. Breakfast was set for 8.30am and then a half hour of indoor manual work. This consisted of being assigned cleaning of a certain area of our living quarters. By 10.00am our lectures or class time began up to 12.45pm, where we would break for mid-day prayer and lunch at 1.00pm. The afternoon was less structured depending on the day. It could consist of outdoor cleaning of the grounds or a sports activity like football with a team from the senior students. I had always liked to keep the weight down with a bit of jogging and there were plenty of runs available all around the side roads surrounding the college. There was a lovely tennis court on the grounds as well, so I soon took to a game of tennis also. Even though as Spiritual Year students we were not facing into any exams, nevertheless it was always recommended that we get into the routine of studying for future years of preparation. We were advised also to take on a bit of spiritual reading from books recommended by Fr Sean, our Spiritual Director.

About three weeks into my seminary life, Fr Sean informed me that I had an appointment in Dublin with my solicitor regarding the closing of the sale of my house. I was really looking forward to my day in Dublin. Imagine having lived there for nearly 11 years and here I was now looking forward to my day trip. I travelled up by bus to Dublin and arranged to meet my parents. I did all the legal stuff with the solicitor and then I had a few hours with Mammy and Daddy before I caught the six o'clock bus back to Kiltegan. It was lovely just to have the few hours with them and share the experience so far.

The next day was Saturday and the day designated to the Colonel. Yes, Colonel Con O'Sullivan, a retired army colonel was our communications, speech and drama teacher. Con was a big man, a larger than life character, with a very posh almost British accent even though he lived in Newbridge, Co. Kildare. Con was unique. I loved the man; he taught me so much over the years in Kiltegan and gave me a lot of confidence when I needed it. I can still see that big broad smile with a glass of whiskey in one hand and a cigar as thick as his wrist in the other. He would spend the morning with us spiritual students and then the afternoons with the senior students. I remember, on one of his first Saturdays with us he put on a CD of Strauss waltzes and encouraged us to waltz around the room either with each other or by ourselves. Most of us did it by ourselves, however, there were a few macho guys who rebelled. The rebellion only lasted for about two Saturdays before they joined in. Of course his idea was to encourage us to get over any inhibitions we might have. He would invite us to speak for five minutes on a chosen topic as well. He always finished up the sessions with a bit of meditation. As soft background music played, he would gently tell us to close our eyes and get in touch with our breathing. The more relaxed we were the better, indeed a few snores were often heard too. He encouraged us too that every morning we got out of bed to take a good look at ourselves in the mirror and say to yourself, "I am beautiful". I am not sure how many of us believed that at seven o'clock in the morning. He informed us that after Halloween we would be rehearsing for our musical *The King and I*, and he would be holding auditions very soon.

As we were first year students it was always tradition that we dine at all meals in our own separate dining room in the "Middle House". The Middle House was the original home of John Hughes in High Park and the building housed the priests who were on the council in charge of the society. However, as it was being redecorated we joined the senior students at mealtime. So in a sense, we got to know them pretty well over the months. There always seemed to be a bit of rivalry between us first years and the senior boys. And I think that rivalry was heightened more because many of us first years were more mature students and similar in age to the senior guys. The rivalry was always on display on the football field. There were times as well when we would try to take the piss out of each other as well.

An occasion like that arose at the dining table one evening. There were a group of six of us at the table. James, a Scottish student, was complaining of a pain in his back. John Trout, my class mate, was sitting beside me and he suggested to James to get a bit of acupuncture. James thought that was a great idea. John went on to say, "Why don't you get Ray Kelly to do it for you, he's a qualified acupuncturist". I nearly choked on my food when I heard that, but I knew what Trout was at. James looked at me and said, "Can you do acupuncture Ray?" "Sure," I said, "Last year my brother had a lot of back pain like you and after a few sessions he was better; my father too had a problem with his shoulder and it worked for him." "That's great Ray, would you try it on my back?" he asked. "Yes, I will," I said, "the only thing is I haven't my needles with me, but it's equally effective with sewing needles." At this stage I could see Trout's face and he was ready to explode. However, I kept quite calm. So I arranged with James to call down to our quarters, "Proboland" as we called it because we were probationers, on Sunday about three o'clock.

Sunday came and about 3.30 James arrived to us in Proboland. All our guys were on alert for what was about to happen. I brought James up to my bedroom and got him to lie on my bed on his stomach. He pulled up his shirt and I gently tapped his lower back where he said the pain was. I explained I was going to put some iodine on the spot to sterilise it. In the meantime, I had asked Ray Milton, another class mate, to place four sewing needles on a saucer with water as if they were just sterilised. Ray arrived at my room and I asked James to stay very still and that he would feel four prods. I gave James four prods of one of the needles then gave them back to Ray. "James, please stay very quiet now for about 20 minutes and I'll be back to you to take out the needles". Well during that 20 minutes I can tell you all my classmates were coming up in their droves to take photos of James lying on my bed. Of course, he couldn't see his back so he didn't realise there were no needles sticking out of his back at all only a big blob of iodine there. After the 20 minute were up I returned to my room with the four needles on the saucer and asked James not to move as I removed the needles. I gave him four little prods again and said, "There ye go James all done, how do you feel?" James got up off my bed, straightened himself up, rubbed his back and said in his most distinctive Scottish accent, "God,

Ray, ye know I think I feel a big improvement already, thank you, thank you." I promised to give him another session the following week, knowing too well it was never going to happen. Well as word got out that Kelly, Trout, Milton and the rest of the 'Proboland' boys had pulled the wool over James and the senior boys, they were not happy. One nil to the boys from Proboland. Of course I knew there would be payback in some form or another, so I was always on the alert.

There were many other pranks carried out on some of the classmates as well. I wasn't always the culprit. Let's just say I may have assisted in some of the procedures. Like attaching a walkie-talkie under someone's bed and they waking up to hearing weird voices during the night. Or when we felt our senior student John O'Sullivan was getting a bit bossy or out of hand and we decided to unscrew his bedroom door so when he opened it the door just fell in front of him. It wasn't necessary to say or do anything more, the message was received loud and clear.

Our daily two and a half hour lectures were very easy to stay with. Most of them were introductory lectures in the subjects we would be studying for the following five or six years. Therefore, I was introduced to courses in fundamental theology, scripture, moral theology and a taste of canon law. Occasionally, some mornings after Mass we were informed we would have no lectures and we were taken on a day trip. I have to say I felt like a child off on a day trip to Glendalough, or maybe the Japanese Gardens or the National Stud in Kildare. They were always fun trips which helped us bond together as a group.

Sunday night was always the entertainment night, and since we had not any access to TV we had to make our own entertainment. I was on the entertainment committee with three other guys, so every Sunday night we had to come up with a two hour entertainment programme. It might be charades, or a card game, or putting two or three teams together to create their own five minute sketch; then the entertainment committee would decide on a winner. There were music nights too, and it was soon discovered that we were a pretty talented bunch. There were at least four guitarists, a few pianists and plenty of pretty good singers too, so our Mass liturgies were always full of music, and we were always learning new hymns. I was in my element when getting together to sing or perform.

As I mentioned I have always been left-handed and indeed left-footed. I remember one priest approached me having observed me genuflecting with my left knee before the Blessed Sacrament in the chapel. He suggested to me that I try changing the genuflecting to using my right knee. When I asked him why he said sometimes doing things with your left hand or left leg/foot can be seen as alien or even evil in some African cultures. When I investigated it further I read about a French sociologist Robert Hertz who wrote that in his travels to southern Africa, the Zulu tribes would pour boiling water into a hole, then place a child's left hand into it, scalding the hand and preventing its use. Of course I have no problem conforming or trying new techniques or ideas. So for about a month I would enter the chapel and as I genuflected on my right knee I was holding on to the seats each side of me. I felt like a geriatric. It worked and didn't take too long. Now of course I can alternate. However, there was never hope in hell of me trying to write with my right hand.

On the first Saturday after Halloween, the Colonel arrived as usual and began auditions for parts for the musical *The King and I.* The show tells the story of a widowed Welsh mother, Anna Leonowens, who takes up a position as a governess and English tutor to the wives and many children of the stubborn King Mongkut of Siam. Anna and the king have a clash of personalities as she works to teach the royal family about the English language, customs, and etiquette and then rushes to prepare a party for a group of European diplomats who must change their opinions about the king. Despite the many female roles in the musical, the entire main cast would comprise of all of us males - yes, all 18 of us "Proboland boys" would have to take part. The children for the March of the Siamese Children would come from the local primary school. Con knew who the good voices were in our group. He encouraged us to audition for all the singing parts. I remember auditioning for the part of the governess Anna. At this time, I was singing in my falsetto voice. Indeed, I thought that type of voice would be more suitable for a female role in the show. Con didn't like it or want it. "No Ray, no we have to bring out your tenor voice." I genuinely didn't think I had a tenor voice. During the following few days I know I developed a sore throat and laryngitis. I was in bed for almost a week with it and genuinely could not speak. I was dosing myself with plenty of hot drinks. It took about two weeks before my speaking voice came back fully. When I started to sing again, amazingly it was my tenor voice that I heard. The colonel had got his tenor voice and I got the part of the King's first wife, Lady Thiang. John Daly got the part of Anna the governess. Many of the songs are so catchy and well known: "Shall we Dance",

"We Kissed in a Shadow", "Hello Young Lovers". "I Whistle a Happy Tune" and "Getting to Know You". My big song was "Something Wonderful" where I sang about the King. The first few weeks of rehearsals right up to our pre-Christmas retreat were concentrating on the music. I loved it. Once we started rehearsing the music I knew it was where I wanted to be. As we rehearsed the songs we, particularly the soloists, were gaining more and more confidence with our singing and harmonies, and roll on the new year when we would start adding choreography and movements to our singing.

Meanwhile, our five-day silent retreat was about to begin in preparation for Christmas and the celebration of the birth of Jesus Christ. The silence was not alien to me. I would have had a number of one-day silent reflection days. Indeed, every evening after night prayer from ten o'clock all of us were encouraged to keep silent until the next morning. Now a five-day silence was something new, but then it was seen as a preparation for our 30-day retreat which would begin on Tuesday 8th March 1983. My retreat was beautiful. In a sense it brought me back down to earth and it took about two days to leave *The King and I* music in the background. I knew I was in the zone of prayer and with Fr Sean's spiritual direction and scripture passages to meditate on I found real peace. The long term silence took a little longer to accept particularly if I was making a cup of coffee and enjoying it in our common room as other guys did the same. We would eye each other and smile, but generally we learned to respect each other's space and silence. I usually disciplined myself with daily routine. After morning prayers and breakfast I would take in a long one hour walk.

The winter had definitely begun as snow fell heavily in Kiltegan. When it snows in Wicklow, we were almost assured of having it as we were surrounded by the mountains. There is nothing more beautiful than walking in the snow. The beauty of the whiteness all around me with the sound of my feet crunching on the packed snow was relaxing and prayerful. After mid-day prayer and lunch we were always encouraged to switch off and even have a siesta - something which I didn't really need encouragement to do. Before supper time I often liked to get a jog in. During our retreat, daily Mass was held most of the time in the evening and as always it was a beautiful prayerful moment.

The retreat ended on Tuesday morning 21st December and I would be going home on Thursday. I wasn't sure yet if Mammy and Daddy were driving up for me as the snow had continued and the roads were very dangerous. However, by the next day, the decision was made that I would get a bus to Dublin and get the train to Mullingar. Mum and Dad met me at the 3.15 arrival, and once the hugs were exchanged I knew I was home.

When we got to the house in Tyrrellspass all my family was there to meet me. I couldn't believe how some of my nieces and nephews had grown. Then I was introduced to the newest member of the family, my nephew Jude. It was so good to be home; my heart was leaping out of my chest with excitement. Every year on TV, I had watched with emotion and joy so many young people arriving home for Christmas from foreign lands and being met at the airport by their parents and family. Now I knew exactly what that felt like. When I joined Kiltegan in September I wasn't sure if I would get home for Christmas, but I guess I was prepared to make that sacrifice; now I was so glad I didn't have to. In fact, as I learned, our group was only the second year that the Spiritual Year students got home for Christmas.

The next morning at home was Christmas Eve and I had no Christmas shopping done. It was another first for me because when I was working in Dublin I would be Christmas shopping over a period of a month. So I asked Mammy for her car to head to Tullamore for a few hours. Here I was, another first for me having to ask my mother for her car. After a few hours around the shops I had more or less everything I wanted. The fastest Christmas shopping I had ever done was complete.

My Christmas day was not any different to any other. I didn't want it to be. After morning Mass there was a visit to my Aunt Kitty and Uncle Ger. Since my granny died over two years ago they were now on their own in the Gavigan house on the green. There was the exchanging of presents, the customary cup of tea and Kitty's homemade Christmas cake followed by a shot of Jameson whiskey. Since my granny had died, Kitty and Ger travelled to Edenderry for their Christmas dinner with Aunt Angie and her family. After the dinner there they would enjoy a game of poker and the poker would continue in their home on St Stephen's night where I would be joining them. My Christmas day was lovely; many of the grandchildren joined us during the day carrying with them some of their Santa Claus presents. Then there was the exchange of our presents. Somehow in my heart I felt the day was more special than previous years, and perhaps it was as they say that my absence from them for a few months made my heart fonder.

As I only had nine days at home before I returned to Kiltegan on January 2nd, I wanted to spend as much time as was possible at home with my parents and family. I still had a fair bit of visiting to get in. And of course I had to share my new life with so many as well. Many were intrigued by my new lifestyle. Indeed, I could almost read their faces with unasked questions like, "How can you adjust or stick to a lifestyle like that?", or statements like, "You must be mad to change your life like that". Of course I had asked myself that many times too, but somehow I was being driven by a power that I could not say no too. Mammy and Daddy drove me back to Kiltegan on Sunday afternoon 2nd January. Some of the boys had arrived before me and I could now introduce many of them to my parents and vice versa. When my parents left for home we caught up on sharing our Christmas experiences. I was happy to be back with my new-found family. It was good for me to be here. The time table was up on the noticeboard for Monday - a free day. So having an easy Monday many of us headed for Juniors the local pub about two miles away. The pints flowed, the guitars were out, the music started. It was indeed a happy New Year.

We were all back and there were no drop-outs. There is always that fear, you know? It has happened many times in the past during Spiritual Year and would happen again. A student might just have decided after three months that this life was not for him and would not be returning. Indeed, it is perfectly understandable that having tried the spiritual life for three months he was able to discern he had enough. But not the class of '82. The first few days were easing us back into routine again particularly with prayer times. Of course our spiritual director would request an individual visit from each of us too to see how our holiday went at home.

The Colonel would be arriving on Saturday for rehearsals for *The King and I*, and to give us a timetable of rehearsing and of course the all-important date of the staging of our musical. I was anxious to know the date as I could invite some family and friends to the show. The Colonel arrived on the Saturday and announced that the show would be performed on the 19th February 1983. We had six weeks to get our show on stage. It was full steam ahead. Needless to say we were a fair bit rusty with ours vocals and movement after our Christmas break. Our classroom was turned into a marked out stage for rehearsing with the floor being taped out to more or less the size of the stage. This was necessary, especially for choreography as our choreographer was now on board as well. We used tables, chairs, stools, anything convenient as temporary props. One of our class would also act as a stage manager and have one or two small parts in the musical. The set for the show would be designed around the palace of the King of Siam with various changes for the different scenes. Some of the theology students in the senior house, where the show would be staged in the main hall, were brought on board for the painting and decorating of the set. We were back in our own dining room now at the middle house, so we were mixing less with the senior boys, nevertheless we were up and down to see how things were progressing on stage.

No matter how well I knew the music and indeed many of the movements, still putting it all together created a whole new challenge - a challenge which I loved. I can still hear Con the Colonel speak sometimes with a cigar in his mouth,

"Remember boys on stage many of you are ladies, so small steps please. Forget you are men when you are up there, get into the image, boys, image, all the king's wives and children take small steps. It is part of their culture, so small steps boys, small steps please." As we got closer and closer to D-day the pressure was on. There were many pep talks to make sure the lines were known, the harmonies and songs perfected. There was the fitting for the costumes. We did have a costume room in the college which catered for most shows. However, with such a big production we had to borrow costumes from Carlow college. Pat McCallion, one of my class-mates, was in charge of costumes and sewing where necessary. Mind you, I was asked to help out in this area since it was known I was handy with sewing needles, however I declined.

The last week coming up to Saturday night was frantic. It was hands on for all of us. I was going to bed "Whistling a Happy Tune" and waking up with "Shall We Dance". I was completely taken over by it all and loved it. I was tired but I didn't know it. The dress rehearsal was on Friday night and all our costumes and wigs were ready and our makeup team was on board. The sound and microphones were superb. We would have a full house of an invited audience at the rehearsal with some of the residents from nursing homes nearby, as well as many local people from around the village of Kiltegan. A few teething problems showed up at the dress rehearsal. Nothing major and mostly out of the cast's control like lighting and special effects. I don't think the audience was aware of it as most of their focus was on seeing how well the class of '82 compared to other shows from previous years that they had attended.

Saturday arrived. It was show time. The buzz around the college was electrifying as the last bits and pieces on stage were set and a final dress-rehearsal without an audience was carried out. By six the makeup room was buzzing as the entire cast got their time for makeup. Our families were arriving and being entertained in the main dining room. I got a chance to greet my parents and sister very briefly when they arrived, but there was no time for chat as the show must go on. And it did. The curtain went up, the overture of *The King and I* started; there was no going back. Here I was fulfilling a long-time dream - my first ever musical theatre performance. I had to join a seminary to do it and I was playing the part of one of the leading ladies. God was definitely testing me and having a right good laugh.

CHAPTER 8

Philosophy & Cork

The Rochestown Park Hotel is situated in a busy suburban village of Douglas about four kilometres from Cork City University and the city itself. It was formerly one of Ireland's most important historical houses. Before being sold by the Kiltegan Fathers as a hotel in the mid-1980s, it was the accommodation college and formation house of their student priests who were attending University College Cork (UCC). It was here I would attend and begin my Philosophy studies for the next two years in preparation for priesthood. As I was quite a mature student like many others of my class of '82, we didn't have to attend UCC rather we attended lectures in the college itself. It was a very cold building in need of a lot of restoration. Its setting, just outside Douglas village, was beautiful. The towering evergreen trees as you entered the grounds created a beautiful calmness and relaxing atmosphere.

While I looked forward to my new surroundings in Douglas, I was also hugely apprehensive. The cause of this apprehension was mainly my fear of getting back into the routine of serious study again. I questioned myself and my ability again and again. However, I need not have worried. I was assured that all the help I needed would be provided to help me succeed. So once I set my own standard, was able to maintain that standard and hopefully improve on it, then all would be fine. Since our lectures and exams would be held in the college there was really no major pressure. But I still knew I would have to put the work in. The Spiritual Year had introduced me to study again after a 12-year gap since my Leaving Certificate.

I loved the idea of being in Cork for the next two years, mainly because it was a city I was very familiar with having worked at Collins Barracks at the top of Patrick's Hill for a few weeks every year during my years with the Department of Defence. Mary and Kate O'Gorman, my two very good friends, lived close by the barracks so I looked forward to visiting them and vice versa. So mid-September of 1983 came and my parents decided to drive me to Douglas in Cork. While I suggested that I would travel by train, my mother insisted she was going to see where her son was holding up for the next two years. I wasn't going to argue with that – in fact I was very glad. I was able to bring my bicycle also which was my only means of transport around the city. Indeed, the last time I travelled around the city I had my car; now I was on two wheels. There were 21 students residing at the college, and some were on a three-year degree course at University College Cork. The rest of us were having our lectures in the house with visiting lecturers as well as lectures from our Rector Fr Seamus O'Neill, our Dean of Studies Fr Denis O'Rourke and our Spiritual Director Fr Micky Murphy.

The first week was taken up with settling into our new surroundings as well as spending the first couple of days picking spuds. Oh yes, picking potatoes. Residing at the gate lodge on entering the college was Eugene O'Sullivan and his wife. Eugene was the caretaker to the college, but he also had a few acres of potatoes in the fields in front of the college and since September was the time to get the potatoes off the ground what better way to do that than to have all hands on board? The odd potato went flying through the air too, and often got Mr Eugene on the head at which he would issue a choice litany of curses.

After settling into the college and the spud picking, there were a few days assigned to a silent retreat and a chance to catch up on some sleep and rest. As soon as our lectures began, daily routine set in very quickly. Morning prayer, Mass, a half hour of house cleaning and then into lectures for a few hours up to lunchtime. The afternoon was given over to an hour of outdoor manual work, maybe a football game or a bit of jogging. And after evening prayer and supper it was expected of us to spend a few hours in study.

Each of us took on some form of social work as well. I know for my two years in Cork I would visit The Lough. In The Lough was an active retirement centre where senior citizens would gather a couple of times a week and socialize. I loved my visits there getting to know many of the older folk, meeting them on a weekly basis, hearing their stories and vice versa. They took a great interest in my life as a student and always assured me of their prayers. And you know I always felt that was important to me knowing that because there were many times, particularly during my time in Cork, that I questioned my ability to continue in studying for priesthood. Not because of the studies and exams, which I was doing fine at, but just the whole idea of being a priest at all. I think I missed my family most of all. There had been so many years of routine of being home every weekend, visiting of my brother and sisters and their families. So it was understandable I felt I was missing out. Sure I would catch up at Christmas and Easter and summer holidays, nevertheless the ache was there and I could not deny it. The letters and phone calls to and from home always kept me in touch with my family. Of course one of my mother's great worries was if I was getting enough to eat. Indeed, I was and if I wasn't there was always a take-away in Douglas village. We called our cook in the college Mrs W. She was an elderly lady and assisted by an even more elderly one called Mary. They resided at the college and had done so for many years. Our dinners and suppers were always placed in a hot stainless steel oven and I remember one day finding more than food in the oven. It seemed as though a pair of women's tights were drying in there as well. It was a Friday and fish was on the dinner menu. So some of the smart boys exaggerated the situation and said they were "fishnets". How appropriate. Saturday nights sometimes involved sneaking out to the pub in Douglas village, staggering home after midnight.

It was also part of our year in Cork that we would pick a play to stage and perform for a weekend before we would break up for Christmas 1983. I was always in my element when it came to anything to do with the stage. "Brr…" was the official name of our little theatre on the grounds of the college. It was nothing more than a shed really with a stage and seating for about 100 people. And the title really summed up what the place was – freezing! Of course having donned the skirt as Lady Thiang in *The King and I* ten months before, it was inevitable that was going to happen again and it did in the comedy *Don't Bother to Unpack*. However, the following year I took on a new role as producer in another comedy *A*

Problem Solved. Our friends, along with many of the local people always came to our plays.

There were many other distractions too from our studies like our sports days where we formed three or four teams and competed against each other in events like high jump, long jump, speed cycling, penalty shooting, cross country running and road races, volley ball, tennis and tug-o-war. As many of us were musical, there was always the odd singsong taking place. Indeed, often while passing along the corridor, I would hear guitar strumming coming from Eric or Michael's room; I would tap on the door and a session would start up until we were told to keep it down as some guys were trying to study. I remember one Saturday morning Michael O'Connor was supposed to be dusting and cleaning the lecture room. However, at the back of the room was a beautiful grand piano, of course Michael could not resist. As I walked into the room Michael was starting to play the cords of "New York, New York". "Do you know this one Ray?" he asked. "Sure," I replied and started singing the song. It got better and better after that as he played and I raised the roof. Little did I know that was the first of many times I would perform that song, even to this very day. So Michael, thank you.

In February of each year I looked forward to a weekend in Kiltegan for the annual Spiritual Year Musical. It was always lovely to be mingling with the senior theology students again. Sometime there would be one or two of the guys that would have left the college permanently having decided that further studies for priesthood were not for them. It always created a huge sense of sadness when that happened, even though I believe it took a fair bit of courage and discernment on behalf of the guys to come to that decision. The Spiritual Year guys however, were all psyched-up in preparation for their big show with the Colonel Con O'Sullivan. As we were the previous year Spiritual students it was important to chat them and encourage them as they journeyed through the year.

The week after our trip to Kiltegan I was paying a surprise visit home to Tyrrellspass. The occasion was my mother's retirement party after 40 years of dedicated service as the midwife for Tyrrellspass and surrounding district. The party was being held in one of the local pubs in the village called Gonoud's. In fact the mother of the owner of the pub was a first-cousin of my mother and indeed it was a fitting place to have the celebration. Once I was assured that everyone had arrived for the party, I walked into the venue to the surprise of everyone there except my brother and sisters. There was loud applause and hugs as I greeted Mammy and Daddy and circled the room greeting everyone else especially all my nieces and nephews. It was so good and special to be there.

One of the principal guests was Fr Sean Deegan, St Patrick's Kiltegan, who freely admitted that my mother was, "The first woman and the first face I ever saw since she played a big part in bringing me into the world". Indeed, Sean would be lecturing me in Scripture in about 18 months time when I returned to Kiltegan to continue my studies for priesthood. Fr Sean also pointed out that Mona not only administered in Tyrrellspass but that her area also included Kilbeggan, Milltownpass, Dalystown, Croghan and so on and every place in between as well. "Her duty involved tremendous hard work as she was often called upon to attend in two or three places in the one night," said Fr Deegan. "Her work progressed throughout the 40s, the 50s and the 60s with her transport initially being a bike, then a scooter and eventually a car." He concluded by praising her for the enthusiasm and energy she put into her work, and for all the joy she helped to bring into the world. He also mentioned her husband, my dad Joe, who he recalled was the first person he had a business transaction with when he sold a sheep to him for £3.00. This was indeed a night for both Mr and Mrs Kelly he said.

A number of presentations were made to my mother during the night; the first being made by Ena Gill, the last child delivered by my mother. Also a presentation was made from the very first child she delivered who was now a grown man, Seamus Eighan. Another presentation was made by Alice Gillespie, who explained that it was "On behalf of all the women who kept Mrs Kelly busy!" Family photos were taken on the night especially with her children and her four sisters. After loads of thank-yous from Mona and Joe, the music started with the Kellys supplying plenty of it including Mona and Joe who were no strangers to the microphone.

I was so thrilled to be part of this celebration of my mother. I know as children growing up we often did not get the chance to say thank you, but that celebration on Saturday night 11th February 1994 said it all from all of us. After 40 years of dedicated service and delivering over 1,000 babies into homes, Mona could relax a little bit. But I knew in my heart that she would never really let go and indeed she would not be allowed by many of her previous expectant mothers. I know for years to come after that retirement party some of those expectant mothers again would call to her for a brief external examination just to be assured that all was ok in their pregnancy. Mona was always happy to oblige. I returned to Cork on the train the following evening, full of joy, love, memories and thankfulness for what I had experienced.

I got through my first year in Cork with no major issues. I was assured by the team of priests in our care that I was doing ok and on the right track. I know I didn't get all A+'s in my exams, but I was assured I did ok with C's and B's. I was welcomed back for a second year in Cork, which I was happy about. I always said I would take it one year at a time and if, following a lot of prayer and discernment, I was still happy with my progress then I would stick at it.

Many of the students would get summer work to keep them in pocket money throughout the year. I was fortunate that I had enough money from the sale of my house in Cabra to keep me going throughout the year. However, I always loved to travel. So before we broke up for our first three-month summer break I, along with Michael O'Connor from Portrush, Co. Antrim and Gerry McDonnell from Belfast, decided to try out the experience of working in a kibbutz in Israel. Sean Mac Suibhne, another student at our college, had tried it a few years before and assured us it was a great and cheap way to see The Holy Land.

Kibbutz volunteers are people who come from all over the world to live and work in the kibbutz community contributing to the running of the kibbutz. In return, their basic living necessities such as food and accommodation are provided free. One also gets a very small minimum wage, pocket money really, at the end of each month. If people from the kibbutz have jobs in the city, then they are meant to submit their wages to the community. So we applied through an agency in Ireland to spend six-weeks over the summer in Israel. Our applications were accepted and we flew into Tel-Aviv where we were met by a representative from the kibbutz beside a town called Migdal Immac located about 5km from Nazareth. At this kibbutz there were many students from other countries: Germans, Dutch, Greeks, many British and a few Irish. In our particular kibbutz there was a swimming pool, a gym, some tennis courts and most important of all a pub. The highlight of the entertainment offered by the kibbutz was the volunteer disco held every Friday night. I have to say it was one of the best experiences of my life. It gave me a lot of confidence in myself and I had the opportunity to meet some fantastic travellers from around the world.

My work included mainly working in the dining room, cleaning tables and emptying the dish-washer, where aside from taking out the dishes after washing I would often have to remove some giant cockroaches that got scalded in the machine. Sometimes, I was assigned to help out in the garden though I often stayed clear of that because of the heat. I liked the copper-wire factory too as the work began at 6.30am and finished by 11.45am. I remember the worst job that I was assigned to, that lasted only about one hour, was to turn up to a giant shed as big as a football field full of thousands of white feathered chickens. It was night work from midnight and I was dreading it. I was supposed to catch seven chickens in each hand by the legs and put them into a cage to be taken away for food. As my hand could barely hold one, the supervisor said to me, "No, no, no, the count will be wrong, you cannot do that, you must catch seven in each hand". At that stage the smell was getting to me and I was very close to vomiting. I told him as politely as I could where to go and walked out. I arrived back at my cabin to my two friends Gerry and Michael still drinking beer and related my story. They fell around the place laughing. I was back on dishwasher duties the next day. Of course as a volunteer kibbutz life was not all work. There were lots of parties and trips around Israel. One such trip was on the back of a lorry to the Mediterranean Sea shore of Rosh Hanikra beach on the border of Lebanon. After about a month in the kibbutz we decided to travel a bit around the country and see all the holy sites, sleeping in hostels and the cheapest accommodation we could find. There were a few days in Tiberrias by the Sea of Galilee and an overnight stay in sleeping bags on top of Masada in the sweltering heat of the Negev desert. In 73AD this 20-acre plateau was the scene of one of the most remarkable and tragic stands for independence made by the Jews against the Romans. Needless to say the highlight of our trip was a week-long tour of Jerusalem. We stayed in Maison D'Abraham, an incredible, low-priced, tree surrounded hotel - like a boarding house for Christian Pilgrims.

My second year in Cork was very similar to the first. In September of 1985 I was back in Kiltegan in the senior house for Theology studies. Of course as I said already, every year has its casualties and two of my very good friends, Kevin and Gerry, were not continuing. But we always kept in touch. Gerry, unfortunately passed away a few years ago at just over 50 years of age. May he rest in peace.

CHAPTER 9

....

Theology in Kiltegan

In September 1985, I returned to Kiltegan, Co. Wicklow for the beginning of my theology studies – so far so good. I was about to begin my fourth year of studies for priesthood and I was still enthused by my vocation and loving my time of preparation. Of course there was a lot of questioning by myself and by my family as well; they wanted to be sure that I was happy with what I was doing. My mother and father knew I was in a good place and they were happy that I was happy. Over the previous three years I had grown very fond of community living. I loved the camaraderie with the other students, my friends. I loved the interaction with the other priests in the college. Aside from the college staff and lecturers, there were many priests coming and going from the missions throughout the year, some home on holidays, some home on medical grounds, and it was always so interesting to hear their stories about their life and work in Nigeria, Kenya, Malawi, Zambia, Brazil and Central America where many of the Society priests were working.

Our year always began with a few days of recollection before we began our lectures. Then we were into new subjects like Moral Theology with Fr Vinny McNamara, Scripture with Fr Sean Deegan, Cannon Law with Fr Paddy Gallagher and Fr Tom O'Connor on Fundamental Theology. We had visiting lecturers as well for other subjects. And of course the

Colonel was back. Yes, Con O'Sullivan would be taking up every Saturday morning for speech and homiletics and drama. I liked the fact that we communicated with each other on a first named basis with no titles, which personally I would say helped me in my studies and in communicating on a professional and a friendly basis.

In 1984, Bob Geldof formed the super-group Band Aid. The televisions all over the world played a major role in capturing the poverty affecting Ethiopian Citizens and influenced Bob to take action. The Band Aid group was composed of 40 artists to raise awareness and funds for the famine. The artists recorded a Christmas No. 1, "Do they know it's Christmas", depicting the poverty stricken Africa of that time. However, Bob was not finished. Realising that a lot more was needed to aid famine relief in Ethiopia, he and Midge Ure set about having another music-based fundraising initiative. The Live Aid concert was held simultaneously at Wembley Stadium in London attended by 72,000 people and J.F. Kennedy Stadium in Philadelphia attended by about 100,000 people. And on the same day, concerts inspired by the Geldof/Ure initiative happened in other countries such as the Soviet Union, Canada, Japan, Yugoslavia, Austria, Australia and West Germany.

Meanwhile, soon after I returned to Kiltegan in September 1985, Fr Tom O'Connor approached me and Eric Armour to ask if we would be interested in writing a song for a local lady, Kathleen Cullen, who was taking part in the Dublin City Marathon to raise funds for Youth Aid in Africa. Kathleen had raised over £100,000 the previous year for the Ethiopian famine relief. So she was at it again because 1985 was the

International Youth Year, and Youth Aid was born. Kathleen was hoping to reach the million mark and make sure it went to financing youth education, training and employment schemes in Kenya, Nigeria, Malawi, Zambia and Sudan. All the money raised would be channelled through St Patrick's Missionary Fathers, Kiltegan, who were administrating the project. Kathleen got interested in the idea of educating people in Third World countries after her visit to Ethiopia. On her return she wrote, "We will keep giving, but we have to teach the people to look after themselves. If not, we are going to witness one famine after another." With that in mind Fr Tom came to us students, Eric and myself, and asked if we could write a song in that theme to help Kathleen raise her funds. I remember the excitement of being asked to write a song for such a worthy event. It was also hinted that if the song was good enough there would be a chance of going to a recording studio and recording the song. Wow, I was on high. The thought began to take over every moment of my day. I have to say I thought about the theme of helping people to help themselves for some time, as did Eric. I would be at a lecture and a line might hit me. I would scribble it down and refer to it later. I would be at my daily meditation and a word or a line would take over my mind. I would run out of the oratory and scribble it down on a bit of paper. Even during my daily Mass, something would cross my mind. I'd hold it in my head until Mass was over and then put it on paper. Eventually, I had so many lines and words and started putting them together, and with Eric and his guitar we began to put the lines to a melody. The obvious title "Help Me to Help Myself" came very quickly to me and Eric started putting the music together. We had a song. As word filtered out among students and priests that we had come up with a catchy tune and words, everyone wanted to hear our song. They liked it. Cullen then suggested we would have to record it. However, since CDs and tapes were not very common our only option was to record on a single vinyl record.

But we needed a B-side, and before long we had a song called "On the Wing". I wrote the words and music with a South American/Latin calypso beat and flavour to it. Kathleen set up a date in a recording studio in Slane, Co. Meath. The excitement of going to a recording studio consumed me. I was totally wrapped up in it. I couldn't sleep. I couldn't eat. Here I was about to fulfil a life-long dream of putting my voice down on vinyl, and I had to join the seminary to do it! Was God messing with my head or what? My first musical on stage was *The King and I* while in the seminary and now my first ever chance to record a song while in the seminary. It was like I had given my life to God and now he was giving me back my dreams. Oh boy, oh boy, I loved it.

Of course, if we as clerical students were going to release a single record, we needed to officially form a group and put a title on our group. In hindsight, we already had formed a group of singers and musicians because we performed daily at out liturgies and often as entertainment for visitors to our college. So we had the group and now we needed a name. Hence Rafiki was born. 'Rafiki' is a Swahili word meaning 'friend'. The perfect title since so many of the Society priests worked in Kenya where Swahili is widely spoken. Rafiki consisted of Eric Armour on the guitar, Mick Madigan on the tin whistle and flute, Martin Smith on the vocals and bongos,

Michael O'Connor on the guitar and myself as lead singer. For the recordings at Slane we drafted in Joe McCullagh, Damien McManus and Kieran Flynn. So, long before Take That, or Boyzone, or Westlife or even One Direction, we were up there – Rafiki, a group of clerical students formed in 1885. The songs were recorded and the finished products needed to be ready for the end of October, the Bank Holiday weekend, when Kathleen would take part in the Dublin city marathon. I remember when the record came to the college for the first time. Fr Tom informed us it had arrived and we all gathered for the first listening. Oh, it was magical, I was gobsmacked! Was that really my voice? I couldn't believe it. The harmonies and guitars, bongos and tin whistle all blended beautifully. I felt on high and so proud.

The record was sent to all the local radio stations to promote such a great cause. I did several radio interviews by telephone from the college. Indeed, there was as much interest in the group Rafiki and its formation as there was in the song. The day of the marathon came and some of our students in the college were taking part along with Kathleen. I didn't run but was standing cheering at various locations throughout to race, and all the while the announcers were playing our song "Help Me to Help Myself". I couldn't have been more proud. After the marathon when things settled down, everyone was asking, "What's going to happen to Rafiki now?" I guess many would have expected us to go on and make more records, but we didn't. However, we stayed together as we were still clerical students. We did a few concerts in the college to invited guests and visited some of the local pubs entertaining as well. I know our Rector Fr Paddy Gallagher was worried in case there might be a mad exit of five or six students from the college launching a new career for themselves. It was a new experience for him to deal with so I could understand his anxiety. But he grounded us all fairly easily so as not to get too carried away by it all. Indeed, he need not have worried, as we were all pretty much mature students who had another focus. I never actually found out how well Kathleen did in her fundraising, however, I do know it generated quite a respectable sum for the project. It also focused much further attention on the wonderful work that young people in Ireland were doing for Third World countries.

Once the novelty of Rafiki had passed it was back to the grindstone to study for Christmas exams. I admit concentration was a little difficult because my head was still full of Rafiki and the thrill of recording. The songs would still be requested and sung at concerts in the college and sometimes on a Saturday night at Juniors Pub in Rathdangan about two miles from the college. So the talking of the event and the memory would live on for a long time.

After Christmas I returned to for the usual three-day silent retreat before I was to go on my two-week placement on social work. During the first term I had been assigned to volunteer a few hours every Monday afternoon to Baltinglass geriatric hospital. The hospital itself was located about five miles from the college on the outskirts of the town of Baltinglass. The residents of the hospital were mainly geriatric though some were younger with mental or physical disabilities. It may have been a district hospital at one time, but now it was regarded more as a nursing home. So, after my retreat I would be assigned to my own living quarters at the hospital and move in there for two weeks. My work involved helping out the nurses with the patients or residents. I would also spend time chatting with many of them, listening to their stories and sharing mine as well as the general news of the day. Because I could sing, I always had to entertain them with a song or two every day, get them to join in and maybe sing a song themselves. I got to know many of the staff too; sometimes when my work for the day was done and the staff was going off duty I would be invited to go to their home, meet their family and share in the hospitality offered. One such family I got to know very well was the Jackman family from Paulville, near Tullow, Co. Carlow. Mary and Todd were the parents and they had three sons. Though for a long time before I was ever invited to their home, I didn't think Mary was married or had a family as I always felt she was "coming on to me" and "making passes" at me. When I tell her that now she has a great laugh at me. We have been great friends for almost 35 years and we meet up for our annual outing at Punchestown Races at the end of April. During my two weeks stay I think she set me up on more than one occasion. For example, she asked me to run a bath for one of the elderly residents, and as I was running the water and had the bath nearly full she came up behind me and pushed me in to the water, clothes and all!

Another job I was assigned to during my two-week stay was feeding some of the residents who were unable to feed themselves. One such man was an 89 year old called Jimmy. For my first week there I fed Jimmy his dinner every day. He didn't eat much but slowly, taking about half an hour, I would get his liquidised dinner into him. He didn't share much conversation either because of dementia but I would talk to him as though it was a normal conversation. It was coming up to my own lunchtime when I was given Jimmy's dinner to feed him. So I brought it over to his bed and duly sat down and said, "Now Jimmy, I have your dinner open your mouth." His head was resting back on his pillow and his mouth was closed. I got a small amount of food on a teaspoon and tried to get it into his mouth. Nothing was happening, so I thought he was resting. Meanwhile the bell went for my lunch time, so I left Jimmy's dinner on the tray and thought I'll go and have mine and then come back and try to feed Jimmy a bit more. I guess I was back in about 20 minutes and when I returned I noticed the curtains pulled around Jimmy. I peeped in and Mary was there with another nurse. I said, "What's wrong?" "Jimmy's just after dying," Mary said. "But I was trying to feed him 20 minutes ago and he wouldn't open his mouth for me." I said. Mary nearly choked on her teeth as they nearly fell from her mouth. "Oh for God's sake," she said "will you start saying the rosary." "Hail Mary full of grace, the Lord is with…"

I knew I would never live this one down when word got out that I was trying to feed a dead man. Indeed, the staff of the hospital, as well as the priests and my fellow students, got plenty of mileage out of it for many months, resulting in plenty of puns as well as some entertaining sketches.

CHAPTER 10

....

Final Year

The day after my diaconate ordination, I learned I was going over to the UK in August to spend four months working in a parish. I was assigned to St John the Baptist Parish at King Edward Road in Hackney. I was delighted my classmate Eric from Scotland had been assigned to St Mary of the Angels Parish at Moorehouse Road, Bayswater. The Parish Priest there was Fr Michael Hollings who was famous for setting up a centre where homeless people were offered breakfast and other services every day. Having Eric in London meant we would meet up on a regular basis. My parish in Hackney included St Joseph's Hospice beside the Catholic Church. The Parish Priest of St John the Baptist was Fr Paul McGinn, a Dublin man who lived in Bray, Co. Wicklow, and at the age of nine came with his parents and sister to the UK.

Hackney was a very culturally diverse part of London. About one third of the Hackney residents were Christian. However, there were significantly more people of Jewish and Muslim faiths and indeed a high proportion of people with no religious affiliation. After being at Thornton Heath Parish in Surrey the previous summer, I found Hackney much more challenging. The poverty and unemployment in the area brought its own problems. Fr Paul was a real gentleman and soon got me involved in the parish activities.

I would spend a few hours each day visiting many of our

parishioners. Calling to Hannah and Charlie Mulhall on the 14th floor of Macron Court was a weekly ministry. Hannah was a native of Cork and pined for the 'ould sod' almost incessantly. She always felt I needed fattening up and went out of her way to make sure I ate well by providing my second dinner of the day. If I needed a bit of quiet time I would call to Kathleen and Seamus Dunne on Victoria Park Road. Our friendship has continued even to this day. Another house of respite for me was at Kathleen O'Gorman's who lived at Layton House apartments. I know Kathleen died about two years ago. I loved to call to Maureen and Frank Lyons and their young family, and to Eileen and Martin Burke, who lived in apartment blocks at Pavelley House, and two Galway families whose young children went to the local Catholic school where I would visit weekly as well. Margaret and Charlie Carter-Leay lived in Valette House. They were elderly parents of a severely physically handicapped son, Richard. Richard loved for me to take him out for a walk in his wheelchair and treat him to some ice cream.

As a deacon I could preach at weekend masses and read the gospel at the daily Mass. I would lead the pre-baptism courses and then baptise the babies on the appointed dates. I would lead funeral services without Mass and attend services at the local crematorium. I remember one of the most nerve-racking services I performed was my first wedding. Of course not having Mass in the service meant that it was a much shorter event. No, I wasn't asked to sing at this wedding and indeed I didn't offer to do it either. I really felt it was enough just to get through the liturgy correctly and at the end of the day make sure the couple were married in the eyes of the Church and the

State; above all to make sure the couple were relaxed and enjoying this part of their big day. As the community centre was beside the church, every Sunday after Mass everyone gathered in the centre for a cup of tea/coffee, or even a drink as there was an alcohol licence there. Nearly every Sunday there was a cake sale raising valuable funds for some local event or charity. I would visit St Joseph's Hospice on a weekly basis and got to know many of the terminally ill patients there. It's amazing to listen to people who know their time is short. Some are so open about it and ready to go – their faith is strong and they believe they are going to God. Others who have no faith just see their demise as the very end. The sad part was often visiting to find that some of the patients might have died before I would have returned the following week. After my four-month experience of parish life at Hackney, I returned home for Christmas to be with family. In my head I had thoughts of that this might be my very last Christmas at home with family, and being honest it scared the living daylight out of me. I chose to block it out and not entertain such thoughts and focus on the present moment at home. It was beautiful, lovely, and as special as all previous Christmas family times were.

Then I was back in London on the second week of January to begin my Clinical Pastoral Education Course. I was about half way through my CPE (Clinical Pastoral Education) course at the Maudsley Hospital in London when the letter, dated 3rd February 1989, arrived via the Chaplain's Office. The date of the letter was significant as it was my mother's 70th Birthday. I already had spoken to Fr Peter Finnegan, Superior General of the Kiltegan Father's about a week before so I knew what the letter contained:

Following the consultation I had with you on the phone, I am happy now to be able to give you your mission appointment. I am appointing you to the new mission territory of Tzaneen. As it takes time to process visas for South Africa, it would be good to start the process fairly soon, and for this you can get in touch with George Corr. I hope you will be happy in your new appointment and pray that the work may be fruitful in every way.

Yours Sincerely,

Fr Peter Finnegan, Superior General

So this was it, I now knew, this is what my previous seven years were all about. I was going to work as a priest in South Africa. I held the letter in my hand and read it over and over again. Tzaneen, where was Tzaneen? I couldn't Google it; Google didn't exist. So I got an atlas and a map of South Africa and located the town. I had heard of other cities like Johannesburg and Pretoria the administrative capital but never heard of Tzaneen. I soon discovered that Tzaneen and the capital were about 420km apart, in other words about a four and a half hour drive. I found the distance hard to comprehend. South Africa must be a huge country I thought. While the thought of travelling, living and working in South Africa excited me, there were a lot of questions in my head; however, I didn't entertain them very much as my focus was on completing my CPE course.

The society of Kiltegan Fathers had introduced this course to all of its students during their Ordination Year. The course was designed to teach Pastoral Care as a method of training hospital/hospice chaplains. Each unit of the course lasts about three months. During those three months each participant is part of a structured group with six people on the course under individual supervision in clinical practice for ministry. While many of my seminary classmates were able to avail of the course either at The Mater Hospital in Dublin or the regional hospital in Cork, I was asked to attend the course at the Maudsley Hospital in London. The Maudsley Hospital is the largest mental health training institution in the UK. During my three-month course I would be given recommended reading in the pastoral care ministry and then write a synopsis of what I read from the book. My supervisor was Rev John Foskett. John was famous for some great work in clinical pastoral education, teaching both clergy and mental health professionals about pastoral counselling. I loved his ability to listen and share when necessary, and supply compassion and wisdom when required.

I would spend about four hours every day on the wards among the patients and residents. I would try and make conversation with them and reflect on their story. I clearly remember chatting to one gentleman as he shared with me how after a domestic with his girlfriend, she jumped out the window and landed on railing spikes in front of their building on the main street. He sounded convincing but I wasn't sure. I had my doubts. So that evening I wrote up a report on what was going on for me as he shared his story about his girlfriend. Later I would share my thoughts and feelings with my supervisor. Were my thoughts and feelings full of compassion? Or were they full of doubts?

Another day I was on the ward when I heard screams coming from the toilets. One of the patients had gone in there and found a man who had committed suicide. Needless to say there was almost a lockdown then with patients and staff as the police were called in to investigate. Each staff member was questioned at length by the police because of what happened. That particular episode gave our daily meetings with our group plenty of food for discussion as to how we felt about what had happened. However, the focus was on me and how I was feeling through the entire situation as I was on the same ward where the tragedy had happened. Needless to say, I was shocked, as I had been speaking to the young man only hours before he took his life. And during the conversation there was not an ounce of indication that he was about to end it all. In fact, as I shared with our group, I finished our conversation feeling very positive about the young man and his dreams and plans with his girlfriend when he was discharged. I was so happy for him. It took me a few days to come to terms with my experience, but with the help of Rev John my supervisor, I was able to unravel for myself and cope with what happened on Ward C.

My CPE course concluded on Friday 17th March, 1989. I left London two days later on Palm Sunday and went back to college. Being very honest, I was really looking forward to being back and Holy Week and above all a little quiet time to pray. I was also looking forward to going home on Easter Sunday to catch up with family though I knew it was going to be a hectic ten days at home as I had decided to have my ordination in my home village of Tyrrellspass. Fr Tom Farrell was our local priest there and was delighted I had decided to come home for my ordination, though it was a lot of extra work for him in the planning and organisation. He was there also in 1969 when Fr John Byrne from the village was ordained. That was the last ordination in our local St Stephen's Church. Fr Tom came to Tyrrellspass in December of 1963 and on his first Sunday mass announced that, "I'm what Santa Claus brought you for Christmas". He loved Tyrrellspass and the people loved him. He didn't mince his words; he said it as it was and people loved him for that. I know he was offered a parish to take over on a number of occasions but declined as he called Tyrrellspass his home, and when he died he often said he wanted to be buried among the people he served over the years. I think he might have had a few health problems as well and so decided against taking on the role of running a full parish. The local people loved him for staying with them.

Three of my classmates, Pat, Frank and Alex, opted to have their ordination to priesthood in St Mary's Church, Killamote, Rathdangan, Co. Wicklow. This is the church about two miles from the college where the Kiltegan Fathers opted to have many of their students ordained. John Trout opted to go home to Athy, Co. Kildare for his ordination, as did Eric Armour in Bannockburn in Scotland. I was the last – my date was set for June 18th 1989 so as not to clash with the other dates and to make it possible for each of us to attend the other Ordinations and/or First Masses.

Planning for an ordination is very similar to planning for a family wedding except there is only "the groom" i.e. the priest, and there is no "bride". However, I knew my mother particularly wanted to be involved in every aspect of the planning and preparation, and my father too, though to a lesser degree. My sister Regina and my brother were there to support. Of course there was the added work of planning for two celebrations. The first was the Ordination itself, which was a very formal occasion with invited guests, and the following day would be the First Mass, a much more relaxed community event. For both ceremonies there were the invitations issued and the Ordination booklets and First Mass booklets to be printed up once the liturgies had been prepared and planned. I also chose to print up some small memorial cards for people as a reminder of the occasion. Bishop Michael Smith of my diocese of Meath had agreed to be my ordaining bishop. He would be accompanied by the retired Bishop Johnny McCormack. I choose the music along with my brother Joe and his wife Olive and we got Sister Geraldine from my old school in Rochfordbridge, who taught me for a short time, to get a choir together. They worked very hard for almost three months preparing hymns and music for the two occasions. Then there was the big decision as to who to invite to the ordination and the formal meal afterwards in Harry's, Kinnegad. This is every bride and groom's nightmare in preparing for their wedding and indeed it was for me and my parents too. I wanted many of my work colleagues from my civil service days there, as well as present friends from my seven years as a student including many of my friends from Hackney and The Maudsley Hospital. My parents had their list too and the line "but if we invite them, we will have to invite them also, we can't leave them out". Oh my head was full of it. But we got there in the end. As for my First Mass, well there was an open invitation to everyone in the village with a function being prepared in the local hall organised at a community level.

I was so glad to get back to Kiltegan for my final few weeks, which was like respite after my ten days at home during

Easter. I also looked forward to the pre-ordination retreat. It was held at the beautiful Ballyvaloo Retreat centre. Fr Micky Murphy would be our Spiritual Director for the week. I found it the perfect place for a week-long retreat; magnificently located overlooking the Irish Sea. I love the sea, I love a beach and walking along it. The long beach and surroundings of rolling terrain was the ideal place for me for prayer and reflection and indeed relaxation. The centre was run by St John of God Sisters and other staff. I loved my week there and after the week I felt very content and at peace about taking on the role of being a priest, after all I had seven years to decide. After our retreat I was back in college and it was hands-on rehearsing for the ordination of Frank, Pat and Alex. Eric and I were called upon to provide the music for their ordination under the direction of Fr Nicky Motherway. After the ordination dinner many of the students broke up for summer holidays. The next day, I attended Pat's First Mass in Dublin and the celebrations afterwards. Meanwhile Eric returned to Bannockburn in Scotland for his ordination on Friday 16th June. John Trout had his ordination on Saturday 17th June in Athy, Co. Kildare. I was unable to attend either as I was caught up in final preparations for my own Big Day on 18th June 1989.

When I returned home after Pat's celebrations, I was in awe to see my home village with an array of colour everywhere. Papal flags, Irish national flags, Westmeath GAA flags and Tyrrellspass GAA flags were everywhere. Bunting strung across the streets from building to building and banners up saying CONGRATULATIONS FATHER RAY. The entire place looked amazing. And to cap it all, the weather matched the beauty of the place with warm sunny days and evenings, and weather predictions were that it was to last well into the weekend and beyond. My mother and father were busy entertaining friends, neighbours and relations each day from early morning to night. I could see they were enjoying the limelight as much as I was. The choir, directed by Sister Geraldine, was rehearsing for a couple of hours every evening and they sounded fantastic. I even gave them a couple of Swahili pieces, which I used to sing in Kiltegan, to include in the liturgy and they had mastered them brilliantly. Sister Pius and the Mercy Sisters from Rochfordbridge, where I went to secondary school, had my stole and chasuble specially designed and made; someone referred to it after as my "wedding dress". I also got another one as a gift from Tess and Aiden Cunniffe. Aidan's sister was a religious sister in Dublin and she and her community made it for me also. It was traditional that each one of us to be ordained would choose a deacon to assist the Bishop on the day of ordination and assist me the next day for my First Mass of Thanksgiving. I chose a classmate of mine from my Spiritual Year, Martin Spillane, or "Scart" as we called him, because he hailed from Scartaglen, a small rural village in Kerry. Scart had fallen a year behind me as he spent three years in Cork completing his degree at University College Cork. He was ordained a deacon then the year after me. He arrived on Friday afternoon and we arranged with Fr Farrell to have a rehearsal of the ordination on Saturday morning with my parents, Michael Maguire who was the MC for the ceremony and the altar servers. On Saturday evening the final visitors left our house by 10pm and I enjoyed two shots of Jameson whiskey with the rest of my family to help me sleep. Indeed, I didn't need them because once my head hit the pillow I was out like a light.

I awoke about 7.00am on Sunday morning with the heat from the glaring sun shining through my bedroom curtains. It was going to be another scorching hot day. My mother cooked a big Irish breakfast for me and the family with a reminder that I needed it as it would be evening before I would be having dinner. I picked at it as best I could just to please her. I was just too nervous, too excited. I just wanted to get on with it, but it would be a few more hours yet. For a while I sat with my dad on the garden seat in front of our house. Wally and Larry Arthur lived across the road and waved to make sure we were all ok as they prepared themselves for the day. It was a very special half hour with Dad, I could see he was very proud as cars passed by on the road beeping their horns and shouting congratulations out the car windows. Da was also very emotional and I could hear it in his voice as he said, "Well Ray this is it, what the last seven years are all about, your mammy and I are so proud of you, it's an amazing thing for me and your mammy about to have a son a priest. God has blessed us in you Ray and you know we love you." I said nothing; words were not necessary. We just hugged and in that hug, I knew I was loved. My mother's voice interrupted our hug as she shouted, "Come in and get dressed". Meanwhile, my friends Kevin Tighe and Martin Smith from my Spiritual Year group arrived. Kevin had left the seminary four years earlier, and Martin would be ordained in two more years. They were in the process of decorating the cars with bunting. Mary Jackman from my Baltinglass hospital episodes arrived with her husband Todd. My friends from Kerry and Cork arrived, along with many of my neighbours and family. There were hugs all around as I hopped into the driver's seat of my mother's car and drove her and Daddy to the church.

The ceremony began at 3.00pm. Fr Tom Farrell began by welcoming everyone on behalf of the parish community, especially my mother and father and family, describing the event as a great occasion for the parish too. All the family, friends and neighbours were in church. The procession into the church was led by altar servers, visiting priests, myself and finally Deacon Martin Spillane with Bishop Michael last. Michael Maguire as MC then explained the different parts of the liturgy as it came along. It was pretty hot inside the church. As I reached the top of the church I sat directly in front of my parents until I was called forward. After the Liturgy of the Word, the Liturgy of Ordination began. A lot of the ceremony was similar to my Diaconate Ordination except of course this was much more daunting as I was on my own. I didn't have my five classmates alongside me, so I felt very nervous. So I was called forward and I announced that I was present. Bishop Michael then gave an instructional homily on the nature of priesthood, according to the teachings of the Second Vatican Council. Then I stood and went before the Bishop as he asked me to make the five promises. As the Bishop sat and read out the questions for me to answer, one of my altar servers Jim Fagan was kneeling before the Bishop holding his missal. I noticed he was wavering a bit as the Bishop got to my final promise. The wavering seemed to go on for a few minutes as the young lad was trying to hold it together. Obviously, the heat got to him and he collapsed book and all into Bishop Michael's knee. Whatever nerves I had at the beginning of the ceremony completely evaporated as I watched my deacon Scart take on a role never seen before at an ordination ceremony. He really came into his own. He calmly got up from his chair, lifted the young lad across his shoulder like a sack of potatoes and carried him into the sacristy. In all the ordinations I had attended over the last seven years this was definitely a first.

I can't remember the Bishop asking me, "Do you promise respect and obedience to your Ordinary?" Indeed I don't remember answering either, but I presume I answered, "I do". After I supposedly made my promise of obedience and just before I prostrated myself on the floor of the Church for the Litany of the Saints, Deacon Scart returned to the sanctuary to assure us that the young altar server was fine. The Bishop then continued with the Laying on of Hands, which happened at my diaconate ordination also, but unlike then all the priests present would also lay their hands on me including Bishop Emeritus Johnny McCormack. Then followed the Prayer of Ordination and Investiture with Stole and Chasuble. These are the vestments the priest wears as he celebrates Mass. Then Bishop Michael anointed my hands, which symbolizes the priest's distinctive participation in Christ's priesthood by the sacrifice he will offer with his hands. Then my mother and father brought forward the bread and wine and presented them to Bishop Michael who in turn presented them to me saying, "Receive from the Holy people of God the gifts to be offered to God. Know what you do, imitate what you celebrate, and conform your life to the mystery of the Lord's cross." In fact this gesture ties the rite of ordination directly to the Eucharistic context and to the priest's service on behalf of the people of God. Finally, the Bishop and all the priests present give me the kiss of peace accepting me as a co-worker in their shared ministry. I was now a newly ordained priest and able to concelebrate the Mass with Bishop Michael. There was a huge round of applause and a bigger one when my young altar server Jim Fagan came back onto the altar. He was fine. The first two people I gave Holy Communion to as a newly ordained priest were my mother and father, as was my first blessing when I, along with the Bishop and priests, processed out of the church. Many more queued up for blessings too and indeed for photographs. Seamus Kelly (no relation) was my official photographer on the day and Eamonn Gillane, owner and manager of Harry's where we held my evening function, took loads of video footage too.

All the family and invited guests arrived at Harry's for the evening dinner and entertainment. I was starving at that stage, but before the food was the official family photographs and then food glorious food. There was the cutting of the cake along with my mother and father and then the speeches. My brother Joe was my "bestman" and Da was the first to speak:

> Reverend fathers, reverend sisters, ladies and gentlemen, it is a great honour for the Kelly family today there is no question about that. I suppose it's eight years ago since Raymond told us he was going to Kiltegan to study for the priesthood. And we didn't pass much remark on it to be candid. But when he finally went in seven years ago I still didn't pass much remark on it because I said God knows where I'll be in seven years. But the first thing I want to say is thanks be to God that God left us our health, my wife and myself, to celebrate Ray's day today. Now the next thing ye know, people meet ye on the street and talk to ye and say Ray's a grand fella he'll make a great priest.

Then Da continued by telling a joke or two about priests hearing confessions. He finished up by saying, "Ray was a good boy and a great son and if he makes as good a priest as he was a son, he'll make St Patrick's in Kiltegan very proud". A round of applause followed and then my brother Joe called on Fr Tom Farrell to say a few words sharing how well he knew my mother and father over 31 years. Then Fr Martin O Reilly representing the Kiltegan Fathers congratulated me and said:

We are all partly products of our environment and it's true that Ray, as well as his vocation, is in some way part of this family, part of this community and I think today is a very happy occasion and special for his parents Joe and Mona because it was from them that he saw the first example of what faith is about, it was from them that he first learned about his faith and nourished in his family and parish with Fr Farrell and the people of Tyrrellspass. And today we can all look on that with pride and rejoice in this day as Ray reaches priesthood.

It was very moving during the ceremony to see tears of joy coming from Mona and Joe and they had every reason to be so joyful today. I'm sure for a lot of young people, the idea of having a secure job, and the civil service is supposed to be a very secure job, having a car of their own, a house of their own and being ready to set up a family of their own, I'm sure this must be the aims of young people. They were the aims and in a sense the achievements of young Ray Kelly some years ago. But something seems to have happened in the meantime. And Ray probably had a feeling like Bono's "I Still Haven't Found What I'm Looking For", so Ray began to search and that took him to Kiltegan, St Patrick's Missionary Society seven years ago.

I suppose since then in Kiltegan we have seen a lot of the qualities of Ray, I suppose first of all the fact that he made that decision, it took great courage and faith and trust in God and his part and Ray seems to have a lot of that. Secondly, he wouldn't have made this decision in a hurry. He is very thorough, he prepares things well and that's a quality that has stood to him in Kiltegan. He is also somebody who has been very dedicated to his duty, somebody who cares for people, who's good with people, who's concerned for them. And he was a good example to students and people down in Kiltegan. He did all those things in a very quiet unassuming way, but it was only when he got a microphone in his hand and when he had some musical backing that we saw the other side of Ray Kelly, Ray the public performer or maybe I should say the "New York" side of Ray. I'm sure we will hear that again before the evening is over.

Joe, Ray's dad, said that he hoped Ray would be a credit to Kiltegan. Well Kiltegan are very happy to welcome Ray as one of their priests, and we can assure his family that Ray is entering into another family now which will always look after him and which will regard him as one of their own. Seven years ago he took a big step and he is about to take another big step now by going on the missions to South Africa and Tzaneen Diocese.

It's a place that is very far away, they speak a different language there from what we are used to and the divide between black and white is as severe and even more so than the divide between Protestant and Catholic in Northern Ireland today. And Ray goes into this situation with a different sort message, a message of Jesus Christ that there should be no divisions between people, that all are equal, that there should be peace, there should be harmony, there should be unity between people. It's quite a mission to go into, quite a difficult one but I'm sure if Ray enters that with the same courage and trust and faith that he has shown in the last seven years then it will bring him great joy, contentment and happiness.

On the back of his ordination booklet he has a little piece about the fact that he is not going alone to South Africa, he goes as your representative, representative of his family, of his friends and of his relations and of his community in Tyrrellspass. So I think it is important that you keep him in mind when he's away and support him through your prayers, through your interest and through your help. I should also mention somebody else who I'm sure has been an influence on Ray, especially his coming to Kiltegan and that is his cousin Fr Joe Pettit whose fine example would have helped Ray along that road. So finally, I wish to ask God's blessing on Ray's ministry that it will be a long and fruitful one and that the Lord will guide him every step of that way.

I guess Fr Martin's speech summed up really everything about me and told the story of my journey so far. I was the last to speak and it was really a time to say thanks to all the people who journeyed with me throughout my seven years in the seminary and even before. I know when I started that part of my life with Kiltegan, very few people gave me a real chance of reaching this day of ordination. I guess they thought, *let him get it out of his system and he'll be back in the civil service in a year or two at most.* And you know I didn't give myself much of a chance of lasting the course either. In all honesty though I grew more and more into my new role of a student and more and more confident as a young man as my giftedness became more and more apparent. The joy of that and my faith in God's call for me kept me going and got me to this day. After concluding my thanks to so many in my speech I said, "You know today is Father's Day and I became a Father today. But I'm going to change the title of the day just for today and call it Father and Mother's Day." I then presented my mother and father with gifts for the special occasion. Well the evening continued with music and plenty of dancing and singers to entertain. My brother Joe gave a great rendition of Joe Dolan's songs "It's You, It's You, It's You" and "More, More, More". Next was my mother with her waltz rendition of "If We Only Had Old Ireland Over Here". Then she was joined by my Da as the two of them sang out their medley of waltzes with "Irene Goodnight, Irene", "Springtime in the Rockies", "Let Me Call You Sweetheart", "After The Ball Is Over" and finishing up the medley with "Good Luck, Good Health, God Bless You". The turn of my niece Lorraine came then with her quickstep rendition of "Top Of The World".

My good friend Eddie from my civil service days entertained with "Come What May". After a few more songs from the band it was my turn. The chants went out for "New York, New York". The "singing priest" was born.

Monday 19th June 1989 was as warm as, if not warmer than, Ordination Day. Even at 7.00pm in evening there was no respite from the heat. I loved it. Many of the priests who were at my Ordination were back for my First Mass. Following the Mass, my mother and father were first up for the traditional first blessing. Aside from me wanting them to be first, I knew they would be anxious to get outside the church for a cigarette. My aunt Kitty and her husband Ger were next and the queue then just lengthened right to the back of the church and indeed outside too. The heat in the church was intense and with the aid of a few glasses of water I kept it going for a good hour or more.

The celebrations continued then in the local parish hall. This was the community event part of my Ordination. The entire village was out. It was wonderful to see such community spirit in action as all the organisation and hard work by the local people fell into place. There was another cake to cut with my mother and father. There were loads of presentations made to me from the Tidy Towns committee, the gardening club and by the principal Mrs Ann Buckley from the local school primary school. The dancing started up with music provide by all the local talent of the village. Fr Tom Farrell took to the microphone to welcome me and my family on behalf of the local community referring to me as, "The finest baby Mona had ever delivered and she delivered quite a few around this area I can tell you. And I know in their heart and soul Raymond is the pet of the whole lot and I congratulate him and his family." He then made a presentation to me on behalf of the people of Tyrrellspass. The dancing went on into the early hours with plenty of local singers to keep the celebrations lively. Needless to say the night would not be complete without "New York, New York" getting another rollicking from the Singing Priest.

I guess it must have been well after 3.00am when I finally got to put my head on the pillow. Fr Tom Farrell had me booked to say 10.00am Mass on Tuesday, Wednesday and Thursday morning. He was gone for a few days' retreat to St Finian's College in Mullingar with many other priests from the Meath Diocese. The Mass was indeed more than well attended as word got out that I was saying Mass in the local church. The village was still buzzing after all the weekend celebrations with the Ordination being the main topic of discussion. The banners and bunting was still decorating the place. I still had celebrity status.

My first Mass outside the village was with the Mercy Sisters in Rochfordbridge. It was really an honour to be asked back to celebrate Mass with the Sisters. They had been so good to me all through my secondary school years and even more so now in the build up to my Ordination. After the Mass my parents, brother Joe and his wife Olive, and my sister Regina, had a lovely evening supper with them.

Saturday morning the village of Tyrrellspass woke up to the sad news of the death of our beloved priest for many years Fr Tom Farrell. To say I was shocked was putting it mildly. It seemed as though after his retreat at St Finian's he came home on Thursday evening. On Friday he was helping some young men throw in some turf into his shed when he got a pain in his chest. He was rushed into Mullingar Hospital where he died sometime later that evening. The entire village was transformed from a state of celebration to a state of mourning. The gift that Santa Claus had brought the village in 1963 was gone. Fr Tom, over his 26 years with the people, had shared so much of life's uneven burdens with so many families. He was there for happy events like baptisms, First Holy Communion and Confirmation day, he was there for the joy of wedding days and indeed the sad days of the deaths of so many old and indeed not so old parishioners. He was part of all our families, part of our community for all those years and now he was gone. I could not help but wonder was the burden of the last week in the village of ordination fever too much for him. Yet I knew he was in his element, I'd never seen him so proud and so happy than over that last weekend. This was his second ordination in this little church in the village; his church and I knew he was very proud. Now we would have to gather in this little church to say fond farewell to our beloved priest and friend. Within hours the village was transformed from a state of celebration to a state of mourning and all the banners, flags and bunting were quickly torn down. His funeral was on Monday 26th June and the funeral Mass was led by Cardinal Tomas O'Fiaich, as well as Bishop Michael Smith, Bishop Emeritus Johnny Mc Cormack and most of the priests from the Meath Diocese. The big topic of conversation among people was how quickly we are forced to shake off the cloak of celebration and put on the cloak of grief.

Meanwhile, each day I was fulfilling invitations for house Mass, and on the Friday morning after the funeral I offered

Mass up in Tyrrellspass for the happy repose of the soul of Fr Tom from the altar society.

Following my ordination and lots of pictures and articles on the local papers, I got the surprise of my life. A lady named Kitty Cox wrote a lovely letter to my mother inquiring was I the same lad that she used to baby-sit over 30 years before. It was of course Kitty Allen whom Mam got to look after us as children while she was out delivering babies. She was now Kitty Cox, a widow with two grown-up sons Ronald and Alan living in Scramogue, near Strokestown, Co. Roscommon. After more than 30 years we met and remain very fond and good friends today.

On Saturday afternoon I was on a plane to London for a six-week phonetics course, along with some of my ordained class. This was a compulsory course that our superiors in Kiltegan insisted that we participate in, in order to help us to pick up some of the local African languages when we got to the missions. I was not a happy man. This was the last place I wanted to be. I know my fellow ordained priests felt the same. Two weeks after being ordained and I was now sitting in a classroom again studying phonetics. It seemed as though it had been traditional that all the newly ordained Kiltegan priests had to take part in this course. So there was no way out.

Phonetics comes from the Greek word phone, which means 'sound' or 'voice', and is the science of the sounds of human speech and the practical application of this science to language study. I found a lot of the course way over my head and I know I was not the only one. However, I lasted the course with a struggle with the help of being in London, taking in a few musical shows on the West End and visiting many of my friends at the Maudsley Hospital and Hackney.

When I returned home on 13th August, I continued my cycle of house masses, to my Aunty Bridie and Aunt Angie and Caroline Gonoud's, then my neighbours across the road Wally and Larry, and my brother Joe and his wife Olive's home. Having these masses in so many homes was also an occasion to invite in neighbours and friends and relations for a party afterwards. Then it was off to Kerry to my friends Michael Holly and his family. The house parties and family masses continued in my Auntie May's home in Cumminstown and my friends Lipsey and J.J., my cousins Richard and Aileen Walsh, my good friend from our Rome trip many years before Nora O'Sullivan, Mary Jackman or Baltinglass Hospital Mary and her husband Todd. Then a few days in Trabolgan, Co. Cork with Mary and Tony Kelly, and their boys, and Tony's mother Josie and Fr Alex who would travel to South Africa with me. Of course I was touching base with Kiltegan also as my visa for South Africa was being processed and I didn't know exactly the date I would be travelling out there. There were the dental appointments and medical appointments to fulfil as well.

Finally, my date of departure for South Africa came through for Thursday 28th September. It would be an overnight flight from Dublin to Amsterdam and then an overnight to Johannesburg arriving at about 8.00am on Friday 29th September. The last couple of house masses were fulfilled in my cousin's home of Breda and Micky Marshall, and Marian and Eamonn Dolan's home in Dublin. I worked with Marian in the civil service for many years. On the Tuesday of the week of my departure I went to Dublin airport to see off one of my ordained classmates Pat Mc Callion as he departed for his mission to Malawi. On Wednesday morning I celebrated Mass with my Aunt Kitty and Uncle Ger in their home. I offered the Mass up for my grandparents, Theresa and Joe Gavigan. This was their home and my second home growing up, the house I was born in.

The morning of my departure, a few of our neighbours and family gathered at home as we celebrated Mass together. At this stage, I was feeling very emotional. I knew tears were not very far away. However, I would hold back. There would be time for tears later. It was decided that Mam and Dad and my oldest niece Lisa Coyle, the first-born grandchild, would come to the airport with me. My bags were packed and in the car so I was ready to go. I walked around the house for one last look, looked into each of the rooms and said my goodbye to the homestead. I drove to the airport and played the radio and purposely kept the chat going to avoid moments of silence and maybe emotion. I knew Mam and Dad and Lisa were struggling with facing the next two hours or so as I was.

When I reached the airport, almost straight away I met Alex and some of his family whom I knew pretty well; there were two of the Kiltegan priests there also to bid us bon voyage. Alex and I checked in our bags together and had secured seating beside each other. There was about a half hour to spare and time for a coffee in the restaurant. I began to feel that I didn't want that half hour to end and wished for time to stand still. I knew everyone else felt the same. Mam was the first to speak and said, "Isn't it time for you and Alex to be going?". Indeed, it was. We all went upstairs to where Alex and I would go through security. This was it. Hugs all around and tears held back. Parting is always painful so I knew the next few minutes would always linger with me. I was leaving home for the next three years. I would not see my parents again for the next three years, and, as they were in their early 70s, maybe I would never see either of them again. I know now that was not the case and I would see them much sooner than I ever thought. As I held Mam and Dad and Lisa in a tight hug, the tears of joy that I shed on my ordination day returned as tears of sorrow. I couldn't help it. Before my boarding pass was checked I turned back for one last look and a wave. I could see Mam and Dad and Lisa as they held each other were letting the tears flow now. Alex and I were gone from our families. We patted each other on the shoulder as to say, "Let's do this". We did.

The call that I heard all those years ago, that little voice, "Ray, you know you could be up there doing what that priest is doing". The departure from the civil service after nearly 11 years; the seven years of preparation for priesthood; the summer of '89 celebrations of Ordination; all those chapters were now over. Tomorrow I would be in South Africa and another chapter in my life would begin.

CHAPTER 11

....

South Africa - 1989

Our flight from Dublin took us to Schiphol Airport in Amsterdam where we then had a two and a half hour stop over. We then took the 8.00pm KLM 747 flight to Jan Smuts airport, now called O.R. Tambo after Oliver Reginald Tambo in memory of one of South Africa's national heroes. This was my first ever experience of a ten-hour overnight flight anywhere. Alex and I settled into our flight very relaxed and shared many of our summer experiences since ordination. At some stage during the flight Alex said "Ray, I have a favour to ask you. When we get to Luckau to begin our language course I want you to cut my hair and shave it all off", "Are you serious, haven't they got barbers in South Africa to do that sort of thing?" I joked. When I realised he was serious, I said "sure, no problem".

Fr Pat Deegan and Fr Sean Mac Suibhne, two familiar faces from Kiltegan, met us at the airport. I got an opportunity to phone home that evening just to tell Mum and Dad that I had arrived safely. I could still hear the emotion in their voices so I didn't stay long chatting and assured them I would phone in a couple of weeks when I was settled into Luckau, Witbank Diocese, where I would be studying the language Northern Sotho. After a great night's sleep we set off on a four and half hour drive to Luckau. Johannesburg is very much a first world city but as we travelled through the countryside apartheid in South Africa became a lot more obvious. We got to Luckau just in time for the generator in the parish to come on at 6.00pm The parish had no phone and no electricity so the generator was the only means of power. It goes off at 9.30pm and after that everything is done by candlelight. The evening we arrived, the generator only lasted about 20 minutes before everything went black, candles were lit immediately, and supper was prepared and eaten by candlelight. It was a first time experience and a beautiful one, but how long would the novelty last? Alex then said to me "Are you ready? Time for my hair cut". "Are you mad, all we have is candles and no hot water" I said. But I got some good sharp scissors and started clipping as close to the scalp as I could. The next evening when we had some hot water via a generator I clean-shaved Alex's scalp, leaving a few tiny cuts. The job was done. Alex was a happy man with a very tender scalp. He wore a green and red cap, the Mayo GAA colours for the next week or so to protect his scalp from the sun. That was my first and last time as a barber.

Alex and I were introduced to our new language teacher Johannes. Our daily lessons would be about two and half hours. The real learning was of course when we would mix with the local people, especially the children, and try to put into practice the few words we would learn each day. Once I saw the children or their parents laughing at me I knew I had made a mistake and probably a fool of myself as well. Many of the children had never seen a bald white man before and as Alex's hair began to have a little bit of stubble they loved to touch it and rub their hands across it. After a week in Luckau, Alex, Pat Deegan and I set out for the town and diocese of Tzaneen where I would be working the cathedral parish. Tzaneen is a large tropical town situated in the Mopani District Municipality of the Limpopo province. It is located in a lush, fertile region surrounded by mountains and hills. It is a town like any town in Ireland with shopping centres, schools, football pitches, 50-metre swimming pools, tennis courts. In fact, living here in the town one would never realise there was a third-world part of this diocese and parish.

We were invited to meet my new bishop, Hugh Slattery, a Tipperary man and part of the Missionary of the Sacred Heart order (MSC). I met my new Parish Priest, a native of from Kerry. He and I would be sharing the parish house together. It was Bishop Hugh's first year as a bishop and he was delighted to have a new priest coming into his diocese. He had a barbecue (*braai* in South Africa) to welcome us, with many of the other priests of the diocese there also. Needless to say after a few beers Alex set me up to entertain with a few songs. I would spend a week here before returning to Luckau to continue my language course. I got a tour around the parish, which was approximately the size of Co. Westmeath and Co. Meath together. There were four spoken languages: English, Afrikaans, Shangaan or Tsonga and Northern Sotho, which was the language I would be learning. The Diocese itself was huge, approximately two-thirds the size of Ireland with 25 parishes. I was the 23rd priest to arrive and work in the diocese. At this stage, I had no concept of the volume of work involved in my parish and the distance between the various villages and townships where the Catholic churches were located. It would be a few months after I had completed my language course that

I would be back living in the parish house in Tzaneen. In the meantime, I returned back to Luckau.

Living in this isolated part of South Africa, I really felt lonely. When the letters would arrive from home I would read and re-read them almost hearing the voice of the person whom the letter was from. I didn't always get a chance to write to all the members of my family but on a weekly basis I wrote home to Mum and Dad keeping them informed of my new life. If I wanted to make a phone call home I would have to drive to the nearest big town of Groblersdal and call to the German Dominican Sisters convent. They always made me feel welcome. I could talk to them about how I was feeling and particularly the loneliness I would feel. Sometimes I would be lost in thinking of what was going on at home, what my mother and father might be doing and the rest of my family. I was thrilled when I received a 12-page letter from my niece Lisa filling me in on all the happenings in the Coyle family and what happened after she and Mam and Dad bid me farewell at the airport. As they got back to their car they all sat there until the tears subsided. She said *"Bambam [my dad] needed a shot of whiskey to calm him and they pulled into the Spa Hotel in Lucan on the way home and they all got something to eat and Bambam got his whiskey."*

When I wrote home about Alex getting his hair shaved off my other niece Gillian wrote *"I am just after washing my big thick head of blonde hair! Tell Alex I will get my hair cut and I will post him a blonde wig!"*

In the villages around Luckau there was a lot of talk of the break-up of apartheid and the ultimate release of Nelson

Mandela from Robben Island. Such information would probably come from the many husbands that worked in the big cities like Johannesburg or Pretoria and got home to their families the last weekend of every month. In the African culture women seemed to be the backbone of many of the Christian churches. They would be seen working on the roadways building walls. They were cooks, housekeepers, and gardeners. What fascinated me was while they worked they often carried their infant babies on their backs. It seemed to be relatively comfortable for the woman and for the baby. Sometimes the babies would be up to a year old and were carried on mother's back right up to walking age. I guess it was like carrying a backpack.

The language course was going very well. Luckau was Fr Sean Smith and Fr Sean Mac Suibhne's parish, with whom Alex and I shared the parish house, and they had mastered the language fairly well already. I was really envious of them and I knew I had a lot of work to do to catch up. After about a month I had some of the basic greetings and I could read some of the Mass in the language. As for preaching in the language, I would often write my sermon out in English and get Johannes to translate it into Northern Sotho for me. I never received a letter from my Dad in all my years coming and going away from home. So when I received a letter from him around the first week of November I was really surprised and delighted. There was nothing exceptional in the letter except to tell me he was always thinking of me and to assure me of his prayers and to tell me the price of cattle was pretty bad but he was going to sell his anyway because he had no winter fodder for them. He finished the letter by saying:

*Now Ray I will say goodbye and may God bless and save
you always. You know we have to keep our 'ould chin up
and we won't find the time passing, hoping to hear from
you soon. God bless you always Ray. I love you as always.
Da xxxxxx"*

I kept that letter because it was so special and most un-
usual to get it. Hindsight is a wonderful thing and I have often wondered did he suspect anything about himself and his
health. I will never know. About a week later Mam's weekly
letter arrived as usual. The last paragraph of her letter told me
that Dad had an appointment for a week later with the eye
specialist from the Eye & Ear Hospital as his glasses were still
not suiting him and she said she insisted to the Clinic that
he have his appointment with Dr Curtain in Mullingar. Of
course I thought no more about that until I would hear from
Mam as to how his appointment went. I had other letters
from home on a weekly basis after that but there was no reference as to how Dad got on with his eye appointment.

Then on 3rd December 1989 I got a message from home
via the Dominican Sisters in Groblersdal that my dad was
hospitalised and for me to phone home as soon as I could.
The next day I phoned home and spoke to Mum and she
told me Dad had been admitted to Mullingar Hospital on
the 2nd. At this stage he was in for some tests. It seemed as
though he was losing his balance a bit. One day Mum had to
pick him up from the yard outside where he had a fall. She
also told me he went out to the toilet during the night and he
tried to get into the bath along side the toilet as he thought

he was getting back into bed. Another time he tried to take the top off the solid range cooker with his finger to put turf on the fire. I asked her what should I do, should I go home? She said wait until we get the results of the tests and see what the problem might be.

I phoned home every day after that until my family had some idea of what was wrong. The doctor seemed to think it was a form of dementia or Alzheimer's. But if it was it came on him very quickly. The other alternative was a brain tumour. The doctor also suggested to Mum that perhaps I should come home from South Africa as soon as possible. While I felt a bit guilty over having to go home so soon after my arrival, I didn't care as I was going home. So I booked a flight and left Johannesburg on December 12th. I went home via Amsterdam and got into Dublin on Wednesday 13th December. I was late coming through arrivals at Dublin airport as I waited for my luggage. Eventually the carousel containing the entire Amsterdam flight luggage had been collected and my luggage had not come through. The Aer Lingus staff checked and apologised and said my bag was not on the plane but it would arrive in the next flight and they would deliver it to my home. I then went through to greet my mother and brother-in-law Seamus. Aer Lingus compensated me straight away with about £240 punts to buy toiletries, underwear and emergency clothes. All my family were at home to meet me. I was glad to be home.

That evening I went to the hospital to see my Father, I was shocked, he had deteriorated so much in less than three months. It didn't even register with him to ask me why I was home. My mother had told him I was coming for a quick holiday and he didn't question that. Meanwhile over the next week I checked with Aer Lingus about my luggage, as it had not arrived. The word came through about four days before Christmas that Dad had a brain tumour and an operation in Beaumont Hospital would determine how serious it was. As it was the Christmas season, the surgery would not be carried out before Christmas. We would be given a date as soon as possible. Meanwhile, he was too ill to come out of hospital, however, we did bring him home for a few hours on Christmas Day. We ate Christmas dinner at my sister Regina's home along with her young family who were full of the joys of Santa Claus. I knew in my heart, though no one wanted to say it out loud, that this would be Dad's last Christmas with us. It was a magical time for all of Regina and Seamus's kids, as it is supposed to be. And all of us present made sure to make it beautiful for Dad too. I could see the old Dad break into a little smile now and then when some of the children would come over to him and ask him *"Are you all right Bambam?"* At different times during the few hours we had Dad home from hospital I along with other members of family would glance at him and almost well-up with emotion and tears. But we all bravely held back. There would be time for tears afterwards.

By 5.00pm I knew Dad was exhausted and Mam and I decided to drive him back to hospital. We waited until the nurses got him into bed and kissed him goodnight. All the while I was phoning Aer Lingus every couple of days to check on the location of my luggage. The usual apology, "sorry sir we are doing all we can to trace your bag". Over the next few days we all spent time with Dad in hospital along with some of our neighbours and friends. Three days after Christmas day we got the word from the hospital informing us that Dad would be transferred to Beaumont Hospital in Dublin on New Year's Eve for assessment before his surgery. There was a sigh of relief all around as we felt we might get some answers. Mum and I moved up to Dublin to stay with my Mum's cousin, Hester Fallon, who lived very close to Beaumont Hospital.

On the 3rd January 1990, Mam and I kissed Dad as he was being wheeled down to the theatre for his surgery. The nurse had informed us that the surgeon would speak to us after surgery to tell us how everything went. About three hours later the surgeon came to us and informed us that all went well with the surgery. Then he took me aside and used a medical term for Dad's illness that I didn't understand. He then continued to translate it into plain English and called it a malignant brain tumour and inoperable. I asked him what all that meant and he said I'm afraid your Dad has cancer of the brain and I would estimate he has six to nine months to live. I'm sure my face turned to shock as I absorbed what I had heard. While part of me expected to hear something like that, I was nevertheless always clinging to hope. Now at that moment I felt there was no way to hope anymore. I looked over at Mum and I knew she didn't hear what I heard. She only heard that the surgery went well.

Dad was moved to the intensive care unit and we would visit him in a few hours. Meanwhile, Mum and I went for a cup of coffee. I knew Mum was anxious to phone the family at home to tell them that all was well. But before she would make that call I would have to tell her everything. I asked her first of all what did she hear from the surgeon and I was right. She just heard that the surgery went well. I then gently told her the news was not good. I told her exactly what the surgeon said to me. She started to cry and so did I. Once we had regained our composure, I said to wait until we got home later to tell the rest of the family. She still needed to hear Rosemarie, Joseph and Regina's voices so she phoned them to tell them that Dad was over his surgery and we would know more about it later. The phone was not the right way to break news like this to family and Mum knew it.

Dad was still heavily sedated when we visited him in ICU but I think he knew we were there. We told him we were going home and would be back tomorrow. Mum and I drove home to Tyrrellspass to break the news about Dad's condition to the rest of the family. I felt it was important that my brother and sisters heard what I heard. There were a lot more tears as the impact of what I said hit home. We were all in agreement that we would get Dad home and look after him in his own comfortable surroundings.

He was released back to Mullingar hospital eight days after his surgery. His good friend Ned Groome was in a hospital bed next to him. They were friends for years, as was Ned's wife Mon with my mother. Their regular weekly trip to Dillon' Pub on a Saturday or Sunday night was always an occasion they looked forward to. Dad was on steroid medication, which gave him a huge appetite and he regained a lot of strength, which as a family we were delighted with. After another ten days in Mullingar hospital Dad was released to come home with us.

It was wonderful to have him home again. His mobility was slow but with help he was able to move around. He also needed help with feeding as he had lost a lot of his coordination. For example, if he tried to feed himself he would struggle putting the food in his mouth. If we left a cup of tea in front of him to drink he would go through the motions of shaping his fingers to grasp the cup handle and direct it to his mouth without the cup being in his hand at all. We would also hold the cigarette for him while he smoked it otherwise he would just tip the cigarette into whatever was in front of him. That evening after Dad was released from hospital, his good friend Ned had died. The family agreed to hold off telling Dad until after Ned's funeral. Then Mum broke the news to him. He stared hard at her and just said "Well isn't it well for him, he has it all over him." There was no emotion or sadness, and nothing else was ever said.

It was a real privilege to have Dad at home with us for over two weeks before he was hospitalised again. It was prime time, privilege time as a family to be together to look after him and attend to his every need. During those two weeks Dad never lost his sense of humour and smiled and joked as best he could. It was like having the old Dad back again in many ways with plenty of visitors and callers to see him. And he enjoyed his little drop of whiskey every night too as Mum and I enjoyed one with him.

In the meantime, I was still checking with Aer Lingus about my luggage and it was the same old story "sorry sir we are doing all we can to trace your bag". I also received a phone call from my superior in Kiltegan with a view that I should be back in South Africa at this stage after being home for nearly two months. When I assured him that I thought my Dad didn't have that long left he said no more.

The six to nine months that the surgeon gave us for Dad's life was really way off the mark now. By early February he was getting weaker and had lost the power of his legs, however, he still enjoyed his food and he was pain free, which was a huge blessing for us. It was necessary to get him back to hospital in early February. Mum and the rest of us were very reluctant, as we knew his time was short and we all wanted him to die at home surrounded by his family. By 9th February when palliative care was set up, Dad came home. For the next five days he never got out of his bed as the family looked after him round the clock and Mum insisted in sleeping in the room with him. He died in the early hours of Wednesday morning 14th February at 1.45am. I think no matter how well we were prepared for that deadline, you never really become accustomed to it, or the frightening finality which followed that last shallow breath marking the end of his life. For the next few hours until daylight, when the community would find out about the death of Joe Kelly at the age of 72, we stayed in the room crying with Dad, laughing, and recalling many of the events of his life, particularly his last days, and repeating some of the things he said. Somewhere through all my new experiences of grief with my family, I saw either on a newspaper or on the TV that Nelson Mandela had been released from Robben Island on 11th February 1990, three days before Dad died.

On Wednesday morning I went to 10.00am Mass and saw Fr Joe Brilly to arrange to have Dad prayed for at the masses in Church, and to organise the date and time for Dad's funeral. It would take place on Friday 16th February, in Tyrrellspass Church at 12.00pm. The 41st Anniversary of their wedding. I would be saying the funeral Mass and giving the eulogy on my Dad. I was dreading it. Up to 1.45am that morning my role as a priest was always in the distance. Sure as a priest I had offered up Mass for him in his bedroom a few hours before he died, and given him the sacrament of the sick, however, I was also a son sitting at the bedside of his dying dad. After his death it was my duty as his son, but also as a priest, to attend to the organisation of Dad's funeral. Most people when their Dad dies just have to attend the funeral but I had to lead it and try and control my emotions as best I could. But I would do it, I wanted to do Dad proud, he deserved that. It was his wish to die at home and he got that wish. It was our wish to have him in repose at home after his remains returned from embalming. As word filtered out about Dad's death many people started calling to the house to sympathise with the family. His remains returned home after embalming at about 3.00pm. He would now have, as they say, a 'good send-off'.

All the neighbours and relations arrived bearing trays of sandwiches and cakes, many others arrived to help with the washing up and the making of pot after pot of tea. It's at times like these that the stories abound. Story after story was repeated from neighbours and friends about Dad, talking about his life as a sheep and cattle dealer. So it was a constant flow of people, stories, sandwiches, cakes and tea. It was beautiful, Dad would have been so proud of the turn-out over the two days. By Thursday night all my family were exhausted. I knew my Mum was totally exhausted, so we encouraged her to go to bed for a few hours. Some neighbours and friends of Dad would stay in the room with his remains as a mark of respect. I stayed until about 2.00am, but I knew I would need a few hours sleep in order to function for the funeral Mass the next day. I had already broken away from the steady flow of people earlier that day in order to write my eulogy for my Dad. I had it ready, I would talk about his life as a husband, a father, and his devotion to my Mum.

As a sheep dealer and cattle dealer, Dad always practiced honesty in his business. I had also picked up a couple of stories from some of his farming friends that I would share. His love for music, entertaining with a song, playing the accordion and involvement in the local drama society, the Tidy Towns and local football were well known but important parts of who he was so I would mention that too. I would mention his bravery in facing up to his illness. Most of all I would highlight Dad's deep, rich and firm religious faith quoting the line he used at his speech on my ordination day: *"But the first thing I want to say is thanks be to God that God left us our health, my wife and myself, to celebrate Ray's day today"*.

He believed in the goodness and love of God, he recognised his own failures but he knew above all that the life he had was blessed by God; he was blessed with his wife Mona, his children, and his work. And it meant most of all that the life he had would one day end and re-begin in another form, in another life, by virtue of his faith in the resurrection. After the funeral Mass his remains were taken to the local cemetery and he was laid to rest along with his two granddaughters (both Joe and Olive's little girls). Alwynne, who died at 13 months on 11th October 1975, and her sister Naomi, who died at three months old on 8th July 1985. Fr Joe Brilly led the prayers at the graveside as Dad was laid to rest. After the burial there were the traditional afters of refreshments for those who attended the funeral and wished to partake. The following days and weeks were time for me to adjust to the absence of Dad. Plenty of visitors were calling to our home with Mass cards and sympathy cards. I was also thinking that I would have to set a date for returning to South Africa as I knew my superiors in Kiltegan would want me returning as soon as possible but I was not going to be pressurised into returning until I was ready. I would know when I was ready. I would set a date for returning after the traditional month's mind Mass in memory of my Dad. I wanted to help Mum out in any way I could with all the arrangements. There is always a lot of work in acknowledging all those who attended the funeral and sent cards and floral wreaths, and helping Mum sort out all the expenses around the funeral. I had no intention of phoning Aer Lingus anymore about my lost luggage. It was gone; I had replaced most of the contents anyway. One of the final arrangements I helped with, along with my Mum and brother and sisters, was deciding the type of headstone for Dad, and his granddaughters' grave. With that done I departed home for South Africa on 23rd April, two days before my 37th Birthday.

Before I left for South Africa, my long-lost child minder Kitty Allen (Cox) had called many times to our house and I was so happy to have her back in my life. We promised to keep in touch.

I returned to South Africa by the same route as before. My stop-over in Amsterdam was four hours so I had plenty of time to get something to eat. While I was having some food I got chatting to another priest on route to South Africa. We chatted for ages and I shared my story about going home and my Dad's death. In passing I mentioned about my lost luggage. He suggested I check downstairs in the lost luggage room at Schiphol. I admitted I didn't even think such a room existed. Well after a few inquiries I found the room with a small window to communicate with the man inside. I explained to him my situation about my bag never arriving with me from South Africa on 13th December last year. He spoke in perfect English and said there would never be a missing bag here in the room that long. I showed him my passport and asked him could he check giving him details of my bag. He said there was no point in checking, as it was not possible. I begged him once more to take a look. I was about to give up and walk away when I stuck my head in through the window and I was astonished to see a huge room full of luggage. So I could understand why he was not going to even attempt to check for me. As I scanned around the room as quickly as I could, I spotted a green holdall bag. It looked very familiar, but I couldn't be sure as it was about located half-way down the room. Then I said to him look that bag over there looks very familiar. Could you check and see if my name is on the label. He walked over to the bag and read out what was on the label "Fr Ray Kelly, Church Road, Tyrrellspass, Co. Westmeath, Ireland". I said that's me. He brought the bag over. I couldn't believe it. There was my bag sitting there for 100 days and no one bothered to get it to me. I asked him why, and he said it was never reported missing. Aer Lingus never reported it missing in the first place. I was shocked, after all my phone calls to them. Everything in my bag was as though I had just packed it. Now I was returning to South Africa with lots of luggage. Our regional superior met me at the airport and after he welcomed me back he made no bones about telling me that I would not be allowed take my holidays home now for three years from the date of my return. At the time what he said did not impact me greatly, but it would later.

Meanwhile, I was back in Luckau with Fr Alex, and Fr Sean to resume my language course in Northern Sotho. As I settled into it the impact of the last five months began to take hold of me. The realisation of what I had gone through with Dad's death and the leaving home twice in nine months seemed to overwhelm me. I was fortunate that I could grieve with Alex there to listen to me. He didn't have to say anything, I just needed a shoulder to cry on.

I moved officially into my new parish of Tzaneen about a month after returning to South Africa. When I moved to South Africa I learned that the Catholic Church there was a very young church, about 50 years in existence. Moving into Tzaneen, I came to realize very quickly how little had been done over that period of time and just how much still had to be done. I shared the house with my Parish Priest. I was living beside the Cathedral Church that had a congregation of about 80 white people. In the surrounding bush-lands and mountains of Tzaneen town we had two large black town-ships Lenyenye and Nkowankowa and 12 small villages. All of these locations had some form of church building and community with the exception of three, in which case I would celebrate the Eucharist under a large shady tree. And believe me there is nothing more beautiful. While living in Tzaneen the only signs of apartheid were the amount of black people arriving in their black taxis from their town-ships or villages to work as gardeners, cooks and housekeepers. In the evening they would return to their rural homes. Maria was our cook and housekeeper employed

Family photo 1960. Left to right: Ray, his father, Regina, Joseph, his mother and Rosemarie.

Joseph and Ray. His first few days at school with black lamb.

Ray with his sisters Regina and Rosemarie, 1962.

Killarney Jaunting. Left to right: his Aunty Kitty, Ray, Uncle Ger, Rosie
Scally and Bernadette Byrne. July 1965.

Ray's First Holy Communion Day.

Ray and his brother Joseph on Confirmation Day.

Boys from St Joseph's Seconday School Rochfordbridge. Ray seated 2nd from left.

Ray as a teenager.

His grandmother Theresa Gavigan and Ray 1980.

August 1980. Visit to Castel Gandolfo with Pope John-Paul II. Ray standing second from right. His friend Eddie (R.I.P) beside him.

Ordination day 18th June 1989 with his mum and dad.

Ordination Day 18th June, 1989.

Rafiki album cover, featuring the band: Eric Armour, Mick Madigan, Ray Kelly, Martin Smith, Michel O Connor.

Visiting Lesotho.

Ray with altar servers and sadality ladies ready for mass at Lenyenye Church.
South Africa 1990.

Victoria Falls. Zimbabwe 1990.

Ray and children. Village of Motupa. South Africa 1990.

After mass with parishoners at Lenyenye Church. South Africa 1990.

Ray with Dana (taken in the Holy Lands).

Ray performing in a concert *(from the Fr Ray Kelly Facebook page)*.

Ray's first *Late Late Show* in April 2014.

Ray in concert.

Ray and Mickey Harte.

Olly Murs and Ray (*Late Late Show* December 2014).

Jason Byrne, Ray and Louis Walsh (*Late Late Show* December 2015).

Ray with Mary Byrne (at a fund-
raising concert for the late Fr Tony
Coote's Fundraising for Motor
Neurons Disease).

Ray with John McNicholl (Alaska
Cruise 2019).

Daniel O'Donnell (Alaska Cruise 2019).

Ray and Nathan Carter (Alaska
Cruise 2019).

Fr Brian D'Arcy and Ray.

Ray holding his album *Where I Belong* for the first time.

Ray serenading his two favorite pals Biddy and Buddy
(from the Fr Ray Kelly Facebook page).

Family photo at Silver Jubilee Mass 25 years ordained.

Ray and Regina. Toasting the platinum status of album *Where I Belong*.

Gordon Charlton (Ray's Manager) and Ray (after receiving his platinum disc).

at the parish house for many years. She came from the township of Lenyenye and would work for five and a half days every week for the equivalent of 250 rand per month, which is equivalent to about 50 euro. One of the visible signs of apartheid in the town were the public toilets, which were separate for black people and white people.

On the last Friday of the month the black people got paid their wages. They would flood the town for shopping and there would be massive queues at the banks as they lodged their money. Many of them took out insurance for their funerals and paid monthly into it. One Friday I saw apartheid in action as I went to the bank to make a lodgement. The queue was massive and I waited patiently. Within a few minutes one of the bank tellers spotted me and called me forward to deal with my transaction. I left and it was only when I got home I realised what had happened. Because I was white, I didn't have to take the black queue but join the white queue that had no one in it. As I was now living in a white town I had access to electricity and the telephone 24/7. And even though it was expensive to make phone calls from Ireland or vice versa, nevertheless, I felt a lot more secure having these familiar facilities.

I spoke on a weekly basis to Mum and Kitty Allen (Cox). In fact, knowing these weekly contacts were happening helped me to settle down to my new life. I was kept up to date on all the happenings at home. Dad's headstone had been placed over his grave with the design the family picked of the Good Shepherd. Dad being a sheep dealer we thought it appropriate. Kitty sent me photos of the newly erected headstone with Dad's name and his granddaughters' names inscribed on it. My deacon Martin Spillane (Scart) had been ordained a priest now at

Kiltegan and my mother attended his First Mass in Scartaglen, Co. Kerry. Martin was appointed to Zimbabwe along with another newly ordained priest John Kerins and both would be calling to South Africa later in the year on route to Zimbabwe.

Myself and the Parish Priest alternated Mass each Sunday morning at the Cathedral Church beside our house. I loved the English-speaking Mass and we had a great music group. After Mass there was usually a half hour to chat over some refreshments. Then I would head out to some of the rural churches for Mass. We had three catechists in our parish and apart from these the standard of catechetical instruction was very poor. There were never large crowds at any of the village Masses on Sunday's mainly because the people had to walk huge distances to get to church. Though the numbers may have been small in Church, the black congregation really knew how to celebrate a liturgy. They had a very natural sense of rhythm and harmony in their voices, which brought each Eucharist celebration very much alive. Meanwhile at home our society had elected a new Superior General, Fr Kieran Birmingham a Co. Offaly man. I heard he was a surprise appointment but a very popular one.

I was back in South Africa about 16 weeks when on August 16th the phonecall came through with the news of my mother's heart attack. I was starting to get used to parish life and beginning to settle down to the language, people, culture and climate. The news really shocked me and set me back. I knew that going home was what I needed to do. However, I couldn't make that decision. I felt guilty about even having the thought of going home. After all, my local superior in South Africa had told me that I would not be entitled to go home for three years from when I returned after Dad's death. So I couldn't decide. The next day I wrote to Mum and sent her a get-well card assuring her of my thoughts and prayers. I was in constant communication with my family regarding the situation. She was in the ICU in Mullingar hospital and every 24 hours was crucial. I felt so helpless and could not think of anything else. Two days after the news of my mother, two Franciscan Sisters came to visit our house at about 11.00am, they obviously saw how upset I was and I explained the situation of my mum to them. Their answer was direct: "For God's sake go and book your flight home to be with your mother. If she passes away at least you will be with her and please God she will recover and you can come back then."

I didn't need to hear any more. I now knew what I must do. I booked an 8.00pm flight to London and an Aer Lingus flight home. I contacted two of our parishioners Tony and Biebie Warren, and asked Tony if he could do a very fast drive to Jan Smuts airport in Johannesburg. We were on the road by 2.00pm and what normally would take a six-hour drive to the airport Tony covered in four hours. I was home in Tyrrellspass by 3.00pm the following day and at my mother's bedside an hour later.

When she saw me of course she said that I shouldn't have come home that she would be ok as it wasn't a heart attack at all but wind in her stomach. Sure I said "nearly five days in ICU for wind in your stomach, I don't thing so Mum." I spent over four weeks at home with Mum and saw her make a full recovery. I returned to South Africa on 21st September 1990.

Since the release from Robben Island of Nelson Mandela in February, I found on my return so much being said in the media about the "New South Africa". Yet even as the laws, governing apartheid were gradually being removed, that dreaded word APARTHEID would shade everything in the country for a long time to come. I found that when I walked or drove around some of the black villages in the parish I was viewed with suspicion because I was a white man, but the white Afrikanners were equally suspicious of me because I didn't speak Afrikaans which was their first language. I know laws may tumble but those huge barriers between black and white would remain for a long time to come. I found in some very rural areas of my parish some black and white people were involved in forms of devil-worship and witchcraft related killings. Such people believed that the killing or sacrificing of young children can be used as "strong medicine" to ensure success in such areas as business and politics.

My Parish Priest met me at the airport on returning and I was literally thrown into the deep end with about 200 people for Baptism and 350 people for Confirmation ranging in age from 15 to 70 years of age. However, before Confirmation Day the sacrament of confession was administered, and that was fun. As I spoke in the simplest Northern Sotho I could tell many of them hadn't a clue what I was saying. Some of the older ladies and gents came in and kept smiling and nodding their heads. I genuinely didn't know whether I had got the words wrong or was it my accent, but I found out soon enough that their first language was either Zulu or Shangaan. The Confirmation ceremony itself was outdoors and started at 10.00am, but as many of the people had to walk we eventually got started by 11.00am. Bishop Hugh was very patient with everyone. Our cook and housekeeper Maria and her two sons also received the Sacrament and she was thrilled. The entire Confirmation ceremony lasted just over four hours. By nine o'clock that evening I was fit for nothing, only a couple of beers and bed. There were about 150 children for First Holy Communion and I started a Pre-Marriage course for eight couples. Most of them were married already for many years in their traditional tribal ceremonies. Now they wanted to be married in the eyes of the Church. So the work was endless.

One of my biggest scares came when I was driving my four-wheel bakkie through the dirt roads of the village of Motupa. As I was driving along I was stopped by a group of about 20 young lads aged about 16. I really was scared. They opened my door and I thought they might try and pull me out of the bakkie. I kept saying "ke moprista oa k'hatho-like" which translated to 'I am a Catholic priest'. Then luckily David, one of the catechists from the village, came along and explained in more detail and they simply dispersed. As I found out later they had been noted for robbing cars and bakkies off people.

Tzaneen is located very close to a famous game reserve, The Kruger National Park. The size of the park is approximately one third the size of Ireland and home to almost 800 species of animals. To appreciate the park and to see as many animals as possible it is always advised to enter the park about 6.30am, then you can have a full 12 hours there before closing. I always found it a great way to relax and get away from parish life. There is also the opportunity to holiday in the park and then avail of night safaris through the park to see many of the animals hunting. Living in Tzaneen also meant that in the evening I was invited regularly to *braais* and dinners in the homes of parishioners. Martha Costa lived up in the hill on her farm and her pool was always a welcome place to chill out after a hot day. Trish and Robb Orr lived close to Martha on their avocado farm and after a hot Sunday being out in the town-ship all day there was nothing more refreshing that calling there and sharing a beer. Another family from our parish that had made the international media was Karen and George Ferreira-Jorge. The family made world headlines over three years before I arrived in the parish when it was revealed that Karen's mother Pat Anthony was acting as a surrogate mother for her daughter's test-tube triplets. It was the first time that triplets after conception by artificial insemination had been developed in a surrogate mother, the first time that the ova and sperm of a couple had been brought together and then transplanted into a third person; and it was the first time a grandmother had given birth to her own grandchildren. After the furore at that time the family had to go into hiding. Now, three years later, they were more than happy to lead a relatively normal life.

Christmas was coming around fast as I sat in my shorts and T-shirt writing the last of my Christmas cards. As I was writing I was thinking that just over a week earlier I was in Johannesburg after completing a half marathon in two hours and three minutes. I was so excited, proud and happy with myself. Now I was dreading writing my Christmas post. I was filled with loneliness knowing that this would be the first Christmas that I would not be home and the first Christmas without my father. Many letters and cards from home were arriving on a daily basis as well wishing me a happy Christmas. One of the letters was from my Aunt Bridie, my father's last remaining sister. She had lived in the

UK for many years and married late in life to a man named Jack Willis. They decided to retire home to Ireland in the 60s and built a house on my parents' land. Within two years of retiring home Jack died from cancer so my Aunty Bridie depended a lot on my parents and our family in general. Her Christmas letter to me was very sad and I could tell she was tired of living. In the letter she wrote: *"Don't be lonely for your daddy now all his sufferings are over, he is in a happy place, I wish I was gone to join him too."*

Around Tzaneen, only for the date - December 11th - I would not think it was almost Christmas at all. It was so different from home. There was no talk of cakes or pudding, except for the ones I made from my mother's recipes. There was no hype of Santa Claus among the children. And there was no talk about celebrating the birth of Jesus. Certainly it was a time of celebration, but for a very different reason. The men would be coming home from the cities with their wages and gifts to spend time with their families. I had been warned not to expect too many people at Mass on Christmas Day. On Christmas Day I celebrated a 5.00am Dawn Mass with the community in the town-ship of Lenyenye and then went back to Tzaneen for a 12.00pm Mass and Carol Service. After Mass I set about checking out the turkey and ham for the Christmas dinner with the invited guests including Bishop Hugh Slattery. By 5.00pm all of the priests and sisters invited to the dinner had arrived including Bishop Hugh and after the initial pre-dinner drink, all sat down to table. I was really proud of myself, I really was. I never thought in a million years I would be cooking for my Bishop. There were no complaints either, the food was thoroughly enjoyed and chilled soup was made from the avocados in our garden as it was 38 degrees outside on Christmas Day.

After Christmas, Fr Alex and Fr Sean and I decided to take a ten-day trip to Zimbabwe. As the border was only a two-hour drive away, we chose our car as the means of transport. Our plan was to visit Victoria Falls, which is on the border of Zimbabwe and Zambia. Our route took us up to Bulawayo for the first night and we stayed as guests of the local Bishop. Then we headed north-west going through the Hwange Nation Park and Game reserve on to Victoria Falls where we stayed for four days crossing then into Zambia for another two days. It was a fantastic break and I was so happy to share it with Alex and Sean.

When I got back to Tzaneen, there was a message for me to phone home. My dear Aunty Bridie had died, she was hospitalised just a few day after she wrote to me and died on 27th December 1990. She had got her wish. The New Year came and a lot of my thoughts were about home. I was really pining for home in a big way. I was remembering what happened a year ago and the journey of my dad's last weeks. The first anniversary of his death was coming up on 14th February. My grief was as strong as ever. I was feeling very unsettled. I had no energy. I couldn't shake it off. Most of all I was missing my family. I was so far away from them. I just didn't know what to do. The very thought of getting up to work every day seemed to overwhelm me. I tried to shake it off to assure myself that it would pass. It didn't seem to.

Even though my heart was not in it I got through the Easter ceremonies in my parish and actually enjoyed the celebrations with the people. The African people love to have processions and clap and sing and the few days really lifted me. Meanwhile, after Easter I decided to go to Durban for a weeklong retreat. It was a full 12-hour journey there. It was a time to be alone with God. I walked the beach each day, I had my spiritual director to guide me and I shared my story with him. By the time I was back in Tzaneen, I had my decision made. I was going home.

A week after I got to Tzaneen my Parish Priest PJ had got word that his mother was very ill. He was going home to be with her. Indeed, I could empathise with him and I understood what he was going to have to go through. I left him to the airport and wished him well.

A week later I wrote home to share with my mother my decision about returning to Ireland and hoping to get working in my home Diocese of Meath. Having the decision made to go home, the next few months were the most enjoyable time for me in South Africa. I guess the decision was made so there was no internal struggle anymore. The new Superior General of our Society, Fr Kieran Birmingham, called to see me after his bout in hospital recovering from malaria and I shared with him my intentions. He was happy to go along with my decision. I set my date for going home on 16th August 1991. Alex was coming with me for a holiday at home. However, about two months before that he got word his Dad was not well so he decided to go home early. What is it about us guys, three of us going home early because of ill parents? And rightly so after all we only have one set of them. Fr PJ's mother died in June and he would not be returning until the end of July. I also met my Bishop Hugh Slattery and shared with him about my departure. He understood and was very supportive and assured me I would always be welcome back to the Diocese of Tzaneen.

About two weeks before I departed from South Africa one of my last big ceremonies in the township of Lenyene was a mega-marriage ceremony. I had prepared ten couples over a number of weeks for their special day. Over one thousand people were at the ceremony and there was food for everyone afterwards.

CHAPTER 12

....

The Decision

Arriving home on 17th August was the right decision for me. After being away from home for 11 months it was the longest period I had ever been away. I knew I was where I wanted to be. Surrounded by the people I loved and that loved me. Those first 26 months of my priesthood had been turbulent. Indeed, I only realised how turbulent and disruptive it had been after getting home and being in familiar territory. I needed time with my family to grieve over the loss of my dad and to heal. I needed to be assured my mum was ok after her illness, and I needed time to catch up with my brother, my sisters and their children. I just needed time.

After a couple of months at home on holidays I knew it was time also to get back to work somewhere. It was about this time I began to feel the guilt of not being on the missions. Working in missionary countries was what I had prepared for in the seminary with the Kiltegan Fathers for seven years. There was a tug-of-war going on in my head. Did I make a mistake in deciding to come home? No, I knew coming home when I did was the right decision. But what would I do now?

I paid a visit to Kiltegan and spoke to the regional superior there. He agreed that I had two very difficult years starting off my priesthood and that I should try working in Ireland for a time and see how it would work out. Wherever I would work it would be on a temporary basis filling in on an absent priest in his parish. The idea was good but it would not take away the guilt. I was envious of many of my classmates still out on the missions, in Malawi, Nigeria, South Africa, Brazil, and Zambia. Thinking of them gave me thoughts of being a failure, of letting the class of '89 down, of letting the Society down; I was very hard on myself. Why was I feeling this way? Why didn't it work out for me? Maybe it still could in time.

In early December word came through that there was a temporary chaplaincy vacancy in the Curragh Camp, Co. Kildare. This was an army camp and a training location for young men and women joining the army and a Cadet School; it was a place I knew fairly well having worked with the Department of Defence for nearly 11 years. In fact, I went to the Curragh to work in the Command Cashier's Office, and later in different areas of the camp on inspection duties from the Department. I was delighted to be part of a team of priests there working as chaplains. I was familiar with a lot of the army grades and ranks, so the language used was not alien to me. Many of the soldiers lived in the camp with their wives and children in married quarters. There was a primary school on the camp too, to cater for the children. In fact, it really was a parish within itself. Many of the friendships I forged over my six months there still remain today.

As army chaplains we would meet with other army chaplains regularly. I remember one such meeting was held on one of the Naval Ships the LE Eithne, based in Haulbowline Naval Base in Cobh, Co. Cork, and organised by Fr Des Campion the Naval Chaplain. The ship was going out on surveillance around the Irish coast and we boarded it in Haulbowline before departure for our meeting. Following our meeting a helicopter would winch us up and take us back to dry land again. I think we were about an hour out to sea in lower deck having our meeting. The sea was fairly rough and gradually I noticed all of the priests opening their collars including myself. The seasickness was taking hold and the meeting came to an abrupt end as the priests dispersed looking for the nearest toilets. I never realised before that I didn't have sea legs but after that experience I knew better. Within a few hours the helicopter arrived and winched us to safety before flying back to Haulbowline and dry land.

The Curragh Camp was part of the Diocese of Kildare and Leighlin. A team of priests from the diocese often got together and would put on a cabaret show to raise funds for various charities whether it was the Boy or Girl Scouts or a new roof on a church or whatever. It was always a great social occasion, and for the six months I worked in the Diocese I became part of the entertaining clergy or All Priests Show. One of the priests from the show was Fr Liam Lawton, and I remember him singing the song "To all the girls I loved before". Liam; a native of Edenderry Co. Offaly, went on to become a wonderful composer of sacred music. Over the years since he has recorded numerous albums. Indeed, his music has been used in many concerts in places such as the Vatican and The White House. The last show I performed with these guys was at Goff's, Co. Kildare, a major fundraising event for one of the local charities.

My temporary appointment at the Curragh Camp finished in early summer just short of six months. I felt so good about myself, and my time at the Curragh. It really was an enjoyable time of my priesthood. I had the daily ministry of priesthood and the social side of performing with the other priests in the shows. I was also only about one hour drive away from home, and the combination of all three was very comfortable for me.

In the summer of 1992, the Kiltegan Fathers asked me would I consider going to the USA for some missionary appeal work. While I had limited experience of missionary work, the society felt that sharing my experience of South Africa would have a very positive impact. They trusted that the parishes I would make the appeals in would be very welcoming and would love to hear my personal story. It was also my opportunity to give something back to the society for all they had done for me. I landed in Newark Airport in New Jersey on Monday 8th June 1992, and based myself at the St Patrick's Father's House in Cliffside Park. My first weekend of preaching was in a place called Tully, very near the city of Syracuse and about four hours from New Jersey. This little town was very beautiful and fascinated me. The church and the houses were all wooden and it reminded me of the houses in *Little House on the Prairie*. I loved it there, especially because the people were so warm and friendly, and there were lots of 2nd and 3rd generation Irish. After my two masses on the Saturday, and three masses on the Sunday, I was then taken to dinner in the evenings.

The following weekend I drove to a parish in Philadelphia, after which, for the next two weekends, I would be in Houston, Texas. This was an ideal opportunity to visit my cousin Gabrielle and her husband Malcolm and their two girls. I really was enjoying my trip to the US, after all, not everyone is lucky enough to only have to work two days a week. That's the way I felt about it. I was asked then to fly to California for a six-week period staying in the St Patrick's House in San Jose about 50 miles south of San Francisco. While here I visited parishes in Sacramento, San Francisco, Las Vegas, Nevada, and Phoenix, Arizona and my last two weekends were in parishes in San Diego and Los Angeles. What a way to see the United States of America.

During my five days off each week I took in The Grand Canyon, The Golden Gate Bridge, Hollywood, and Waterworld in San Diego. I also had lunch at Pebble Beach Golf Resort near the town of Carmel on the Monterey Peninsula, and of course played some golf while I was there. I continued south and crossed the border into Tijuana, Mexico. I was the regular tourist, although, the most difficult part for me was getting into my car after visiting all of these great places and having no one to talk to and share my experiences with. I was bursting with excitement about where I had been. After my six weeks in California, I returned to New Jersey via Chicago to spend a few days with my cousins, Trish and Frank Sweetman, in the town of St Charles. During my last few weeks I was located at the St Patrick's House in New Jersey. Whilst here I visited some parishes in the States of Connecticut and Massachusetts, and spent a few days in Cape Cod.

On my return to Ireland, after a few days with my family, I spent a week in Kiltegan sharing with them my USA experience. During that week there were priests coming and going from the Irish homes, and from the mission countries. It was always good to chat to them and listen to their experience of their life and work. Somehow, I felt connected to the Society again after my experience in America and listening to their experiences. Much of the guilty feelings that stuck to me for months after I returned from South Africa had disappeared. It was good to be in Kiltegan for these days.

About a month after my visit to Kiltegan the Society asked me would I consider going to work in Aughnacloy, Co. Tyrone, Northern Ireland. The Parish Priest there was gone on sick leave having by-pass surgery. I would fill-in for him for a short while. Another temporary appointment, and this was a difficult appointment. Being a Catholic priest and living and working in a seventy percent Protestant town at the height of the Troubles in Northern Ireland was not easy. Fr Padraig Murphy was the other priest in the parish and he shared the Parochial House with me while waiting to move into his own house. The Parochial House was located just a couple of hundred yards from the border post crossing into Co. Monaghan. Fr Padraig and I alternated our visits to the three churches Aughnacloy, Killens and Caledon for masses. I got to know many wonderful people in the town. In my six months in Aughnacloy I discovered a huge amount of suffering and pain as a result of sectarianism. I witnessed a lot of intimidation of the people and indeed of myself. Many of the Protestant people chose not to speak to me because I wore, as they said, the Roman collar. In some of the shops where I would frequent the conversation was zero. Sometimes I would just force conversation from the people whether it was to talk about the weather or the traffic or whatever.

The 12th July, the anniversary of the Battle of the Boyne, was a day to get out of town for most of the Catholics. Sometimes, when I would be saying the 11.30am Mass in the town on a Sunday, I would have to hold off for a while or re-start the Mass as many of the people coming to Mass had to cross the border checkpoint. While crossing at the checkpoint they would be purposely held up by the British soldiers so as to be late. Even though I would go through the checkpoint a few times every week and particularly when going home, I was often directed in to a huge hangar with nothing in it except a pit in the middle of the building and a desk with a British soldier sitting at. The purpose of the pit was to do a thorough check on my car for fear of carrying arms and as the search took place I would be interviewed by the British soldier at the desk. After about a 15-minute search I was directed to drive out. I only had to drive around the corner to the Parochial House. I saw this as a form of intimidation because those checking me out knew exactly who I was and where I lived. I was advised by some of parishioners to always check my car after it was searched to make sure everything was as it should be. I was glad my time in Aughnacloy ended after six months. While, I loved the work and the people, I could not get used to the coldness I experienced. It just didn't make sense to me.

After my short-term experience of the Curragh and Aughnacloy, I was enjoying working in Ireland. I knew Kiltegan were happy to give me short-term appointments, with a view to not settling anywhere in order to encourage me to go back to missionary work. However, I felt after three years of ordination I needed a more long-term appointment. So I asked to have an appointment in my own Diocese of Meath for at least a two-year period. Bishop Michael Smith who ordained me was happy to take me into his Diocese.

Meanwhile, before I took up my next appointment, I saw advertised in the local papers about a talent competition taking place in the Bridge House in Tullamore, Co. Offaly. It had been a long time since I had got involved in anything like this. I attended the first round heats and easily got into the second round. About six weeks later I was called to participate in the second round. I was surprised I was still in the competition and made it to one of the three semi-final nights. As far as I was concerned I had gone as far as I expected. The results of my semi-final surprised me, it really did. I made it to the final. There were eleven contestants in the final and I was the third act to perform. I began with a song from the musical *Porgy and Bess* called "Summertime", next I sang "The Wind Beneath my Wings", and finally I finished up with the Frank Sinatra classic "New York, New York". All my family were there, and I was delighted to see my long time friends Ann O'Sullivan, Marie Gough, Annie Purcell, her daughter Pauline Powell and lots of other friends from the Curragh where I had worked the previous year. By 1.00am the result was announced and the judges were escorted onto the stage. The place went wild as my name was called out as the overall winner. The cheering continued as I walked from the back of the ballroom to the stage to the congratulations of everybody and to receive my prize. I got a cheque for £750.00 as well as a silver trophy and set of crystal glasses. Even 26 years on, my performance in the competition can still be viewed on YouTube and has currently had over a quarter of a million views.

A temporary appointment came up in the parish of Drumraney near Athlone, Co. Westmeath. My mother's cousin Fr Joe Pettit had retired home to Ireland after over 30 years in Nigeria. He was working in a small rural area of Tang, Drumraney parish, and was about to undergo by-pass surgery which would put him out of action for about three months. I was happy to fill in for him there. I was so well looked after by his housekeeper Kitty Feeney and many of the parishioners, there was no pressure and it was so lovely after my time in Aughnacloy.

In September of 1993, I began working in St Mary's Parish, Navan, Co. Meath. About a month before I took up the appointment Bishop Smith requested to see me to tell me where he was appointing me. When he mentioned Navan I realised it was a town I was not familiar with at all. As a child, I would drive through the town with my family on route to our annual weekly holiday at Bettystown to Ryan's Caravan Park. Other than that Navan meant nothing to me. However, Bishop Smith assured me I would like Navan as it had a history of great church choirs and a great Musical Society.

Fr Peter Mulvany was also taking over as the administrator of the parish when I began that September. We were a team of five priests working in the parish and living in the newly renovated parochial house, all with our own apartments within. From the beginning Peter and I got on very well together. He was a former Columban Missionary priest who had worked in South Korea for over 12 years. I often think the reason we clicked was the fact that both of us came from a missionary background of priesthood and had similar charism.

My nine years in Navan were perfect. I could not have asked for a more wonderful parish to help me settle into priesthood, and I loved it. I loved the people, and I loved the communal living at the parochial house where we were all one team along with the staff there. The two Marys in the office were always so helpful, Mary McCabe an avid Meath football supporter and Mary Cuffe who worked part-time. The rest of the staff were so easy to be around and always made sure us priests wanted for nothing. I was thrown into the deep-end of all of the parish activities. I was on the daily rota of masses in either St Mary's Church in the town where Peggy Owens was the sacristan who kept everything, including the priests, in top shape, or St Oliver's Church at Blackcastle where Josie and Patricia were the sacristans. On Saturdays I had confessions over a three-hour period and then the chaplaincy role at Our Lady's Hospital, which often meant being called during the night if a patient was deemed to be close to death. I was chairperson for two primary schools in the parish: Scoil Mhuire, a former De La Salle Primary School for boys, and St Ultan's Special School for children with mild general learning disabilities, ages ranging from four to 18. My work in these schools varied from the role of chaplain to decision making, along with the other members on the Board of Management. I was also chaplain in St Michael's All-Girls Secondary School established by the Loreto Sisters in 1904. Sister Elaine, who was the principal, welcomed me and I felt very much part of the staff there as I provided chaplaincy services for the staff and pupils.

Navan was a town famous for bingo. There were at least three different sessions of bingo each week for various organisations in the town and Navan Parish ran a parish fund-raising bingo every Monday night. As none of the other priests were too anxious to be involved, and as it was important for a priest of the parish to attend, I volunteered to help out any way I could. Using my limited experience from attending bingo with my Aunt Kitty and Uncle Ger for years, I would help sell the books, chat to all the customers and then call a few numbers during the evening. Usually the entire bingo hall was a sea of smoke as smoking and playing bingo went hand in hand. In fact, many bingo players would confess to smoking at least ten cigarettes during their one and a half hour bingo session. Sometimes I would have to waft my way through the bingo hall to find the person who had shouted. When smoking was outlawed in public buildings, it included bingo halls and there was a huge outcry. In fact I thought it was the end of bingo. I heard lots of people saying, "that's it, I'm never going to bingo again", but they did continue to come and play. We would have an interval for 10 to 15 minutes to give the smokers a chance to ease their withdrawal symptoms and go outside for a few cigarettes.

When Bishop Michael Smith mentioned to me that Navan had a great history of church choirs and a great Musical Society, he was certainly right. And while I loved Church Choirs I also had a passion for rock-gospel music. Soon, I was in contact with other singers and musicians with a similar desire. Evelyn and Kathleen Sheridan and I got together to pick some popular songs and along with other members of their family we formed St Oliver's Rock Gospel group. We had a brilliant sound and would rehearse every week for a couple of hours before our 12.30pm Sunday Mass in St Oliver's Church at Blackcastle in Navan. The Mass became so popular that on a regular basis many people came from other parishes to our Sunday Mass. There was always a constant stream of phone calls to the parish office to see if our rock-gospel Mass was scheduled for a particular Sunday. The church was always jammed, and whilst Ireland did not have a tradition of people being early to church for Mass, or indeed staying in the church until the end of Mass, this rock-gospel Mass was an exception as many people got there early to guarantee a seat and stayed until the last note was played as a round of applause rang out.

I was about a year in the parish of Navan when I joined St Mary's Musical Society. The society was formed in 1967 staging their first show a year later. When I joined it was a new experience for the committee as I was the first priest ever to be involved on the stage with other members of the cast. They just didn't know what to call me. Was it to be Fr Kelly, or Fr Ray or just Ray? I think I put their mind very much at ease as I mingled with everyone and joined them after rehearsals for a pint in Paddy Fitzsimons' pub across the road from the community centre where we would rehearse.

The first show in which I was on stage was *Jesus Christ Superstar* in 1994. I auditioned for the part of Jesus but I didn't get the part. William Byrne got the part and was brilliant. In fact, William went on to play the lead role afterwards in London in the West End, and when the show came to Dublin. I got the part of Simon Peter, my favourite part of which was singing the song "Heaven on Their Minds". The following year I played the part of Reuben, the eldest half-brother to Joseph in *Joseph and the Amazing Technicolor Dreamcoat*. The big song I had was "One More Angel In Heaven". The next production was *Fiddler On The Roof* in 1996, where I played the role of Motel, a poor tailor who gathers the courage to ask Tevye for his eldest daughter Tzeitel's hand in marriage. He feels that "even a poor tailor is entitled to some happiness". On the show we get married in a traditional Jewish style wedding and start a family, which also includes the new arrival of a sewing machine. My big song on the show was "Miracle of Miracles". The last show I took part in was *Guys and Dolls* where I played the part of Nicely-Nicely Johnson and performed the song "Sit Down, You're Rockin' The Boat".

One of the founding members of the musical society was Jim Byrne. Jim was the local barber in the town and a genius with regards music. I always regarded barbershops and hair salons as places where many clients would pour out their personal stories to the barber or stylist. Jim Byrne was a man who would listen as his clients chatted to him, and the information was always held in strict confidence. I would have my hair cut with Jim on a monthly basis, and we would usually spend our time discussing music and songs that might suit my voice. When my hair was cut, Jim would take me to the kitchen area for a cup of coffee and possibly we would end up trying out a song or two on the piano. I often got the chance to perform a few songs at weddings if Jim's band was playing. Jim died before his time in November 2010. However, I know all his family continue to perform and play music and one of his sons, Brian, went on to become a very famous film score composer living in Los Angeles.

I enjoyed my priesthood whilst living and working in Navan; I loved the parish, the work, the people and the musical outlet of the rock-gospel group and St Mary's Musical Society. As far as I was concerned it was perfect and as a priest I really felt this was where I wanted to be. During the first few years in Navan, I decided I wanted to stay working at home and not go back to South Africa or indeed any other African missionary country. I was happy and fulfilled; there were no more feelings of guilt or regret with this decision. I knew it was the right one for me. With that in mind I applied to my superiors of Kiltegan Fathers to leave the Society, and be incardinated into the Meath Diocese with Bishop Michael Smith. Bishop Michael was delighted to accept me as part of his Diocese and in 1996 I became a member of the Meath Diocesan clergy.

CHAPTER 13

....

Mona

In 2002 when I was transferred to Rahan, Mucklagh outside Tullamore, Co. Offaly, I thought my heart would break. I was devastated. Before I left Navan there was the usual goodbye parties and gifts showered on me from so many of the parishioners. The guys in our rock-gospel group presented me with a mini-disc playback machine with some backing tracks on. At the time I hadn't a clue what I would do with it, but I later learned how to use it and record with it. My last trip from Navan with my car loaded up with all my worldly goods was the most difficult; I cried all the way home.

I called into my mother and she knew I was upset. She was in her usual spot lying stretched out on her favourite couch in the kitchen with her favourite companion Ben, her seven-year-old King Charles Cavalier lying beside her, or "her little man" as she called him. I convinced her back in 1995 to get a little dog as a companion. Mammy was reluctant for a long time, but one day I took her for a drive and told her we were going to Carlow to collect her new dog. She didn't even argue with me, I think she was happy that the decision was made for her. We picked up the cutest little King Charles Cavalier puppy and I knew she fell in love with him straight away. He was born on 29th July and was eight weeks old when he became part of our family. The initial few months of the increase in family were stressful enough for Mammy as

she went through the toilet training and the tearing of cush-
ions, armchairs, and anything he could get his teeth around.
Many times when I would arrive home for a night she would
tell me to take Ben away with me. I knew she would never let
him go. On a Sunday night when I would stay over at home,
the first opportunity Ben got to dash through to door and
to my bedroom he was on top of me and licking my face all
over to wake me up. He was as much my Ben as hers, but if
I mentioned about bringing him back to my parish, Mammy
would just look at me and I knew I dared not. Arriving home
from my last trip from Navan, Ben jumped all over me as he
usually did to greet me, this time licking my tears. Mammy,
seeing how upset I was, consoled me by telling me "it is ok to
be upset after leaving nine happy years behind you". She was
right of course; the only positive aspect to it was that I was
located much closer to home.

Mammy was 81 years of age now and I knew her health
was slowing up dramatically. She suffered a lot of pain in her
back and legs from arthritis and consequently had to take a
lot of painkillers. She always said the tablets never worked,
nevertheless, she continued to take her usual daily dose. She
spent most of her days now lying on her couch with her faithful pal Ben. She was able to cook a little for herself, and my
sister Rosemarie would come from her home in Tullamore
faithfully every Tuesday and stay overnight with her. She
would clean the house, and get any shopping she needed,
as well as stocking up her cigarette supply. She had given up
the driving about a year before, indeed, we as a family were
all delighted over that because she had a few scrapes with the
car driving in and out of our gate. When she was assured that

we were all there to 'dance around her' she agreed to let go of her driving licence, which was a very happy relief to all of us. I was glad to now be that bit closer to home where I could call into her a few times in the week, stay over night, and take on my responsibility of looking after her as well and be back in the parish in 20 minutes if needed. I was now living in a house on my own which was a totally new experience for me, it was a house that looked like it needed a fair bit of decoration and painting, but a house that was liveable. With the help of family, especially my sister Regina and her husband Seamus, who was a painter and decorator, it didn't take that long to get it into the way I wanted it.

There was great community spirit in Mucklagh. The parishioners and neighbours around the church were very welcoming and helpful. Timmy Dillon across the road kept the grounds of the church and house in ship-shape. Along with his wife Anne, Timmy was always on hand and so helpful. Marie White was the sacristan and she kept everything spick and span along with her husband Ray. They were so lovely and I knew I could call on them 24/7 for anything. Marie just wanted to 'mother me' as much as she could, and make sure I never went hungry with constant invites to dinner.

One day while rooting in one of the presses in the sacristy, I came across a little machine like a CD player only smaller. I'd never seen something like this before. There were loads of little mini-discs as well beside it with titles on the discs like Classical Church Music, Christmas Hymns, recorded albums by Andrea Bocelli, and some instrumental church music. When I asked Marie what they were for, she explained that Fr Martin McErlean, the previous priest in the parish, would connect the system up through the speakers in the church from the altar and he would often play some music in the church if the choir was not available. I tried it out myself a few times when the church was quiet and I was really impressed by the system and how it worked. Soon after that the penny dropped and I realised that I had one or two mini-discs given to me, along with a much larger backing track machine by my friends of St Oliver's Rock Gospel Group from Navan. Indeed, at this stage I hadn't even taken the gift out of its packaging except for a quick look after it was given to me. I found the mini-discs and set about listening to them in the church. There were Elvis songs on it, Bruce Springsteen songs, Neil Diamond songs, along with loads of other great backing-tracks of songs. I remember getting excited about it all. Straight away in my head I was imagining myself singing to some of the tracks, I just needed the words of the songs. While some of the tracks were in the wrong key for my voice, there were plenty of songs that suited me perfectly.

Now that the thought of possibly being able to sing in church with the aid of backing-tracks was firmly planted in my head, I couldn't let it go. My large 'gift' backing track machine was out of its box and I started to devour the instructions as much as I could understand. This machine could record tracks as well. All I needed now was to find some tracks to record, ones that would suit my voice to sing. Before long I was downloading from iTunes. I remember one of the first pieces of music I downloaded from iTunes was "Panis Angelicus" from an Andrea Bocelli album. I rehearsed it in the evening when the church was locked up and no one was around. I went over it and over it and was reluctant to make a decision as to whether I would sing it at a Sunday Mass. One evening when rehearsing, Timmy Dillon, who lived across the road, heard my singing coming from the church. He had a key to the church and while I was singing away Timmy was listening in the porch. When I was finished, he walked in clapping and I knew then my secret was out. "Are ye going to sing that at Mass" he asked. I said "maybe". "You should," he said. The following Sunday I sang "Panis Angelicus" after Holy Communion and finished to a reluctant round of applause. I say reluctant because I think the local congregation wanted to clap but were unsure whether they should clap or not in the church. However, despite their reluctance, they did. And so Ray Kelly singing in church was born. Gradually, I began to build up my repertoire of songs. Thanks to iTunes I found the tracks of "Ave Maria", Garth Brooks' "The River", "The Old Rugged Cross", "Love Changes Everything" from the musical *Aspect of Love*, "My Forever Friend" by Charlie Landsborough and many more. Within a few weeks, the word had spread and I was attracting many more people from outside the parish to weekend Mass.

During my first year in Mucklagh, I was going back to Navan parish occasionally fulfilling some wedding commitments and other events from time to time. It is something that happens to most priests when they are moved from one parish to another one. Tom Fitzsimons from Navan also booked me to lead a pilgrimage to Fatima with a group of pilgrims from their parish. The pilgrimage was for one week from 23rd June 2004. However, Mammy was hospitalised about a week before our pilgrimage departed.

She had not been eating a lot for weeks, had been in a

lot of pain, and there were times when she would have a loss of blood. During her hospitalization she was receiving blood transfusions and platelets. After she had received these transfusions, she was full off energy. Within a few days, however, her energy levels dropped again. This process continued for a few weeks. I was assured that there was no danger of her condition worsening and I left with my group for Fatima. I kept in touch with home a couple of times every day. At the beginning of my third day in Fatima my sisters phoned me to inform me that Mammy had deteriorated and perhaps I should come home. I was on a flight out of Lisbon on Friday evening and I was at my mother's bedside early on Saturday morning.

I was really shocked to see how she had deteriorated. When I walked into her room she was surprised to see me, as she knew I had gone to Fatima. I told her I came home early. She didn't really question me on that but knowing her she probably did in her own head anyway. After sitting with her for about ten minutes she surprised me when she said "I'm dying you know". I was completely thrown by her statement and wanted to say straight away, no you are not you will be fine and home soon lying on your couch with your little man in a few days but I didn't. I said nothing for a minute or more. Then I said, "so, you're dying, are you? How do you feel about that?" She looked at me with her deep blue eyes and said, "I'm ready to go, I'll be with your daddy". "Ye you will," I said, "you will be together again after being separated for over 14 years, make sure you tell him I love him and miss him still." There was silence then between us for a long while as Mammy closed her eyes to sleep. She wasn't asleep. I asked her reluctantly "Mammy would you like to go to confessions?" Her eyes shot open and said "Go to confessions with you, you must be joking, anyway I have nothing to confess." Well I said "I'll say the prayer of absolution and give you the blessing of the sick and Holy Communion." I had given Mammy all of these sacraments before, many times in the comfort of her own home when we would celebrate Mass together, although, there was no danger of death then. Now it felt very different for me. Somehow, I felt inadequate, and uncomfortable doing this. When my sisters and brother came in to visit later that day Mammy never mentioned anything about dying to them. In fact, it was never mentioned again.

Later that day she was given another transfusion of blood and platelets and as usual it perked her up greatly. She also asked us to arrange to get her home as soon as possible. I knew the reason, in fact we all did. We agreed it was the right thing to do to have her home for her last days and weeks to die in her own bed and home. We had been through all this before and would face into it again with one intention, just to show Mammy how much we all loved her.

The doctors and nurses were reluctant to let Mammy home because of the nature of her illness. They did agree that there was nothing more they could do for her, and that her days were few. They wanted us to wait until Monday until such time as they could set up some home services to cater for her illness, however, we persuaded them to let us take her home and bring in palliative care on Monday. They agreed, but warned us that there may be some bleeding from her body and to be prepared for that. They would give her one more transfusion of blood and platelets on Sunday morning.

In the afternoon, the ambulance took her home with my sister Rosemarie accompanying her. She was wheeled into her own home and her request was to be put on her couch. She was now in her happy place with her "little man" Ben resting along side her. It was the picture we as a family all longed to see and treasure. She drank a little cup of tea and smoked a few pulls from her Silk Cut cigarette. Her sister-in-law May came in to see her and chat, as she had often done before. The chatting was very little but it didn't matter, it was just good to be here. Having her home on the first night was not easy, as the hospital staff had warned. My sister Regina agreed to stay with Mammy and sleep in the bed with her, whilst I was in the room next door. At about 2.00am Regina called me in; the bed was covered in blood and Mammy was bleeding from her nose and mouth. We gently cleaned her up, and changed the bed and we all settled down. However, within a few hours we had the same problem and carried out the same cleaning up again. After that most of the bleeding had stopped. By early morning my sister Rosemarie and my brother Joseph were on hand to help us, as well as our neighbour across the road Wally who was a nurse and my mother's first cousin.

The next few days were what I like to call prime time, or privilege time, as we all got the chance to shower Mammy with love and care. During those days Mammy was confined to bed, she enjoyed sips of tea and took a few pulls from her cigarettes. She enjoyed the presence of her "little man" Ben as we sat him beside her in her bed for a while. However, Ben wanted more attention and rubbing than Mammy was able to give him. I offered up Mass for her in her bedroom each day and she was able to receive a small particle of the Eucharist. She welcomed her sisters from Edenderry; Patsy, Nancy and Angie. However, Mammy was sleeping a lot too and while many neighbours, friends, and women whom she had been the midwife for wanted to see her and thank her for all she did for them, as time went by we felt it was now so important to just have family around her. Sometimes either my brother or I while sitting with Mammy would sing one of her favourite party songs. It might be a verse or two of her medley of songs like "Daisy Daisy", "My Bonny Lies Over the Ocean", or "I'll be your Sweetheart". Of course her favourite was "The Old Refrain". *"I often think of home Dee-ol-ee-ay, When I am all alone and far away; I sing an old refrain, Dee-ol-ee-ay For it recalls to me a bygone day."* While her eyes might be closed most of the time, sometimes they would open and a little smile and movement of lips would follow as she tried to join in.

The palliative care team came on board on Monday, which I was so glad of as I was not sure I could face another night of what Regina and I had faced on the Sunday night. Kathleen Guinan, a native of Tore outside Tyrrellspass, was the palliative care nurse. Our family knew her and her family well so it was really like having another member of the family around. She was brilliant. As a family we were able to get some valuable rest, as we would need it in the days ahead. Kathleen administered an injection to Mammy to stop any more bleeding. Occasionally Kathleen would need a little help just to change Mammy's position in the bed or freshen her up a little. For her last few days her only intake was a little water on a sponge, which helped to cool her mouth from dryness.

Meanwhile, in my own head I was preparing for what lay ahead too. I had been through all this with Dad over 14 years ago as a newly ordained priest and I felt totally inadequate then. Now I guess I had over 15 years of priesthood behind me so just like I did for Daddy; I would carry out my role as a son and as a priest to the best of my ability. I would be saying the funeral Mass and giving the eulogy on Mammy, and I was dreading it. I would share about her life as a district midwife, and about the many hardships she endured, as she was called out during the night and attended to her patients, even at the side of the road for the travelling women. I would share about her life as a wife and mother, and her devotion to her family. Then she became Mona the entertainer, when she got a microphone into her hand. I would mention the suffering she endured from arthritis over many years, and how through her strong faith she coped with all the pain.

Kathleen kept us up to date on Mammy's weakness and by Wednesday morning she told us it would not be long. All that day we were there at her bedside, and all I wanted to do was pray, but I couldn't. Mammy was not responding now and she would never open her eyes again. Her breathing became more deep and intensive by the hour. Sometimes the change in breathing pattern created a rattling sound; commonly know as the death rattle. By 10.00pm, Kathleen told us it would be very soon. We were all there, sitting on the bed, kneeling on the floor, holding her hands. All her 15 grandchildren were there too. She was Gigi to all of them; she loved all of them deeply and was the midwife for at least two of them. Her eldest grandson Paul Coyle called to say farewell to his Gigi too. Paul was very ill at the time with liver failure. He loved her deeply and she loved him; what we didn't know at the time was that 24 days after Mum's death, death would visit our family again with the sad death of Paul. My sister Rosemarie would have lost her mother and her son within 24 days.

At 10.45pm, Mum opened her eyes wide, took one last look at everyone and breathed her last breath. She had let go. That last shallow breath marked the end of her life. Someone said to me "Ray start the rosary", but I couldn't. It might have been the time for the rosary but I was not able to begin it. It was a time for tears and more tears and I held Mammy's hand in mine and cried and cried and cried. The person who had given me life, the person who had protected me from the teacher who tried to make me write with my right hand, the person that told me who Santa Claus was, had died. Mammy had died. I'm going to stop now and take a break from writing. I haven't cried for Mammy in many years, but I am going to now. Isn't it strange more than 15 years since she died and there are still tears? I guess there will always be some un-cried tears.

I was exhausted, my whole family were exhausted, but there would be plenty of time to catch up on sleep. Meanwhile, Wally our neighbour across the road would lay out Mammy's body. I know Gillian, Mammy's grand-daughter and a nurse wanted to help Wally but she felt it better for her not to be involved. We made tea, we made hot whiskeys, and we began to speak about Mammy, re-living many moments of our lives together as a family. We remembered her last words, what Mammy might have said or done, when she had her last cig-arette. We began to speak about Daddy too. They were to-gether now after being separated for over 14 years. I guess in these hours until morning we were really prolonging both their lives for ourselves. We were grieving.

After 9.00am, I contacted Paddy O'Brien, the undertaker,

to set in motion Mammy's embalming. It was our wish to have her reposing at home after her remains returned from embalming. It didn't take long for word to spread around the village about Mammy's death, which meant many people started calling to the house to sympathise with the family. Mammy was returned to us about 5.00pm after her embalming. The same ritual began, the same as when my Dad died. The wake would begin, and all the neighbours and relations arrived during the evening and well into the night bearing trays of sandwiches and cakes. Story after story was repeated; neighbours and friends spoke about Mammy and her life as a mid-wife on the local district. It was beautiful, Mammy would be so proud of the turn out of so many over the couple of days. As she reposed in her bedroom some neighbours and family stayed in the room over night as a mark of respect to Mammy and to the family. The removal of her remains would take place on Friday evening.

It was a short ceremony with my friend from Navan and St Oliver's Rock Gospel group Rosemary Hussy providing some beautiful reflective singing. The next day, Saturday, her life would be celebrated in the Eucharist in thanksgiving to God for her 85 years of life. During those two days of my mum's wake, I was able to put together the eulogy that would be delivered at her funeral Mass. However, because of the great sense of sadness and loss that I now felt, I knew I would not be able to share it. So I asked my friend from Kiltegan, Fr Martin Smith, to share it on behalf of my family and me. On Friday night tiredness hit me like a ton of bricks. I was exhausted, and I knew I needed a few hours sleep in order to celebrate the funeral Mass the next day.

The funeral was beautiful; every aspect of Mammy's life was talked about and celebrated. So many people came up to me afterwards and were proud to say "Mona delivered me". It was calculated that over her 39 years as a midwife in the district she delivered over one thousand babies to families. Indeed, it was a wonderful testament to her, and a great privilege to share these very special times with families. While I was consumed by a huge amount of sadness and loss over the passing of Mum, I was also very thankful for having such a wonderful, hard-working, and loving mother. As a family we were truly blessed in having her with us for over 85 years. During the few weeks after her funeral, while I was in organisation mode regarding all her affairs, some days I really felt she hadn't left us at all. I would go home to an empty house in Tyrrellspass and sense her presence everywhere. I remember about six months after she died, my sister Regina convinced me to get rid of the kitchen table and chairs. She had been given a lovely new table and chairs that she didn't want. Seamus her husband brought them over and removed the old one from the kitchen and brought in the new set. As soon as it was in place, I said, "No, no, no, bring back the old ones". It was too much change, too soon for me and I wasn't ready. I wanted the old table back, the table beside the couch where Mammy sat. The table that held her ashtray and Silk Cut, the table that she leaned on with her left elbow as she smoked her cigarettes.

My mum has never really left me. I find her when I'm officiating at funerals of ladies of similar age. I find her when I go home to her house in Tyrrellspass, or when I pass by the house in the village where she was born. I find her especially when I go to light a candle or say a prayer in her local church of St Stephen's in Tyrrellspass. I find her when I hear her songs such as "The Old Refrain" come on the radio. I took care of her 'little man Ben' after she died, who was also a constant reminder. Recently, I came across another strong reminder; her soap bag which I kept and put away for safe-keeping. Inside it was an empty bottle, which once held her favourite perfume Chanel No5, and her hairbrush with a few strands of her hair in it. All I know is that all through my life so far I have found little reminders of the lives and experiences of both my parents, that awaken memories for me of the people Mum and Dad were. Reminders of things they said, the ways they had: little bits of times gone by that will forever keep the memories alive.

I guess it was a few months later when a lady named Anne Corbett from Tullamore, about three miles from my parish, contacted me. She knew about my mother's death and as she said knew I was going through a difficult time. She had organised a pilgrimage to Medjugorje and had a vacant seat if I would like to come. Once I had organised cover for my parish while away, I kindly accepted her invitation. It had been 18 years since I had been to Medjugorje and I expected a lot of changes since my visit in 1986. The apparitions had been happening for over five years then, and now 18 years later, the young children to whom Our Lady appeared all those years ago were grown up, and still receiving the visions of Our Lady Queen of Peace. During this visit, I would learn a lot more about Medjugorje. Our group was under the guidance of one of the Irish travel agencies that organise the pilgrimages. So on arrival at Dubrovnik airport in Croatia we were met by local guides who would spend the entire week with us in order to make a success of our trip. Our journey to Medjugorje would take about three hours.

The town is located in the country of Bosnia and Herzegovina. When we arrived in the town, my eyes were opened. I couldn't believe what 18 years of pilgrimages had done to the town. There were hotels and guesthouses everywhere. The small houses that I had remembered were now two, three and four floors high. There were restaurants everywhere, while on my previous visit I struggled to get a bag of chips. Everywhere, there were souvenir shops selling all kinds of religious articles. 18 years before, all I had seen was one lady selling some rosary beads on a kitchen table outside her small house. There were thousands of people all over the town. I recognised St James' Church from my first visit and the parochial house where Our Lady was appearing at that time. What there was no doubt about was the holiness of the place, the volume of prayer that was being prayed every day, and the amount of healing for thousands through the sacrament of reconciliation. Aside from the daily masses at St James' Church in many different languages, the main daily Mass was in the Croatian language at evening time. The rosary and then a holy hour of prayer around the cross usually followed this, or sometimes an hour of Adoration. I was completely overcome by the solemnness of all the ceremonies. The evening holy hours always filled me with tears of grief, which were sometimes uncontrollable. However, it was ok as I was among many other tearful people too. My tears brought me comfort but sometimes complete exhaustion. Our group visited all of the sites that Our Lady appeared at during those early days of apparitions.

The Blue Cross is a very popular location at which Our Lady appeared to the six visionaries in the early days when they hid from the Communist policemen trying to apprehend them. Climbing from the Blue Cross up towards Apparition Mountain or Mount Podbrdo one reaches the site where Our Lady first appeared to the visionaries. After the apparitions began, it became known as Apparition Mountain. Climbing to this site with the group, I led the group in the rosary. I really felt a deep, personal, intimate and life changing moment through my praying the rosary as I climbed.

Another beautiful spot which draws pilgrims is the statue of the Risen Jesus Christ. I love it here. This larger than human form statue made of bronze has been oozing water from the right knee, a liquid that is chemically similar to human tears.

The biggest climb of all for us pilgrims is always the steep climb up Cross Mountain. Whilst climbing I led our group in the Stations of the Cross. The cross was constructed in 1934 by the parishioners in remembrance of the 1900 years since the death of Jesus. It is said that relics from the true cross as a gift from Rome are embedded in the cross. At the beginning of our climb to the High Cross our guide encouraged us to carry a stone(s) in our hand or pocket attributing each stone to the name of a person either living or dead and leave the stone there at the cross. I carried one stone representing my Mammy. I reached the cross with my group and I prayed my rosary in tears conscious of what I was going to do, praying to Our Lady "Mary, my mother take Mammy in your hand and never let her go". As I left I took the little stone from my pocket and was about to place it at the cross, but I couldn't, I felt it was me saying I had to let her go and I wasn't ready, I wasn't ready to let go of my Mammy yet. It was too soon. Some day when I return I would leave that stone at the cross for her, but not yet. I carried the stone back down the mountain with me.

I have returned to Medjugorje almost on an annual basis since that time. I have carried up many stones up to that mountain, remembering them, praying for them in an effort to let go of those with whom I have shared my life. I think of Eddie Fitzgerald, Fr Oliver McDonagh, Trina Keoghan, Peggy Owens, Fr Peter Mulvany, Joe Rabbette, my Aunty Kitty, my nephew Paul, my nieces Allwynne and Naoimi, my father Joe, my mother Mona, and many other relations and friends and parishioners over the years.

A few year ago as I was returning from a pilgrimage there, I met Anne Corbett at the airport. Anne was leading another pilgrimage out there. She was in a wheelchair. She was terminally ill and had little time left. She was on her last pilgrimage to Medjugorje and indeed as she told me at the airport she was uncertain if she would survive the week. She would have been happy to die out there and indeed it would be a fitting place for her to pass away as she had led so many pilgrims over the years to this holy place. She asked me to hear her confessions. I did. She made it home and died a few weeks later. Anne brought me back to Our Lady Queen of Peace when I needed her most and found it hard to find her. Often, I carry a stone to that High Cross Mountain for Anne too and leave it there and simply say "Mary, my mother take Anne in your hand and never let her go".

I was glad to be back in my parish of Mucklagh united with Ben, my mother's 'little man'. As long as I had him with me I felt close to my mother, part of her was with me too.

I had always had a strong desire to record a CD, but I didn't know exactly how to go about it. I spoke to Joe Rabbette a good friend of mine from Clara, a great musician and singer with whom I had travelled to Lourdes and Medjugorje with many times. Joe put me in touch with Peter Kelly at Penny Lane Recording studio in Tullamore. Thanks to the parishioners of Mucklagh, who encouraged me with that extra little push to record the album, and to all of the people in the parish who sponsored me, *Simply Me*, my first ever album, was born. My niece Tara sang a duet with me on the beautiful song "The Prayer". I had a big launch night at the Bridge House Hotel in Tullamore, the scene of my talent competition win. I was so excited having recorded my voice on a disc at last; it was a dream, a long time ambition. I had a feeling, just a feeling, that I would record again sometime. When, where, or how, I didn't know, but I had got the itch for recording and I liked it. The launch night was in aid of local charities and lots of CDs were sold. I dedicated my album in memory of my mum and dad, my nieces Allwynne and Naoimi and my nephew Paul.

Soon after my launch, I got a phone call from my Bishop Michael Smith in Mullingar. I called to his house and after four years in Mucklagh I was on the move. I was being appointed Parish Priest in a small town called Oldcastle, Co. Meath. This was a town that I was not very familiar with. I had been in the parish church once before at the funeral of Bishop Michael's sister. Fr Eugene Conlon had been the Parish Priest for over 20 years there and now as he was approaching 80 years he was about to retire and live in the parish house at Dromone/Moylagh, the out-station part of the parish. All the parishioners of Oldcastle and Dromone/Moylagh loved

Fr Eugene. He had served the community very well over the years, and was indeed entitled to put his feet up. When I arrived in the parish in October 2006, I got a huge welcome and a round of applause. Many of the people knew I could sing and it wasn't long before I got my backing track machine connected up on the altar just like in Mucklagh. They liked it. As in all cases when a new priest arrives at a parish, the masses are hugely attended, mainly to have a good look at the new PP and hear what is he like. Does he say a quick Mass or a long one? All of these little things determine whether I would be liked or accepted. Of course I knew I could never fill the shoes of Fr Eugene or indeed would I ever try. I would just be my own man and they would have to accept it. So being a singer and saying a relatively quick Mass, I would be ok.

Meanwhile, Mum's 'little man' Ben was slowing up. I always thought that after getting over the death of my mother I would never have to experience such intense grief again. How wrong I was. Ben was my link with her. He was over 13 years of age and had lived a couple of years above the normal length for his breed. I prayed that I would never have to do what I had to do in the end. I had to have him put to sleep on 17th November 2008. In all honesty it was the hardest decision I had to make. The decision was mine alone. I didn't want him to suffer any longer. I had to let him go. It broke my heart; it was like Mum dying all over again. I always felt that if I minded him, protected him and loved him as I did he would live forever. I found a lady who had a website to help people who were grieving over the death of their pets. For months I would write to her and share all the happy memories of my pal and Mum's 'little man'. It helped, it really did. I knew I could never replace him but in time I would get another King Charles Cavalier when I felt I had honoured him by grieving sufficiently.

One day I was speaking to Oliver Callan who had a recording studio called Castle Studios. He encouraged me to call and consider recording a few songs. Well we got together and within a few months my second album, *More of Me,* was created. I launched it in Clonmellon and raised some funds for the North Westmeath Pallative care team. I know it seemed to be the case that every time I have been bereaved I resort to recording a new album. Definitely that had been the case. Someone said to me after I recorded *More of Me,* I should call the next album *No More Of Me!*

Just over six months after Ben's death, on the June bank holiday weekend, I drove to Tullow, Co. Carlow to collect my new dog. Before I left, my sister Regina said to me, "since you are out of the house so much, why don't you think of getting two dogs, to keep each other company." I wasn't sure, I think in my heart all I wanted to do was get a male to replace Ben. When I arrived to collect him, he was the only male left and there were two females. One of them in particular was looking up at me almost saying, "take me as well". How could I say no? I took her. Buddy was always going to be the name of the male. Regina put a name on the little girl. Biddy and Buddy came to live in Oldcastle. Life would never be the same again.

I was fortunate that when I would be out of the house for long periods of time or going away for a few days I could depend on my dog-sitters Esther, Bridget Flynn and May Farrelly. When I would return home, I would often find May asleep with the two puppies beside her. It took them a few days to move out of their little bed, but once they got going, the arms of my chairs began to get chewed. The couch in the kitchen was torn to shreds where the white filling was falling out of it. Buddy liked to go for a walk but Biddy wouldn't, so I would have to carry her. Their personalities were total different. Buddy would cling to me, Biddy was Miss Independent, hearing me but ignoring me. They loved to drive in my car in the back seat. More often that not Biddy would try to sit on my knee while I would be driving. Eventually, I got harnesses and could secure them in the back seat but that was only after Biddy had chewed the arm off one of the back doors of my new Toyota Avensis. I would know she was up to something when Buddy would come running to me barking. There I would find her sitting on my kitchen table. If there had been biscuits on a plate on the table, they were gone. I would often find her asleep on my kitchen table as well. On one occasion Oliver Callan called to me with a CD to listen to. He left a package on my kitchen table. We went upstairs to play the CD. When we came down Oliver said "Where are my pancakes?" When we looked at Biddy there she was after carrying the paper bag from the table and comfortably seated on the mat enjoying her sixth pancake. I could write a book about my girl Biddy, maybe someday I will.

She was diagnosed with multiple tumours on 1st November 2018. I was devastated and heart broken. She was given 3-6 months. She lived just two weeks beyond the three months. I had to let her go on Thursday 14th February 2019, the feast of St Valentine and the 29th Anniversary of my father Joe's death. My little family at the Parochial House was broken forever. Buddy is still with me and will be looked after like gold dust as he always is. Needless to say, like Ben, Biddy will be remembered forever in my heart.

CHAPTER 14

....

The Hallelujah Story

In January 2010, John Pakenham and his wife-to-be Mary Magee asked me to perform their wedding ceremony. They were to marry in the parish of Tempo at St Joseph's Church in a little rural area called Craiden, very close to Enniskillen, Co. Fermanagh, in Northern Ireland. It was an honour to be asked, but I was reluctant because of the workload in my parish. Generally I try to avoid attending weddings outside my parish. However, I did know John's parents very well. His father was the local postman so I knew him from when he would deliver mail to the parochial house. The wedding was held on 23rd July 2010. Everything went beautifully.

John and Mary had asked me to sing "You Raise Me Up", which I sang after Holy Communion. Before they processed down the aisle we all signed the state civil document. As we were doing that and posing for photographs, a young girl aged about nine, named Lucy, who was a junior bridesmaid ,began to sing a personalised version of Leonard Cohen's famous song "Hallelujah". I was listening very carefully as were all the guests in the church. Her sweet voice was beautiful and she sang the song with love and feeling. When she finished singing there was huge round of applause. Afterwards, I approached her to congratulate her. She told me she had written the words along with her parents. I asked her for a copy of the words and she generously obliged.

I put the words into my suit pocket and forgot about them after that. I guess it was probably about a month later when I was taking out my suit for dry cleaning that I emptied all the pockets and found the personalised words for a wedding song. I put them in a drawer for safekeeping. And once again forgot about them.

Meanwhile, I was being invited at all the weddings in my parish to sing a song after Holy Communion. My usual repertoire of songs for such occasions included "Ave Maria" and "Amazing Grace" among others. However, when I thought about adding to my repertoire of songs I then remembered Lucy's version of "Hallelujah". I searched and searched for the copy that Lucy gave to me and came across the words hidden away for safekeeping in a drawer. I read the words again and I thought I would need to get a backing track made to sing this song at weddings using my old reliable mini-disc player.

I read about the history of the song and how Leonard Cohen wrote the song about a love that had soured and gone stale, a bitter lament about love and loss, making it an inappropriate choice of wedding song. But the melody was simple, haunting, and addictive. Combined with Lucy's words it could be a real winner. So I purchased the backing track and recorded it on a mini-disc to use in my mini-disc player. The first time I sang it at a wedding it was very well received with a huge round of applause. After that the bride and groom, if they were local and from my parish, often requested me to sing it. Some couples liked it; others still wanted one of the other songs in my repertoire.

2014 was to be a big year for me. On the 18th June I would be celebrating my Silver Jubilee in Priesthood, 25 years. When I met many other priests over the years celebrating in such a manner, I always thought it would never happen to me. It was always way out there. To celebrate the year, I planned to have a parish function around the date and invite many of those who attended 25 years ago to get together again. Also it was my intention to have a celebration in my home village of Tyrrellspass and have an open invitation for people to come along. I also planned to record an album for charity around the date. What happened in early April 2014 changed a lot of my plans.

Before all that towards the end of 2013 a young couple in their mid-twenties phoned me about the possibility of having their wedding in St Brigid's Church, Oldcastle. They were Leah Crowe and Christopher O'Kane. They had already booked the Crover House Hotel in Mountnugent, Co. Cavan for their wedding reception after the church service. Now they wanted a church convenient to the hotel. They had visited a few churches in the locality and when they saw our parish church they knew this was the one that they wanted to get married in. I agreed to take on the wedding and they booked it for Saturday 5th April 2014. They visited me before Christmas and I directed them as to what they had to do and the amount of paperwork that had to be completed in preparation for their big day on 5th April. I also sat down with them to plan their wedding liturgy, the readings of the wedding Mass, the words that they would exchange to each other and the music and hymns that they would like. They had booked a beautiful group called SonLight Music Ministry, a Christian Band based at the Sacred Heart House of Prayer, and assured me that the group had a huge amount of experience and were very professional having played at many weddings and funerals throughout Ireland.

I always insist on having a wedding rehearsal and I set Thursday 3rd April at 7.30pm for Chris and Leah's. I always try to make sure all those taking part in the ceremony turn up to make sure everything runs smoothly on the day. We rehearsed ever aspect of the ceremony. I quickly looked through the music chosen for the wedding and thought it was very appropriate. If this was a local wedding i.e. the couple were from my parish here in Oldcastle, at this stage of the wedding rehearsal they would ask me to sing a song at the wedding for them. Chris and Leah didn't do that because they were not local and they didn't know I could sing. So just before we all left the church I quietly said to them "I might sing an 'auld song for you myself". They looked at each other in amusement and possibly confusion, which seemed to say 'Is he off his rocker or what'. I didn't say anything else after that. I presumed they were happy enough for me to sing a song at their wedding.

The 5th April 2014 arrived. The wedding of Leah and Christopher would begin at 1.00pm. As is usually the case the wedding never starts on time. Usually, the bride is late due to no fault of her own. The photographer and videographer are often responsible, as they want to get the best photos on the day. Just before 1.30pm Leah walks up the aisle arm in arm with her dad Patrick to the beautiful singing of "Ave Maria" sung by SonLight Music Ministry. She was indeed a beautiful bride. All the rehearsing on the Thursday evening had made everything run very smoothly. It was perfect. As the ceremony continued, no one expected a thing as I pressed my mini-disc player to begin the sound of the backing song "Hallelujah" and began to sing Lucy's vocals:

We join together here today
To help two people on their way
As Leah and Chris start their life together
And now we've reached their special date
We've come to help them celebrate
And show them how much we all love them too yeah

Hallelujah, hallelujah, hallelujah, hallelujah

As Leah's walking up the aisle
And Chris looks up and gives a smile
The love that flows between them fills the Church yeah
With Leah's friends and family at her side
She really is the blushing bride
With love and pride they lead the Hallelujahs

Hallelujah, hallelujah, hallelujah, hallelujah

With the priest and the family who lead the prayers
We say our lines and they say theirs
I guide them through the ceremony oh yeah
And in this house of God above
They join their hands to show their love
And say those most important words
I do yeah

Hallelujah, hallelujah, hallelujah, hallelujah
Hallelujah, hallelujah, hallelujah, hallelujah
Hallelujah, hallelujah.

During my singing of "Hallelujah", a lot was happening in the church that I was not aware of at the time. It was only after watching the video of these five minutes in the church that I could put it all together. First of all, I hadn't realised that I was being videoed by Tom and Matej, members of the SonLight team. I wasn't aware that for a while the wedding guests in the church were wondering where the sound and the voice was coming from. For a while they seemed to think that it was coming from the SonLight Music Group. However, they were seated and unsure themselves for a while until they looked over at me. I think at that stage the wedding guests realized 'oh my god the priest singing'.

I know I was totally immersed in the song but I could hear the rumbling of talking and whispering coming towards me from the wedding guests. After the first verse of the song I smiled at Leah and Chris. I could see Chris smiling but Leah seemed to be getting a bit teary eyed so after the second verse during the instrumental piece I quickly flashed my eyebrows at her to lighten the situation and relax her. The people in the church spotted it and laughed and at that moment Leah seemed to relax and enjoy the moment. Moving into the last verse of the song I realised I had everyone with me and enjoying my rendition of "Hallelujah". I finished the last note to a rapturous round of applause and a standing ovation. Before I left the altar during the applause, I quickly gave Leah and Chris a little wink, just to say that's for you guys, congratulations. I returned to the mic at the chair and pointed to Chris and Leah saying "I think they are a little bit in shock". A huge round of laughter followed. After the signing of the civil register Leah and Chris walked down the aisle to the beautiful recessional hymn "I Love You More And More" sung by SonLight Music Ministry.

It was a beautiful wedding and made especially beautiful by the prayerful participation of all those who had a role to play, but especially by the beautiful bride and groom.

Three days later on Tuesday 8th April, Leah sent me a message. It read:

Hello Fr Ray
Thank you very much for a beautiful mass. Your lovely song was put up on YouTube, I have attached the link for you. People are still talking to us about it and it's memory that both myself and Chris will cherish.
Thanks again for making our special day even more memorable! Chris & Leah

I hit the link and I watched the five minute video. I watched it again and again. Dale Weston, my niece Gillian's husband who was doing a bit of painting in my house, came in to the office. I said, "look Dale, look at this". We watched it again at least twice. Then I sent a reply to Leah and Chris who I knew were about to embark on their honeymoon to Mexico.

Dear Leah and Chris
Viva Mexico. What a lovely surprise, thank you so much, never thought I'd be on YouTube. Sounds great too even if I may say so myself. Have a great honeymoon. And if you are ever this way do call in for a cuppa and a chat.
Slán,
Love, Fr Ray

By evening the phone was hopping, the text messages were flooding in. *Fr Ray, you're on Facebook, you're on Twitter, you're on YouTube, you've got 1,000 hits, you've got 2,000 hits, you've got 3,000 hits* and it went on and on like that all evening. The next morning Ray Darcy on Today FM was the first one to ask for me to take a live telephone call. I did and while I was very nervous, I did not let the nerves get the better of me. Ray and I had a great chat, I shared the story of what had happened and he concluded by saying this could go viral. He was right it did, although he also said it could reach a half a million hits on YouTube; he was a long way off the mark there. As I write this piece it currently stands at 68,745,894. I guess by the time this book is on the shelves it will be over 70 million. Indeed, I have spoken to Ray many times since and reminded him how far out he was.

The next 24 hours were crazy. Emails of congratulations were flowing in. Many people sharing how emotional they got and how it brought back so many memories of their own wedding day as they watched the YouTube clip. My phone was hopping as Esther my housekeeper was dealing with calls and taking messages. The radio stations were queuing up for me. The next phone interview was with Ryan Tubridy from RTÉ 2FM on the Thursday morning. Then there were interviews with the BBC in Northern Ireland and of course the local radio stations like Louth Meath FM, and Midlands Radio 3 in Tullamore. The big news was that the researchers for *The Late Late Show* phoned to see would I be available to be on the show with Ryan Tubridy on Friday night. My God, what was happening! I was always a big fan of *The Late Late Show* and often thought I'd love to be singing on the show and now it was going to happen. My dream was going to become a reality. My sisters Rosemarie and Regina, my brother Joe and my niece would be in the audience with me. Regina was full of suggestions as to what I should wear, I told her I would wear my one and only suit. I opted to sit in the audience in the front row along side my family rather than be introduced and come from behind the set. At least in the audience I could enjoy the whole show and besides I would also benefit from being in the audience for the weekly "one for everyone in the audience" prize. My sisters were hoping it would be an overnight stay in a hotel. However, being close to Easter, it was always going to be chocolate and Easter eggs; I was right.

I arrived by 5.30pm at the RTÉ studio and was greeted and taken straightaway to the set of the show where the house band was setting up. The nerves were beginning to kick in at this stage; sometimes I felt like pinching myself to see if this was all happening or was it a dream. I was introduced to all the different managers and production team of the show. There were the sound checks and after about half an hour of hanging around I had the first of two runs through the song. Soon after that Ryan Tubridy walks over to me dressed casually in his jeans and jacket. We chatted and he said 'let's have a real fun interview together', which I was really pleased to hear. After that I was called for my second rehearsal, which went really well. As I was going to be sitting in the audience, I was then taken to the hospitality room where all the audience were welcomed with a glass of wine or a soft drink. I spotted my family and filled them in on everything. Then among the crowd I spotted two Oldcastle faces, Ollie Gilseman and his mum, Agnes, whom

I was delighted to see. Just after 9.00pm we were whisked into the main studio and directed to our seats for the show.

The Late Late Show music started up; we were going live. Ryan opened the show by saying, "This week 11 million people have watched one Irishman on YouTube. I am of course referring to the priest who took a wedding by storm." Then they played a clip from the YouTube video. "More of that later" - I was going to be interviewed from my seat in the audience on Part 2 of the show. Ryan would sit on the step beside my seat and chat. I was ready, and then Part 2 of the show began.

"Welcome back everybody, well my next guest shocked wedding guests when from the altar he burst into an extraordinary version of Leonard Cohen's "Hallelujah". And soon afterwards the video went online. On Monday the clip had been seen by 120,000 people. Currently, this night over 11 million people have watched the same clip. The man of this musical moment is Fr Ray Kelly."

Following Ryan's introduction, I told Ryan about the amazing week I had and how this night last week I had been at home texting in the answer to your quiz and now I'm on *The Late Late Show*. I explained to Ryan and the audience how I decided to sing the song for Chris and Leah. Then a clip of Leah and Chris while on their honeymoon was shown as a short interview by Skype sharing with us the surprise they got when I started to sing. I had already given RTÉ Leah's phone number to make contact with them. Their interview was lovely, highlighting how special I had made their day. Ryan asked me what was so special about this video that so many people were watching it? I said possibly because the couple and the congregation were not expecting it. Indeed, many thought it was the SonLight Music group, but as I said they were all sitting as surprised as everyone else. I went on to explain to Ryan where I got the song and the words. I shared also of how as a child I would sing, as all the family were musical. Then I talked a little bit of my late-vocation to priesthood and how it came about. I told him also how taken back I was with all of the media interest. I explained how just before I came up to Dublin that evening, I'd a call from Brazil, they wanted to put something on some religious programme tonight. And how I had checked my emails the night before and discovered I had been invited to weddings in Japan, Lithuania and Croatia. I joked that "I think I get a first class ticket to fly out anywhere. I'm going to have a great time. I'm not sure what my Bishop will have to say about that!"

In Part 3 of the show I was to sing. Ryan introduced me while I was standing on the platform in front of the audience ready to sing and waiting for the lights to come up. The cameras were on me, there was no escape, I was nervous, very nervous, I started going through the first line of the song in my head *"We join together here today..."* BLANK! My mind went blank, I went blank, and I couldn't remember the second line of the song. *"Oh God, what am I going to do. We join together here today..."* BLANK! I had the words in my pocket and put my hand on them, but I couldn't take them out not now the audience were in front of me. Just then Ryan introduced me, "But right now he's going to perform live in this very studio, singing "Hallelujah", would you welcome please Fr Ray Kelly." As Ryan spoke those words, my line came to me *"We join together here today, to help two people on their way..."* I was going to be fine. Once I got going into the song I knew I was fine. I had been a bit worried too whether my falsetto little bits would sound ok having spent so much time talking in the last few days. But, as someone commented on my YouTube clip afterwards, it was "Pitch Perfect". That was it, if nothing ever happened after that, I was a happy man, I had sung on *The Late Late Show* in front of at least a half a million viewers. My dream was fulfilled.

Of course the story didn't end there. I drove home from the RTÉ studios on my own, exhausted, but on a high. My phone was a constant jingle as texts rolled in from all over Ireland. The world had seen me. I wanted to talk to everyone, to family, but that would wait. I got home before 1.00am and my two loyal pals Biddy and Buddy woke up to greet me with waggling tails and barks for a treat. They deserved to share in my joy too. I got to bed about 1.30am and was in a deep sleep when the phone beside my bed went off at about 5.00am. "Hello Fr Kelly, is that Fr Kelly, this is Alfons from Krakow, my daughter Alexandra is getting married in July, you must come to her wedding father, you must come to her wedding." I could hardly speak. I rubbed my eyes, looked at my watch. "It's 5.10am. Send me an email with all the details." I gave him my email and hung up. I got up about 8.00am and after breakfast I checked my YouTube clip of "Hallelujah". It had hit another million reaching over 12 million now. I checked my emails; top of the list was my 5am friend from Krakow, Alfons' lovely letter about his daughter Alexandra. There were another at least seven invitations for weddings now also, two from Ireland, one from the UK, Australia and Germany, South Africa and The Netherlands.

Esther my housekeeper came in for the weekend to take the many phone calls. I was just bombarded with them and requests to be interviewed by various radio stations. Many of the papers that weekend were all about the Hallelujah wedding, with headlines such as 'Singing Fr puts on a Holy show', and 'Hallelujah! Wedding Priest is an online hit'.

Meanwhile, the busiest week in the Church's calendar year, Holy Week was around the corner and I needed to concentrate on my parish. I shut the door on all the media, as I wanted to focus on the week ahead. Holy Week ceremonies are beautiful and while it is a crazy week work-wise, it is also a beautiful week. I love it in many ways. So while I was focused on that I knew I just could not stop thinking of what happened the week before either. So in a sense I could not shut it all out. The annual Chrism Mass in Christ the King Cathedral in Mullingar was held on Spy Wednesday of Holy Week. It is always a beautiful diocesan ceremony and I looked forward to it. However, before that, earlier in the day, I had Joe Little, the religious and social affairs correspondent visiting me for an interview to feature on the Holy Thursday six o'clock news. It was featured towards the end of the news with Sharon Ní Bheoláin. At that stage the YouTube clip had reached over 28 million hits.

Then on Good Friday, 18th April, me singing "Hallelujah" at the wedding of Chris and Leah O'Kane was featured on Fox News USA. The title of the news item was Singing Priest becomes Viral Video Star. It began with them showing a little clip of me singing and the presenter talking about how it made her cry. Many people told me afterwards the reaction to that over six-minute feature on Fox News was enormous. Needless to say it sent the viewing of the YouTube clip soaring once again.

After Holy Week and Easter Sunday ceremonies, I was exhausted but on a high. I went home and as was traditional enjoyed my Sunday dinner with my sister Regina and family. Monday was a bank holiday and holiday time for some families as the schools were closed. I had my two faithful friends, Biddy and Buddy to take for a long walk. I had lunch again with my sister. I visited my brother Joe and his wife Olive at their home in Rahugh. I visited my other sister Rosemarie and family in Tullamore. They were as excited as I was about all that had gone on the previous two weeks. In fact, Lisa my niece, was telling me that over the last week she was getting up in the middle of the night to check the "Hallelujah" wedding to see how many more hits it had reached. Everyone seemed to be getting addicted to it. I returned to my parish on Monday evening to a quiet house. So quiet in fact that I began to miss all the attention, the limelight. In my head I was saying I'm back, come on Easter is over, I'm ready for you once again.

I checked my phone messages and there were loads of congratulatory messages as well as ones from radio and TV stations from the UK, Germany and USA looking for interviews. I already had an invite to headline a New York gig for to raise funds for the undocumented Irish in the US. However, as I did not have a working visa, I had to withdraw from that. After a few more days of constant messages, interviews and requests for TV shows in USA and Germany, I realised I could not handle this on my own. Aside from that there were messages from Annette Donnelly Managing Director of Sony Music in Ireland and Mark Crossingham Managing Director of Universal Music in Ireland. They both wanted to meet me with the possibility of signing a record deal with me. This was now way above my expectations. I was in a world now that I knew nothing about, absolutely nothing. I needed legal advice on where I was heading and I needed it fast. I contacted a solicitor in Navan, I knew from my time there. We spoke and after a long chat he put me on to his son William O'Reilly, who was also a solicitor in the firm. Will as I got to know him by agreed to call to see me and recommended a friend of his to join us Willie Ryan, a barrister who was used to dealing with contracts for musicians and singers. Willie Ryan lived in Kells, so both guys, from now on referred to as the '2 Wills', were very convenient to me. We met, and now with both Universal Ireland and Sony Ireland ready to sign me to a record deal, all was handed over to the '2 Wills' to sort out.

Meanwhile, Willie Ryan wanted to introduce me to a possible manager. So we flew to London for an overnight and I was introduced to Gordon Charlton from Big Life Management Ltd a music management and promotion company in London. We had a great chat and I have to say I felt very comfortable in his presence. We agreed to work together. In the meantime, contract negotiations were reaching a close and it looked like I would be signing with Sony Music.

During these days I had contact from my friends in South Africa telling me I was featured on their News 24 TV show. I was also contacted and featured on Slovakian daily news. Matt Whittemore from Australian television made contact to feature me on their Sunrise on 7 Network. This meant that I had to travel to Dublin late on a Tuesday evening to a Broadcasting House studio and at about 11.00pm Irish time

I was interviewed live for breakfast television in Australia on Wednesday morning. They loved it and the reaction was fantastic. I have been to Australia twice and walked around Sydney Opera House with a dream in my heart to sing there someday. Maybe it will happen and if it doesn't I still love the dream. Sure there is no harm in dreaming.

RTL German TV contacted me with the possibility of coming to Ireland to film me and also if they could have Chris and Leah come down from Belfast and stay overnight in the Crover House Hotel in Mountnugent where they had their wedding reception. Chris and Leah duly obliged and spent a day filming around Lough Sheelin and Crover House Hotel. Then they arrived at my house to have a cup of tea and to show me some wedding photos, all the while being filmed. I think they were very nervous but as I said to them it's a once in a lifetime experience, so enjoy it. There were other local TV shows on which I was also featured. *Meath County Matters* is a programme that delves into the fabric of Irish Culture and characters of community life. Then there was *Entertainment Ireland*, a weekly programme bringing the very best of music, song, dance and fashion while promoting the emerging new talent that Ireland has to offer. Later in the year I was also featured on the RTÉ *Today Show* with Maura Derrane and Dáithí Ó Sé.

As my contract was about to be signed, an email arrived from Steve Crosby, a British record producer, songwriter, and music manager, introducing me to Christian Seitz, an Austrian record producer, engineer and songwriter. Then Christian wrote to me in an email that was like a CV. It was impeccable. He shared with me his experience of working with other artists and selling more than 20 million records specializing in classical-crossover music and working with orchestras - being Viennese this is his expertise. As a music producer Christian specialised in what the business call "adult contemporary music", recording with a real orchestra. He mentioned having a strong vision for me, he wanted to produce an Irish album and had been looking for the right artist. He shared his heartfelt impressions of how much he had liked the videos of me.

When I read the email, I was excited about it; I was in love with it. I felt a little bit in awe of it that someone like Christian would even want to consider working with me. In fact, I questioned my own ability that at my age someone, anyone, a record producer would be interested in me. It was Christian's wish to come to meet me, and Gordon my manager in Oldcastle. However, I had been invited to take part in the German TV RTL for the Stern TV Magazine programme AI&U production introduced by Steffan Hallaschka. The company flew Gordon and I over to Cologne for the show and during that short stay in Cologne, Christian Seitz met us at the beautiful rooftop garden restaurant of the Hyatt Hotel and treated us to dinner. Indeed, I loved the man, his charm, and enthusiasm to work with me was as strong if not stronger than his email. He said when he saw my YouTube wedding clip that he was obsessed with it and in love with me. My warmth, my humour, and my joy for singing was palpable. At the restaurant we had great food and lots of laughter. As Christian said afterwards; we connected. It was clear at the end of the evening that if Christian could deliver a deal that at least matched or topped the Sony offer I would work with him. I know Gordon met him again the following day and Gordon like myself was completely bought over by Christian. One of Christian's assets at the time was that he had worked directly with Max Hole, Universal Music's No 2 man worldwide. Max was a powerful yet a wonderful person, as Christian said he would never sign with a priest but he trusted me, since I had successful albums before in that genre. There was not going to be a contract with Sony Music after all, instead I would now fly to London and sign a five album record deal with Universal International Music.

CHAPTER 15

....

Where I Belong

The contracts were signed. Christian Seitz was going to be the executive producer. He knew that time was of the essence because as he said YouTube phenomenons rise quickly, but they get forgotten just as quickly. So he decided to get a second producer on board to share the workload. He asked David Bronner, a fellow Austrian producer, songwriter, and musician whom he had always admired. David had worked on the production of the winning Eurovision Song for Austria, Conchita Wurst in 2014, and produced the subsequent album *From Vienna with Love* in 2017. Now it was a matter of where, when and how and what to record on the album.

Christian and David came to Oldcastle to set the plan in motion. They were far from even having a track listing but we discussed lots of ideas, checking out songs and seeing if I liked them and indeed what key I would sing them in. The recording of the album would take place during the month of July and possibly into the first week of August but where? Christian was very conscious of my work as a priest in the parish and tried not to interfere with my workload as much as possible. I was not aware of any commercial studio for recording close by. He had a vision of me recording in my own surroundings, the Parochial House and St Brigid's Church. When they saw my house they loved it and found it comfortable and cosy with, as Christian said, Esther my housekeeper being 'super sweet' managing the house and indeed all of us. The decision was made; he would record my voice in my own surroundings. They decided to build a studio in my house. They had an experienced Austrian acoustic designer create the best possible soundproof booth. They sent his drawing and specifications to Brendan Tully, a local carpenter here in Oldcastle.

My dining room would be taken over as the hub of the recording or the hi-end control room, with the dining room table covered with computers and Genelec Speakers for the best sound quality. Leading from my dining room, through the door is my sitting room, and located there, thanks to Brendan Tully the local carpenter, were three acoustic walls with a roof. The entire structure was not much bigger than the old telephone booths. They had brought two Neumann microphones that were set up in the recording booth. Christian and David would work around my parish commitments for weekday masses, weddings, funerals and weekend masses also. Now it was a matter of working out what songs would be on the album. I wanted a mixture of Irish songs, as the album would be available in the USA, so we included "Galway Bay", "Danny Boy" and "Isle of Hope". Two of my favourite church hymns were also included: "Amazing Grace" and "How Great Thou Art". One song I loved and remembered from my rock-gospel days in Navan was called "How Marvellous". Obviously, "Hallelujah" would have to be on the album. However, there was a strong possibility that I might not get permission from Leonard Cohen's recording company to record the song with the special wedding words. So I worked on a shortened version of the original. In the meantime, Christian Knollmuller and Marc Copely wrote another beautiful wedding song especially for me titled "Together Forever". Another original song had a beautiful Celtic/Irish feel to it, and was written for the album by David Bronner, Sebastian Arman and David Mallin. The song was called "Where I Belong", and would become the title track of the album and I loved it.

Although I had never sung the songs before in my life, my two all time favourites were "Tears In Heaven", and "Everybody Hurts". It was always my dream to be able to record them, but I questioned my ability to do so as they are songs with deep emotion and I questioned whether I had it in me to do justice to the songs. I tried them with Christian and David and rehearsed them. Christian and David thought I could carry them, but I still wasn't sure. Eventually, we all agreed; I really loved my version as I loved my emotion in the song. I was a happy man. However, we had 11 songs, and I wanted one more.

I have always had a huge interest in the Eurovision Song Contest; my earliest memories are of the first Irish entries. Butch Moore with "Walking the Streets in the Rain" in 1965, and Dickie Rock with "Come Back To Stay" in 1966. I loved the international flavour of the competition. When Dana won in 1970, the first of Ireland's seven wins, I was sitting my Leaving Certificate. I remember, I was in love with her then, she was more or less my age too. I remember so fondly Sr Columba, my science and maths teacher for my Leaving Certificate, talking about the Eurovision Song Contest in our class. I told her that Dana would win, not because I loved the song but because I was in love with Dana. Sr Columba then said 'ok if she wins you can skip your homework in maths and science'. Dana won, but I still completed my homework as it was coming up to my Leaving Cert and I needed to do it. So when Christian's wife Margit suggested that I record "Love Shine A Light", the last winning song for UK in 1997, I was delighted with the suggestion. First of all, because of my love of Eurovision, but also I wanted an up-tempo song to finish the album. I had my 12 songs.

Everything was set up in my home to start the recording in early July and everything went to plan. As I was recording I was able to keep a lot of my parish work going and with the aid of Esther my housekeeper, she kept the door and the phone in check and protected me from it all. Christian and David would give me periods to rest my voice and drink plenty of hot tea. Yvie Burnett my vocal coach was always on hand to warm up my voice for recording. As a team we all worked well together. Christian then came up with the idea of using our church for some of the recording. It would also be an opportunity for many local people to come in and see the recording. We decided on the songs "How Great Thou Art", "How Marvellous", and the chorus of "Hallelujah". We recruited many from Oldcastle Parish Choir, the Meath Diocesan Choir, and the Clara Parish Choir whom I had travelled to Lourdes with many times. We also invited the combined choirs of Kilbeg, Kilmainham Wood, and Kingscourt under their leader Bernie Curtis whom I had worked with at a concert in Kingscourt. It was a brilliant idea and over 200 voices had a powerful effect. The choirs knew the songs very well, once we got all of them singing from the same hymn sheet it worked perfectly, and the sound was amazing. I think it even surpassed Christian and David's expectations. I remember David telling me that he will never forget how the first hallelujah blew him away. He described it as like a huge ocean wave sweeping over him. My work was nearly done. However, Christian thought it would be a good idea to come to Vienna for any final tweaking that needed to be done on the album. My niece Amy and I spend almost a week in Vienna and I know Christian often says that I did some of my finest recording during that week. The album was recorded. In September Christian and David recorded the orchestra in Budapest and then they started mixing. They were very much aware of having the album master completed on time, as I would be launching the album on *The Late Late Show*. The design of the sleeve would all be handled by Universal in London.

The first Sunday after I returned from Vienna, the early morning saw my dining room turned into a wardrobe of clothes for me to try on for the photo shoots. I spent an entire day around my house and church having photographs taken by Barry McCall and by 7.00pm when I thought I was finished he insisted I travel to his photography studio in Dublin for more photos along with my two best friends Biddy and Buddy. We left there after midnight and I was convinced my face and my body would be changed forever from smiling and posing. Before my recording I had to appear at concerts and shows. One of the first I performed was at Kingscourt Church in Co. Cavan, which was promptly followed by a concert at Curraha Church near Ashbourne, Co. Meath. Then I was invited to perform at the annual Jambouree in Killinkere, Co. Cavan. About a month or so before the release of my album, I performed concerts in Ballyjamesduff, Co. Cavan, the Solstice Arts Centre in Navan, Co. Meath and at the Iontas Arts and

Community Resource Centre at Castleblaney, Co. Monaghan. While I was driving there, Christian phoned me with the great news. Leonard Cohen's company had agreed for us to record "Hallelujah" with the wedding words. I was ecstatic, I felt in my heart this song had to be on the album but it was out of my control, I was pleased to know now it would.

On 5th December, eight months after the famous "Hallelujah" wedding, my album *Where I Belong* was launched. I had received a copy about a month before the official launch. I played it for my family and they all said it was super. Then word came through it would be launched on *The Late Late Show* with Ryan Tubridy. I thought, my God twice on *The Late Late Show* in one year? Wow. This time, I would not be in the audience. I would come from behind the stage like most of his guests and celebrities. I was in dreamland; me a guest and a celebrity on the *Late Late*.

Ryan and I talked about reaching over 39 million hits on YouTube and what attracted people to watching it and about record negotiations. Ryan asked about recording the album in my own house and how it worked out. Ryan was curious about which I preferred 'the Altar or the Mixing Desk'. I told him they were working very well together as I was 25 years at the altar before the mixing desk came into my life. Then he surprised me by playing a clip from the 1993 talent competition that I won in the Bridge House, Tullamore. I couldn't believe that it had been resurrected. Of course Ryan shared that they had watched all the clips of me singing over the years, but they particularly liked my version of "Summertime". My version of the *Porgy and Bess* classic was available for the whole world to see, and now had over 100,000 views on YouTube. We talked about all the invites I had received to sing "Hallelujah" at weddings all over the world and how as a parish priest I just could not drop everything to do that. Ryan asked me about being recognised as well. I told him about how people had looked at me suspiciously when I was in Lourdes and the Holy Land earlier in the year, and I knew that they were trying to remember where they had seen me before. I shared about one of the more funny incidents I had in which I was staying overnight at a hotel in Westport. The next morning, as I was having breakfast two German ladies passed me by as they left the dining room. I saw them looking at me very suspiciously. They moved on and whispered to each other. Then one of them comes back to my table, points her finger at me and says "Mr Hallelujah ja?" I said "Ja, Mr Hallelujah". They smiled and moved on, but when I left the dining room and arrived at the lobby of the hotel, it was like the paparazzi were waiting for me. About 30 Germans with their iPads and iPhones and they are all watching the YouTube clip of "Hallelujah".

The big question that I was waiting for from Ryan was what was I going to do with the money? I always got asked that question and I hated it. Why did I hate it? Well, not because I have anything to hide, but mainly because I always felt I was asked just because I'm a priest. If I was a plumber, a doctor or even unemployed, I would never have been asked the question, what are you going to do with the money? If I were Hozier or Ed Sheeran, Ryan wouldn't have asked that question. It was just because I was a priest I got it thrown at me all the time. As an answer to Ryan's question, I just told him I hadn't received anything yet but should some come my way, it wasn't going to change my life. I explained I had a couple of favourite charities that I liked to support and also had a big family of nieces and nephews that I would help out along the way. In other words, just share it out.

My interview ended with me explaining the hectic week that lay ahead between my parish and my new music life. I was really looking forward to signing the new album at the record store in Navan on the Saturday as I had worked in the parish for nine years. The Saturday evening, I would fly to Cologne in Germany for the German TV channel RTL and their annual show called *Menschen, Bilder, Emotionen.* I would return home via London on the Monday for a Christmas video shoot at St Pancras station. On Tuesday I would travel to Portlaoise for signing, a day in the parish on Wednesday and off to Letterkenny on Thursday for signing. It was a mad week, but a new experience in my life and I loved it. Ryan let the audience know that I would be in the Olympia Theatre in Dublin for a concert on Thursday 19th February. Ryan finally introduced me to perform "Together Forever", which was an original song. The sentiment and feel of this song draws even further on the union of love and marriage. I was in awe as I performed this song; there was no forgetting of words or nervousness. An orchestra surrounded me, with Rob Burke on the piano and a beautiful choir that made me feel I was living the dream. I really was.

Once again, I left the RTÉ studio on my own and needed to talk to share my experience. Luckily, I could phone my family at home to share my excitement. As always Biddy and Buddy were also there to greet me when I arrived home. After my hectic week in Germany and many parts of Ireland, I was so glad to be back in my parish to ground myself for the Christmas celebrations. About a month before the launch of my CD on *The Late Late Show*, I was invited to take part in RTÉ's Christmas Carol Service, which was recorded from Kilkenny Castle on Thursday 27th November. The lovely Mary Kennedy would introduce the entire show. The song the production team chose for me to sing was one of my favourites, "Little Drummer Boy". It was a pre-recorded production and would be shown on RTÉ television on Christmas Eve and Christmas Day. I had already rehearsed my song with the RTÉ concert orchestra at their studio in Dublin. Mary began my section by introducing me and having a chat about the "Hallelujah" story, which had now reached almost 40 million hits on YouTube. I shared with her about the release of my new album and also how sometimes my music life eats into my parish life but that the people of Oldcastle and Moylagh were very understanding and that I also had the support of my Bishop.

Two days after my *Late Late* appearance my niece Gillian gave birth to her fourth child, a little boy; it would seem my family never stopped growing. Always during my life, I longed to have one of my nephews called after me. I guess because I would never have children of my own, it was always an unspoken ambition I dreamt of. It had never happened. However, it happened when my gran-nephew, Conal-Ray Weston, was born on 7th December 2014. Gillian wanted his baptism to take place in the month of February. Indeed, that month was a kind of crazy busy month for me, as Ash Wednesday and beginning of Lent was right in the middle of the month. I was also rehearsing for my first show at the Olympia Theatre in Dublin. I would be joined on stage by the Louise Smith

Academy of dancing and also by a local Oldcastle girl Annie Galligan. I was so excited about this event as I had often been to see shows in the Olympia but had never been on stage performing. It was amazing. I performed to an almost full house and everyone was so pleased for me. On stage I was presented with a Platinum Disc for reaching a certain amount of sales of my album in Ireland. I received a bottle of champagne from my manager Gordon and Big Life management company in London. I remember bringing it home and cracking open the bottle with my sister Regina and her family.

The day after the show, the *Late Late* contacted me to know would I be available for the show on Friday 27th as they were picking a song to represent Ireland at the Eurovision to be held in Vienna. A young girl Molly Sterling won by playing the piano and singing her own composition "Playing with Numbers". While the voting was taking place I was involved in a fun quiz; Ryan spinning the wheel and it landing on the line of a Eurovision song as Mary Byrne, Joe McCaul, Kelly McDonagh-Mongan and I guessed the song title and then sang the song. It was a great bit of fun and I was so delighted to be asked. I mean three times on *The Late Late Show* in less than a year was not bad going at all.

CHAPTER 16

....

Regina

On Saturday 21st February, we had Conal-Ray Weston's baptism at Kilbeggan Church. Afterwards, all of the family went for a lovely lunch at Tyrrellspass Castle. My sister Regina, Conal-Ray's granny was sitting opposite me and I noticed how she wasn't able to eat her lunch. I hadn't noticed that she had lost weight, but some of the family had noticed it. I passed the remark to her about eating and she said she found it uncomfortable to swallow. The next day Sunday, Regina herself asked to be brought to casualty at Tullamore Hospital to be checked out. I know for Regina to request to be brought to casualty she knew in her heart something was wrong. All her bloods were tested and came back as normal. They sent her home and told her to get a bottle of Gaviscon as they thought she had indigestion or heartburn. When it was suggested at the hospital that she have a scope done, she was told the waiting list was about 18 months. I felt, in fact the entire family felt, she couldn't wait that long. So we got a private appointment for the scope test, or the medical term is an upper gastrointestinal endoscopy, to be carried out at St Francis Medical Clinic in Mullingar. This test allows a doctor to look at the inside of her oesophagus, stomach and the first part of her small intestine. Our worst fears were realised. Regina had a tumour at the base of the oesophagus and the top of the stomach.

When she received word, I called to her home and found her in her dressing-gown in her sitting room. I knew she was in a very dark place and anything I would say would make no difference. I sat with her for a while and as I left the room I hugged her tightly. I remember thinking there and then that if I could swap places with her, I would gladly do it. In all our 58 years together I had never seen her like this, it scared me, it really did. She needed time on her own to absorb the news she received, and I knew that. I also knew that once that was done, she would go have a shower, put on her make-up and get back to where her real love was, her family. When she did that Regina the fighter was back. She would now face this head on and fill her head with hope, which would radiate to every one of her family. That's what she did as she faced into eight sessions of chemotherapy every three weeks. The only thing she missed was her work. She adored her work. She was a teacher's assistant in the local primary school and having some of her grandchildren at the school was a very big plus. Mr Rabbitt the principal and all the staff loved her. She loved them too. And even though she was out on official sick leave, she would regularly call up to the school just to keep in touch. She needed to do that, and I think the school needed her too.

In early June, two months after the "Hallelujah" story broke, a nun Sr Christina on the Italian casting show *The Voice of Italy*, won the competition. One of the songs that she was asked to sing was the famous Madonna song "Like A Virgin". The song was chosen for her by some A&R (artist and repertoire) men. These are the guys that are responsible for talent scouting and overseeing the artistic development of recording artists and songwriters. It was a bad choice however, because there was a huge possibility that it wouldn't sell records as it lacked substance and really insulted the feelings of many. At Universal everyone expected her to be a big success. When her sales stalled far below their expectations Universal pulled the plug on Father Ray Kelly. Their argument was when a nun who won *The Voice of Italy* doesn't sell records, why should a priest without such a supporting show sell? I know Christian my record producer was furious and so disappointed. He was told "let it go…focus on your next project". One British A&R said, "I don't think he can sing". As Christian told me afterwards, 2014 wasn't a great year for the music industry. Streaming hadn't compensated for the decrease in sales of downloads and physical records and when there is a danger to miss the year's business targets, then they drop some acts that they consider "less important" or that they don't fully believe in rather than invest more money in marketing them, which can be expensive. I knew Christian was deeply disappointed and he then, after my *Britain's Got Talent* appearance, went on to say:

> You put five months of your life and all your love and passion into one album and then they pull the plug, even worse, you develop a relationship, I'd even say a friendship with some artists due to the very intense, intimate work. With Father Ray that was certainly the case for David and me. I am still disappointed.

> When three years later Ray performed on *Britain's Got Talent* and the whole jury as well as over two thousand people went crazy in the London Palladium after Ray's performance of his version of "Everybody Hurts" and

Simon Cowell called it 'one of the best performances I've ever seen on this show', I was very satisfied…and hoped the British A&R person had watched the show. Ray didn't end up winning the show…But one thing is for sure: NOTHING will EVER stop his passion for singing and performing. When he does, he starts to shine like only few artists I've worked with. God provided him with this gift…and Ray takes good care of it.

In March of 2015, I spent five days in New York on a US promotions trip as I was invited to be a special guest at an evening of Irish music in St Joseph's Church, Greenwich Village, New York. It was a fundraising event for friends of Kylemore Abbey as part of a campaign in the US to raise valuable funds for the huge amount of restoration work. It was a wonderful evening and at the meet-and-greet afterwards I met some people who have remained great friends today, including Dorothy le Blanc, a beautiful lady from a little town called Poultney in the state of Vermont. Dorothy had never travelled much outside of her state but came especially to meet me. Since then she has visited Oldcastle. We have remained very special and loyal friends to this day. I also met Larry and Tracey Coryell who flew from Florida to meet me. Larry was a very famous American jazz guitarist who later died suddenly in February 2017. His wife Tracey organised two US tours for me that same year. Indeed, they both came to Oldcastle and stayed with me for a few days. Unfortunately, my meet-and-greet was short-lived as I had to be at Fox TV for a sound check very early the next morning which was St Patrick's Day. After the 5.00am sound check

I went for breakfast, before going back to Fox TV for a live interview and performance of "Danny Boy" on the *Fox and Friends* breakfast show.

After that I assembled under the Westmeath Banner for the 5th Avenue New York St Patrick's Day Parade, the largest and oldest parade for St Patrick in the world, and in my opinion, by far the best. For over a quarter of a millennium, Irish migrants and Americans have demonstrated Irish pride on the streets of New York on St Patrick's Day. They have honoured St Patrick, the Patron Saint of the Archdiocese of New York and Ireland on the streets of New York ever since 1762. The parade reflects the indomitable spirit of the people of Ireland and its migrants who emigrated to the United States of America. The parade takes pride in honouring St Patrick, preserving Irish heritage, culture, promoting family values, and paying tribute to the Irish past and present. I felt very honoured and privileged to be invited to be part of this great event. It was a very cold, dry Tuesday morning on the streets of New York, but I didn't feel it, I was too excited.

During my five days in New York, I was in daily communication with Regina, anxious to know if she had a date to start her chemotherapy. She had, although Regina had a very funny way of texting, as she couldn't operate predicted text which meant that in her messages she would often leave out some letters of her words. For example, word would be texted as 'wrd', and that as 'tht'. I used to tease her about it, saying it looked like Chinese to me. It always took a while to interpret her messages, but eventually I would understand. Her messages were always something like "I'm fine, don't be worrying, I'll be alright, you enjoy yourself and get home safely". However, when a message would come to me at about 9.00am US time, which was 4.00am at home, I would wonder why she was up. Obviously, she couldn't sleep and was up drinking tea and smoking. I asked her about her early morning texts but I usually got no answer.

If there was anything positive about Regina having her chemotherapy, it was the fact that the hospital in Tullamore was only about a 15-minute drive from her home. What was noticeable all through Regina's chemotherapy sessions was her bravery facing into it. She was always so weak for a day or two after her session. She often complained that her legs were so tired, she would say, "If I could get my legs under me I'd be alright". Every chemo affects people differently; Regina was fortunate she didn't loose her hair. She was told it could affect her toenails and fingernails. A way of helping was to steep her finger and toenails in water and vinegar. One part vinegar, to ten parts water. For a few nights she was doing it the other way around. She was stinking the house out of it until she realised her mistake. One of Regina's biggest struggles was to accept her limitations and learning to depend on others. So within two days of her chemo she was back into the mother role of cooking and cleaning her house. The only thing missing was she was not going to work at the school.

I got an invitation to attend the Eurovision Song Contest in Vienna from David Bronner who worked with me on my *Where I Belong* album. I wanted to bring Regina with me so much but I knew it was not going to happen. So I brought my niece Gillian with me for a few days. It was an amazing experience and even though the Irish song didn't make the final, nevertheless, just being there was really special. It was my fourth

Eurovision Song Contest to attend. Maybe some day before I die I'll be asked to represent Ireland at a Eurovision Final.

Meanwhile I was invited to perform at concerts for "Mary's Meal's" at Croke Park in Dublin and in Kildare to raise funds for a school my cousin Miriam's children attended. My cousin Therese Abbott in Edenderry organised a concert in the church there to raise funds for the autistic unit in one of the primary schools that some of her grandchildren attend.

When it was suggested that I record a Christmas album, my-inner child smiled with joy and shouted YES, YES, YES! My heart jingled as a flood of Christmas songs came to mind. I wanted to record them all. I always felt there couldn't be anything as magical as Christmas. A time full of memories that hold a sense of nostalgia, for good times long gone, and for loved ones no longer with us. Little did I know or contemplate at the time that the coming Christmas of 2015 was going to be much more special than anyone could realise. The two Wills were on board again and I signed a new contract with Universal Ireland to record a Christmas album. Regina was thrilled, I think it gave her another focus for a while to know my music career was still on board despite not being promoted anymore by Universal International.

I travelled to London to record the album with Nigel Wright. Nigel is a very famous record producer who has worked with Andrew Lloyd Webber on many of his musicals and their film versions. When Nigel agreed to work with me and produce my Christmas album, I felt privileged to be amongst his recording artists. It was so fantastic to work with Nigel and his team, Paul and Robin, and to avail of the hospitality of Nigel's wife Deana in London. Yvie Burnett was on hand to provide me with vocal coaching and warming up my voice before recording. The strangest thing about the entire project was singing Christmas songs during the summertime. When I took a break from recording I was sitting in the sun or enjoying the comforts of Nigel's pool. I also found it very emotional sometimes as I recorded some of the songs. I know Regina's illness was playing on my mind. One of the most difficult songs to record was "I'll be Home For Christmas". It knotted me up every time I went for a 'take' to record. I was also missing my two pals at home Biddy and Buddy. Sometimes I just felt I needed to hug them. Many of the songs were filling me with emotion. As two of the songs on the album were written by Keith Getty and recorded by his wife Kristyn, "Joy Has Dawned" and "An Irish Christmas Blessing", we agreed to title the album *An Irish Christmas Blessing*. I got a slot on *The Late Late Show* on Friday 18th December, one week before Christmas singing "When A Child Is Born". It was a great privilege once again to get on *The Late Late Show* to promote my album. I dedicated the album to Regina my sister. I wrote: *"I want to thank my sister Regina who has been "The Mammy" of the family for many years now. She is always a tower of strength and Christmas is her specialty, she pulls out all of the stops for all of us. Reg we are all here for you too, and I dedicate this Christmas album to you for what you mean to all of us. I love you, Ray."*

Regina's second to last chemo session was cancelled. She was very disappointed and low after the experience. It seemed her white blood cells were low, or rather not quite high enough for the shot of chemo. This is called Neutropenia, when the white blood cells that are meant to fight infection are in short supply. So they postponed her chemo for a week. But the following week she was fine and got her session of chemo, and three weeks later was her final shot of chemo. In her head she was feeling good and looking forward to getting back to school. The CT scan showed that the tumour had significantly reduced. Her oncologist was very pleased for her. So were we all, we never lost hope and it paid off; or so we thought.

About a month after her last chemo and just as she was about to return to school, Gillian, her daughter and a nurse by profession, noticed little lumps on her face, under her eye and on her back and arm. It was back to the oncologist and the beginning of a second bout of chemo. We were all so disappointed; the cancer was rapidly growing again and spreading to other parts of her body. This second bout of chemo resulted in Regina loosing her hair very quickly. The cancer was attacking her kidneys too and so she was having difficulty passing urine. She was admitted to St James' Hospital in Dublin where they were able to help the situation by implanting stents to help the urine pass from the kidneys to the bladder. Regina was always a great one for protecting her family from difficulties, and we strongly believed she was told something in St James' along the lines that there was nothing more they could do. She kept it to herself or perhaps she just didn't hear what she was told. We don't know, we will never know. She never spoke about it.

We had her home for Christmas. All her children and grandchildren were there. It was her day. Christmas day was always her specialty and this one was not to be taken from her. She had her three daughters and daughter-in-law on board to supervise and make sure everything was up to her high standard. She was in her element. She sat down most of the time in the kitchen, surrounded by her nine grandchildren whom Santa had visited during the night. It was a beautiful day. We celebrated Mass together in the sitting room, and her granddaughter Mia played the guitar singing "Silent Night". They all loved my recording of "Little Drummer Boy" on the Christmas album and all joined in as we sang it together. I recorded some of those moments and I put it on a DVD of that Christmas.

The next few weeks were very special for our family. Regina was not talking, she was keeping everything to herself and wanted to carry it and we could not stop her, it was her way of protecting us all; she was still in charge. Other tumours were appearing on her body. She must have known deep down her time was running out. Laura, a palliative care counsellor, called to see her and we were hoping she would open up to her. Fr Brendan Corrigan the Parish Priest would also call on a daily basis to see her. When she would see him driving into the yard she would say "for f*** sake is he coming again, people will think we are having an affair!" He was brilliant to her and asked her if she had any worries. Eventually she said to him "I'd like to have a clean sheet before I go". She received all the sacraments and Fr Brendan assured her she would go straight up. Her appetite was very poor at this stage, but she loved her cup of coffee and a cigarette. Over her last ten days she had lost the power in her legs, so she had to use a wheelchair. She liked to go to her living room to watch a bit of TV, particularly if *Fair City* was on. However, she was complaining of her eyes, and suggested she needed her eyes checked or a change of glasses. One of the last programmes she watched on TV was our cousin Dolores Kelly taking part in *The Voice* singing competition on RTÉ. She returned to bed after that and never got out of bed again. A few days after that her eyesight went completely as a result of the growth of tumours behind her eyes. About three days before she died she said to her daughters Gillian and Deborah; as they sat on her bed, that she saw a blue angel all in light at the end of her bed. Reg was big into angels. Afterwards Deborah asked her friend what a blue angel meant and she was told it meant strength and courage. Amazingly, when Regina was diagnosed with cancer she got a tattoo on her arm with the words *strength* and *courage*. At 8.40am on Thursday 11th February, the feast of Our Lady of Lourdes, Regina let go of her earthly life. She needed no more strength and courage.

As she let go and breathed her last breath, my earliest memory of her when I was three years old came flooding back to me as I was brought to the door of my mother's bedroom to peep in at the new baby girl. Mary Regina, who was born on the 31st of May 1956, had now on the 11th February 2016 died. She was my sister and my best friend for over 59 years. I was now the baby of the family once more. I had my title back but I wish I hadn't, I didn't want it.

CHAPTER 17

....

The German Experience

The "Hallelujah" story was, and indeed is, very big in Germany. After the wedding clip went viral on YouTube, I had phone calls, TV interviews and emails from all over the world but particularly from Germany. Every television show on all of the channels wanted a slice of me. Needless to say it wasn't as simple as that to go over there and do all the interviews and sing "Hallelujah". Most of these TV shows thought I had nothing better to do than to get over there as soon as possible. They forgot that I was still a Parish Priest working full time with a busy schedule of weddings, First Holy Communion ceremonies and funerals. But I was very excited about the idea of them wanting me, though a bit apprehensive. "Are they mad that they want a 60-year old Parish Priest from Ireland?" I could not help it.

One of the first shows that German TV RTL flew me over to Cologne for was for the Stern TV Magazine programme, introduced by Steffan Hallaschka. I was introduced first of all by showing a clip of various artists singing "Hallelujah" and the number of hits these clips generated on YouTube - all in their millions, Leonard Cohen included. Finally, they showed my wedding clip of "Hallelujah", which at that stage had generated approximately 39 million hits. I felt like a superstar. So I walk on stage to a round of applause. It was a live TV show and my very first experience of a three-way interview. In other words, Steffan would ask me the questions in German, I would get the translation in my ear piece in English, and proceed to answer the question in English and my answer was then sub-titled on the TV screen. So there was always a delay in my answers to Steffan for a few seconds. However it worked very well, mainly because Steffan was a very gracious man and made me feel very much at ease. As he was also a piano player, he wanted to accompany me singing the song "Hallelujah". I felt my voice was a bit "rusty", but nevertheless the entire interview and song came across very well and there was a huge reaction from the TV viewers as well.

My next visit to Germany was in December 2014 for the very famous show on the German TV channel RTL, called *Menschen, Bilder, Emotionen*, presented by Gunther Jauch - the Ryan Tubridy of German television. Indeed, the three-hour programme is very similar to our *Late Late Show*. The programme features current topics and events that made it big on global TV over the previous year. Some of the guests on the TV show with me were some of the German football team who had won the World Cup in 2014. While I was in the makeup room I met and had my photo with the famous German goalkeeper Manuel Neuer and got his autograph; that was a real honour. My grannephew Ryan at home was very jealous when he heard it, but I gave him the autograph and he was on cloud nine. When I got home I had to photocopy the autograph for many of the children in the primary school as well. It was also the year of the famous ice bucket challenge and some of the more famous challenges that appeared on YouTube were featured. Conchita Wurst was also featured on the show. Conchita won the Eurovision

Song contest for Austria in 2014 with the great song "Rise Like A Phoenix" and a fantastic voice to go with it. I didn't actually get introduced to Conchita on the show, however at breakfast the next morning in our hotel I was introduced to Tom Neuwirth. While he is in drag he is Conchita, but while dressed in normal gear he is Tom. They created a huge production around my singing of "Hallelujah". The entire set behind me was like a church and as I sang I was walking up the aisle of the church scene. After the song, I had a short interview with Gunther. I felt very positive after this experience and I guess a lot more confident. Oh yes, my confidence was building and I was enjoying the celebrity status and fame.

In the early summer of 2016 when the invitation came from the producers of the German television show *Deutschland Sucht Das Supertalent* (DSDS), the equivalent of *Britain's Got Talent* in the UK, I thought long and hard about the invitation. I just didn't see myself going before three or four judges and maybe getting the buzzer to buzz off the stage. No, I didn't fancy that at all. So after a lot of thought and discussion with Gordon my manager, who thought it would be a good experience, I agreed to take part in the competition. My positive feelings built up over the weeks as I thought about it more and more.

I shared my news with my family who were very excited; I think we all saw me as the winner, and in our heads we were quite happy to be spending the winning money. I shared the news with my two special friends on Facebook from Germany, Nicole and Barbara, and my good friend Janneke from The Netherlands. And as I didn't speak a word of German, the ladies proceeded to give me a few German lessons for when

I got on stage. "Mein name ist Fr Ray Kelly. Ich komme aus Irland [I come from Ireland]. Ich bin dreiundsechzig Jahre alt [I am 63 years of age]." And of course the three girls, "Ray's Angels", were going to meet me and be at my audition. I had met Nicole and Barbara before, but I had never met Janneke so I was really excited about meeting her.

I flew out to Frankfurt on Tuesday morning 9th August 2016. Gordon my manager flew in also from the UK. We met at Frankfurt airport and drove the two and half hour journey to Essen where the auditions were being held at the Colosseum Theatre. We arrived at the Ibis hotel where we were greeted by my three friends. Indeed, I was as excited to meet them as they were to meet me. I was scheduled to be at the Colosseum by 2pm. When I arrived there was the usual signing of documents giving the show permission to interview me, and film me at various places and of course to air these interviews on German TV. There were various other contestants as well around the theatre green room. In fact, many of them were also booked into the same hotel. I spent a lot of time hanging around basically being available should the producers need me for anything. I knew they liked to have you within close view at all times. However, I did manage to escape now and then and pop downstairs to meet my friends and fill them in on the happenings so far. I was delighted to hear that they had succeeded in getting tickets in the theatre for the auditions which would begin about 7.00pm. When the auditions began I was brought up to a room behind the stage and waited. I was nervous, mostly that they wouldn't understand my little bit of German. I knew I could perform the song they chose for my audition "Love Shine A Light". I had sung the song many times before and knew I could carry it off. I had also had the track of "Everybody Hurts" in reserve.

There were three judges. First up, Dieter Bohlen who is a German musician, songwriter, record producer and television personality. It was obvious he was wearing a lot of fake tan with his teeth whiter than white. He is the "Simon Cowell" of the judging panel and is noted for his harsh criticisms of contestants often belittling them to make them feel almost useless. The "David Walliams" of the panel was Bruce Darnell an American model, dancer and choreographer based in Germany. The third member of the judging panel was Victoria Swarovski - an Austrian pop singer and the daughter of the famous family owned company Swarovski. I guess she was the Amanda Holden or the Alesha Dixon of *Britain's Got Talent*, or both. Well the show started and I could hear some of the comments from the judging panel on the other acts. I remember thinking these judges are hard to please. There were four or five acts before me and I don't think any of the acts got three Yeses so they were eliminated straight away. I think that made me feel more nervous than ever.

My turn came and as I walked out on to the stage, I could see "Ray's Angels" waving the Irish flags which seemed to relax me. Dieter started speaking to me in German and when he realised I didn't understand he spoke in English. I then proceeded to introduce myself in German. "Mein name ist…" and Dieter stopped me and started speaking in English. So much for my learning my little bit of German. It threw me for a few seconds until I regained my composure and told them who I was, where I came from and my age. They asked me what was the name of the song I was going to sing and

I said "Love Shine A Light". Dieter didn't seem to know the song and I explained to him that it won the Eurovision Song Contest for the UK in 1997 which was held in Dublin.

My backing track started and I sang "Love Shine A Light" to a very warm audience who seemed to clap along. I was really happy with myself at how it was coming along and my confidence grew as I got more and more into the song. I have to say the Irish flags flying with my three girls helped in no small way to make me feel very comfortable. Janneke told me that during the singing of the song some of the audience around them started saying in whispers, "That's the priest from Ireland from the YouTube wedding video". Janneke, Nicole and Barbara confirmed to those around them that indeed it was.

When I had finished singing the audience gave me a wonderful round of applause, however the judges didn't seem over-enthused about my singing or indeed the song, and they didn't know me from the wedding video or indeed recognise me. However, they heard the audience talk and shout "Hallelujah" and clap. I proceeded to explain to them about the "Hallelujah" wedding and what the audience was reacting too. Victoria from the judging panel then said "Oh yes, I remember seeing that on YouTube. I thought it was the most beautiful thing I had seen in a long time". Then Bruce stood up and started dancing around his seat like a child having a tantrum and said, "Hallelujah, Hallelujah, Hallelujah - I'm sick of people singing "Hallelujah"." I remember thinking to myself, what's he on about because I didn't even sing "Hallelujah"; I kept my thoughts to myself though and let him enjoy his tantrum as I'm sure most of it was for the television cameras. The audience continued to shout, "Hallelujah, Hallelujah", and with that Dieter intervened and said, "Would you sing "Hallelujah"?" I said, "I don't have that track" at the same time as a voice from behind the stage said something similar. Dieter then asked me if I would sing it acapella. So I proceeded to sing the song without the track and as I got to the chorus the audience joined in and raised the roof. However, as I was about to go into the second verse Dieter raises his hand for me to stop. I did. He said, "That's enough, I don't want to offend my friend any longer" meaning Bruce obviously. He may have said, "Thank you for coming" but I didn't hear him. I just walked off the front of the stage down a ramp in front of the audience quite embarrassed and disgusted with myself.

I felt so low and cut-up by the whole experience. I went outside the doors of the theatre and just sat there on my own for what seemed like a long time but I reckon only about ten minutes. I know my three friends were anxious to get out to me and were being stopped. They eventually told security they were leaving and they found me sitting alone. I got three hugs and I knew I was not alone and that consoled me. I know the girls were totally disgusted and embarrassed by the way I was treated by the judges and by the TV production company because not one of them came near me afterwards. I know when some major disappointment happens to me like that I console myself with the line, "It's ok, it's not the end of the world, no one died". Being a priest I have witnessed too much pain in the world to equate what happened to me as tragic. All I wanted now was to go to a pub, get a beer and have something to eat.

Gordon has sussed out a restaurant for us just around the corner from the theatre. Soon calmness descended on me and indeed as the adrenaline that kept me going all day was gone, I suddenly became very tired. I was so glad to have the company of Gordon and my friends. I remember saying to them that I would never, ever enter another competition like this again. I meant it. I would never put myself up in front of anybody like that again to be embarrassed and humiliated. I didn't need that at this stage of my life. I was still angry and I knew it would take time for that to pass, but it would and I knew I would be ok.

I asked my German friends to keep an eye out on TV during the showing of *Das Supertalent* series and see if they would show what happened that day in the Colosseum. I believe my audition that day in Essen was never shown or I definitely would have heard about it. Perhaps, they didn't want to show Bruce and Dieter making fools of themselves. In the days after my trip to Essen there was a lot of post-mortem about the event among my friends who had journeyed with me. I know, they were completely disgusted by the behaviour of Dieter and Bruce and very surprised by the production team of *Das Supertalent*. But I knew that when I put myself out there for a reality TV show I would have to be prepared for any consequence. But in all honestly I was not prepared for what happened in the Colosseum in Essen. I was flying off to Lourdes in France the following day for a week with my friend and folk group from Clara Parish in Co. Offaly. I knew that if there was any anger left in me I would be able to leave it behind me there. I did.

Soon after I returned from Lourdes, my manager Gordon let me know that he was planning two big concerts for me in November and December that would be spearheaded by Pat

Egan Promotions. These concerts were going to be similar to the event in the Olympia. The first concert was held at the National Concert Hall in Dublin. I was going to have live music on the stage with me, so I rehearsed with the musicians over a period of a few weeks before the shows. I also invited the young chamber choir from St Oliver Post Primary School to take part and accompany me under the direction of their teacher Dara McSweeney. Their harmonies were just spectacular. My niece Tara Kelly also joined me on stage and we sang the beautiful song "The Prayer". My special guest on the night was a beautiful gifted singer and songwriter Maria Butterley. I felt so at ease and proud to say I sang on the stage of the National Concert Hall.

Three weeks later I looked forward to taking the stage at the Cork Opera House. I had spent time in Cork during my work as a Civil Servant back in the 70s and in 1983 to 1985 during seminary training. During those years I would have frequented the Opera House for many shows and pantomimes. So it was lovely to be back in one of my all time favourite cities. I had the same accompaniment on stage as in the Concert Hall. I was delighted to have my niece Tara back for this show too, I knew she would want to sing again after she got the bug from the National Concert Hall. And Maria Butterley was my special guest once again.

Having theses shows was a real blessing. They helped me through my grief after losing my sister. Every time I sang the song "Everybody Hurts" at the shows I just felt my own pain, my own loss, my own hurt. Still do. Of course there wasn't a day since the 11th February that I didn't think about Reg and cry a few tears for her. I felt so sorry for her family too, her husband Seamus and her children and grandchildren. I mean if I was feeling the way I was what must it have been like for them. Christmas was just around the corner too and for the first time in 26 years the Christmas dinner would not be in Reg's home. Gillian had decided to have it in her home, but we would all be there, to celebrate, to laugh, to cry and to toast our beloved Regina. They say that once the first Christmas is over, the first birthday, the first anniversary, the pain of loss gets less. I don't know. For some maybe. We would celebrate Reg's first anniversary Mass on 11th February and that would be the three main "firsts" over.

Germany was calling me again as I was invited by Fr Niall Leahy to spend the weekend as a guest in Munich for the St Patrick's Celebrations. I spent some time seeing some of the wonderful sights of the city. On Saturday I was the main celebrant at the 6.00pm Mass at St Ludwig Church delivering my homily in English; however, Mary Ronane followed me with a perfect German translation. Over one thousand people attended the Mass. I sang the Gloria during Mass and led the people with "Hail Glorious St Patrick". After Mass there was a short concert with all the artists and I duly obliged with "Hallelujah".

Bavarian TV were making a TV programme featuring myself and the famous Bavarian Chef Fritz Haring. He runs a very popular restaurant on the lake outside Munich in a small town called Tutzinger and he travels the world making TV programmes. On Saturday evening it was off to the Hofbrauhaus for the pre-parade party, a sold out event of over 600 people. I entertained the audience with a selection of my songs from my album *Where I Belong*. In the Irish spirit of the evening, "Galway Bay" and "Danny Boy" were the favourites and I finished up with "Hallelujah". At 9.30am the next day, I was invited to the pre-parade breakfast with the Irish minister for Agriculture Michael Creed. In the big parade I was in a horse-drawn carriage. It was estimated about twenty thousand people lined the streets to cheer us on. I felt like royalty in my carriage as I waved to the people. When we reached the main platform on the Wittelsbacherplatz I blessed the shamrock in the Irish language. Then various speakers including our Irish Minister spoke and the real party started with plenty of entertainment for a few hours. Again, I sang my few Irish songs and finished up with "Hallelujah".

CHAPTER 18

....

Britain's Got Talent

It must have been a year after my *Das Supertalent* experience that the invitation came from Thames Television and Freemantle, who produce *Britain's Got Talent*. I remember the first phone call so very well. The contact explanation was similar to the first request from *Das Supertalent*, in that they had watched my personalised version of "Hallelujah" for the wedding of Chris and Leah O'Kane and thought it was beautiful. She went on to say how good my voice was and then asked, "Would you consider taking part in the auditions for *Britain's Got Talent*, they would love to have you." I think if she was sitting in front of me and saw my face after she asked me that question, I wouldn't have had to say another word because she would know my answer. However, I was polite. I told her I would not be interested as I would not have the time because I was working full time in my parish. She asked for my email, which I supplied, and then thanked me for taking the call. She said if I ever did consider it to make contact with her via email.

The thought and fear of going through something like *Das Supertalent* again came back to me like a ton of bricks. And it would be heightened all the more because of how big a fan I was of *Britain's Got Talent*. While watching it I had often asked myself would I ever audition and the answer was NO, NO, NO! It was so much easier to watch it from the comfort of my own home with a beer in my hand. The thought of going up in front of Simon Cowell, "The God of Judges", did not appeal to me. I mean if Dieter and Bruce could insult me and make me feel small, imagine what Simon could make me feel.

A few months later contact was made again, via email this time. She asked would I take a phone call, and while my answer hadn't changed, I still gave her my number. Within an hour we spoke. This time it was a different person from the previous invitation. She used similar lines from my first invite about the "Hallelujah" wedding on YouTube and how they would love to have me attend the audition. I explained to her my reasons for not wanting to take part, what happened at the *Das Supertalent* audition, how I felt humiliated from the whole experience and how I felt as though it was more about the judges than the talent on the stage.

She listened intently to what I was sharing with her and I knew she understood where I was coming from. She then went on to tell me I would be treated with the highest respect and assured me that my experience would be an extremely positive one, no matter what the outcome. She knew from speaking to me that I was a huge fan of the TV show. She also assured me that I would not have to go through the initial audition, which is in front of a different judging panel without the official judges. The initial audition is shown on TV when you see footage of massive queues of people waiting for their chance. Because of what they had seen of me on YouTube, my first audition would be in front of Simon, Amanda, Alesha and David. They had also listened to my two albums *Where I Belong* and *An Irish Christmas Blessing*. She said she would send me some dates for auditioning and get back to me in about a week. So I sat with the idea for a few days and discussed it with my family. They were very keen for me to do it as long as I didn't take the whole thing too seriously and beat myself up if I didn't get the "YES" from the judges. I also discussed it with Gordon Charlton, my agent in the UK, who knew more than me about the happenings of reality TV shows.

Since there was nothing much happening in my music career after signing with Universal Music and the release of my two albums, I thought it might work out as a launching-pad for something new for me; it would be quite a bit of exposure on UK and Irish TV. The question was would or would I not go for it? I think I had made my decision when the email arrived with the different dates for auditions. There were a number of dates available at The Lowry Theatre in Manchester and at least three dates for The London Palladium as well. The date that was best suited for me was Wednesday 31st January at The London Palladium.

It was easier for me to fly to London as I could meet my agent there. I said to myself, "Ok, let's get this over with once and for all. I'll be home in two days and it all will be history." I didn't want any of my family to come with me, but the thought of travelling alone didn't appeal to me at all. At least when travelling with someone my heart would not feel as heavy, as weighed down, as though I was about to face a firing squad. I therefore decided to invite a friend, Ollie Callan from Oldcastle, to travel with me for the two night stay. Ollie has a small recording studio in his home and I recorded my *More of Me* album for charity there many years before. We flew out the Tuesday evening to Heathrow and checked into our hotel - a cheapy, but adequate - only a ten-minute walk from the London Palladium. In fact, after having something to eat, we decided to take a dummy-run walk to the theatre just so as we would not get lost the next day.

The big day arrived and I was among many other artists signing in for the day. Once I had all the signings done I was given a wrist band and I was in. I introduced myself to some of the crew. There were many of them all over the place on their speakers in contact with each other. I was assigned a "crew person" and then directed to a huge waiting room where there were many other artists: singers, magicians, dancers, a dog or two, comedians and some very colourfully dressed people ready to perform only God knows what. There were cameras set up filming all the time. In fact, I really didn't know when I was and wasn't being filmed. Some interviews were set up; I was filmed sharing my story of "Hallelujah" with at least two or three other artists. I was filmed for *Britain's Got More Talent* with Stephen Mulhern. I must say, I found him very funny and amusing. He pulled off a few magic tricks in front of me too. With the huge amount of filming and interviews, I knew that only about one percent of it, if any, might be seen on TV.

After the filming of various interviews, it was back to the waiting room again and hanging about. What fascinated me was that the crew, by way of walkie-talkie, knew where all the artists were are at all times. At one stage I heard one of the crew asking through a walkie-talkie, "Has Fr Ray done his filming on the street yet?" Within a few minutes another crew member came and brought me to the street for filming. There I was walking along the street, smiling and looking all around me admiring the buildings. Back again for another take; I was walking too slow. Another take; I was walking too fast.

Eventually I got it right and the filming crew were happy they had enough footage.

I knew there were going to be two sets of auditions. The first was scheduled for 4.00pm, but didn't begin until about 4.30pm. The second was scheduled for 7.00pm, but didn't begin until about 7.30pm. I didn't know which schedule I was timed in for and they would not tell me. However, I was still in the waiting room long after 5.00pm so I figured my audition was not going to happen until the later schedule of auditions. By 8.10pm I was brought up onto the side of the stage, ready for my audition. I was told in advance that Simon would be the one speaking to me.

The song we had agreed that I would sing was the R.E.M. song "Everybody Hurts". I could see Ant and Dec over near the side of the stage and I was brought over to meet them and be filmed just before I walked onto the stage. One of the crew was with me and I waited as another artist performed on stage. The next thing I heard was four very loud buzzers following each other. The sound lifted me. I think the young crew member assigned to me saw the fear in my face as I heard the noise. He assured me it was not going to happen to me. I knew of course that Kaptain Rock, a musician and music teacher, had got his marching orders. After that Alex from Romania and living in London was on, a builder who was delivering a holistic healing dance. However, the four buzzers didn't let him finish his dance. As he left the stage, I could hear Simon saying, "I think this is going to be one of those days". The thought quickly entered my head that I'm next for the chop. Then I was directed over to Ant and Dec. We shook hands and the boys were very polite to me. I remember passing a remark to Dec that he looks a lot taller than on television. I was winding him up a bit because I had watched *I'm A Celebrity Get Me Out Of Here* about two months previously, and during the series there was a lot of banter aimed at Dec about his height. The two boys wished me the best of luck and directed me onto the stage.

The stage in the London Palladium is huge, and I had been told to stand on the star. I walked onto the stage to a round of applause which settled me quite a bit. After we finished with my introduction, Simon asked me a question I was not expecting, "Let me ask you a question, do you do exorcisms?" Indeed, I was thrown by it a little. I always knew, however, that there was a bit of banter going on between Simon and David, so when he looked over at David and shrugged his right shoulder, I knew it was a set up. So I joined in the fun. "Yeah, we can work on David whenever you want," I replied as I stepped slightly over towards David and raised my right hand over him, "Do you want me to zap him now or later?" The audience erupted in laughter. I felt comfortable and relaxed. This was not *Das Supertalent* after all. When asked why I decided to come onto the show I replied, "Well, I thought maybe I'd be the first singing priest to win *Britain's Got Talent*." When Simon asked what song I was singing and why I had chosen it, I told them I was going to sing "Everybody Hurts" because "It's a song that's kind of near and dear to my heart. I suppose being a priest you get in touch with a lot of pain, a lot of joy and happiness as well."

I placed the mic back in the stand to another round of applause and waited for the track to start. Once I sang the opening line, *"When the day is long…"*, in my soft falsetto voice

I knew this was going to be ok. I was now in a world where I felt every word I sang. "*Yes, everybody hurts, take comfort in your friends. When you're on your own in this life the days and the night are long.*" Every time I sing those lines, even now, my thoughts turn to my terminally ill sister Regina as she waited out the last, long, and maybe lonely nights of her life. It's what I feel, it's what I have experienced in my life as a priest that takes my voice in this song to a place almost like prayer.

As I continued, I could see I had Simon drawn into my story. Alesha's smile told me she was there too. Simon was nodding to the beat. Amanda was just in a gaze with her right fist under her chin. David sat back, but I knew he was listening very intently. I took the mic from the stand just before I sang the final few words, "*Hold on…*", as I wanted to direct my left hand to the audience clenching my fist to let them know to hold on too. The final words of the song I spoke, "You're not alone". Little did I think the impact those last three words would have on so many people.

The track finished. There was silence. In that few seconds of silence I thought of my *Das Supertalent* moment. It hadn't left me after all. Will I walk off the stage quickly now and forget this ever happened? Hopefully they won't show it on TV. What I didn't realise until afterwards was that for those few seconds of silence, which seemed like an hour, the audience, Simon, Amanda, Alesha and David were coming to terms with where I had brought them in that song. They all felt it. Simon broke the trance by leading the standing ovation placing his hands around his mouth like a megaphone and shouting "Wow", followed by the other judges and the whole London Palladium. I was shaking. Now I was trying to figure out what was happening. I was supposed to walk off the stage and forget about this like *Das Supertalent*. That's what I had experienced and the only thing I knew to do. I couldn't do that now. *Das Supertalent* was put to bed once and for all.

I took in some deep breaths as I moved from one foot to another to relax and control myself. I held on to the mic stand with my right hand for a prop as I held back the tears. Simon gave me the thumbs up and I knew I was in a place I had never experienced in my life before, and possibly never would again. I spoke softly back to Simon, "Thank you". Simon went down the line of judges who gave me their feedback. "Well, that was a beautiful performance," David said, "It really was. I've never seen a priest stand at a microphone and sing like that, you did it with such soul and passion, it just was a really, really brilliant performance." Alesha followed, saying, "So soothing and calming. Everybody was listening to every single word, relating it to things going on in their lives and you just seem like the loveliest man…it was a beautiful audition". Amanda said "For me it was everything, it's just brilliant and honest", then she waved her right hand back to the audience and continued "and the whole congregation was behind you". The audience applauded again and I waved back, thankful for their kindness to me.

Then it all came down to Simon, "Fr Ray, I wasn't quite sure what to expect to be honest with you, but I'm going to tell you something - this is one of my favourite ever auditions." I was stunned. He continued, "I really mean it, I think your voice is beautiful. I love the version of the song. This was everything we've been waiting for genuinely." I thanked him for his kind words.

It was time for the verdict of whether I'd be continuing on in the competition. They went down the line again with their decisions; "It's a YES from me," said David; followed by Alesha, "I'm saying YES"; then Amanda, "Absolute YES from me, well done." It then came down to Simon's opinion. He said, "Fr Ray Kelly, I'm delighted to say you have four huge fat Yeses!" I left the stage with Simon's thumbs up sign and my own back to the audience and a big wave. The audience was brilliant and they carried me and helped me all the way through. I was met at the side of the stage by Ant and Dec who shook my hand in congratulations. When Ant asked how I was I said, "I'm emotional, emotional. I'm an emotional wreck...It was awesome." Dec replied, "That was some congregation out there." Knowing that Dec was a practicing Catholic and had been married by his brother a priest, I knew my answer to him. "We should have had a collection shouldn't we," I retorted. "Always got an eye on it, always got an eye on it," Dec replied.

I handed over the mic to a crew member and was directed to a corridor just behind the stage. Many of the young crew members gathered around me in congratulations to tell me I was through to the semi-finals - the live television show. They asked me if I realised what had happened, that Simon had said it was one of his favourite auditions ever.

After my audition, the judges were having a break and as Amanda was passing me by she came over to congratulate me again and gave me a big hug. As she left, Simon came over to me and congratulated me again. "You blew us away," he said "We were not expecting a performance like that, I meant it, it is one of my favourite auditions ever. If only I hadn't given

my golden buzzer away two days ago you would have got it."
I thanked Simon for his kind words and said, "Hope we meet
again sometime," as we shook hands. He let go of my hand
and started to walk away, but he turned round and said, "We
definitely will be meeting again." I thought to myself "Wow."
He had already told me while I was on stage that he would
have given me his golden buzzer only he had given it away to
Jack and Tim; a father and son duet. However, that line was
cut from Simon's comments and never said on TV because
my performance was shown on TV before Jack and Tim's was.

After all the congratulations had been extended and the
hugs given, I was brought into a room to sign papers and
forms. Officially, I was through to the next round because
any of the artists that gets three or four Yeses qualify for the
next round. That still does not guarantee them a place in the
semi-final and a place on the live TV show though. I was
unofficially told I had made the semi-final and the live show,
but I would have to return to the London Palladium in about
two weeks for the official revealing show.

I know it was very late when I got back to my hotel room.
By the time I got back there, I could have done with some
food and would have loved a pint to toast my success, but
neither was available. I wanted to phone the world and tell
them that Ray Kelly was back, but I couldn't; I signed a document promising not to reveal what happened until my audition was seen on TV and that would not happen for another
80 days. I tried to phone my niece Tara who has sung with
me, but, because it was late, there was no answer. I tried to
phone Lorraine- again no answer. I tried to phone Gillian my
niece, no answer. But I got my sister-in-law Olive, Tara and

Lorraine's mum, as I figured she would still be up and excitedly shared the great news. It was so hard to explain what had happened and only when my audition was seen on TV would the full impact of what happened to me sink in with me, and indeed with my family, friends and my parish in Oldcastle.

Ollie and I arrived home on the Thursday afternoon from London. As I had signed a non-disclosure document concerning the results of my audition, Ollie and I were sworn to secrecy. I was able to share with my family the full details of what happened, but, like me, they were sworn to secrecy. When anyone outside that circle asked about how I did, all I could say was I did well. By the time my audition was broadcast, many people had actually forgotten that I was taking part; that is until the series of *BGT* started on TV on 7th April, which was two weeks before my audition would be seen.

In the meantime, there was a lot of communication with phone calls and emails between the *BGT* production team and myself. I would be needed at the London Palladium for the recording of the revealing show for TV. The show and recording of it would be held on Sunday 18th February at the London Palladium. This is the show where the artists who got three or four Yeses are told if they made the live semi-finals or if their *BGT* journey is over. I felt positive and good about getting through, mainly because I was told unofficially, and I was one of Simon's favourite auditions ever. Nevertheless, when all the judges put their heads together and were vying for their own favourites I may have not made the cut either. I was so glad it was not the previous Sunday 11th February as that was the second anniversary of my younger sister Regina's death. I had a good feeling though because I carried her photo in my pocket all the time and indeed looked at it just before I walked on stage for my audition and said, "Reg, you better root for me."

So, that Sunday afternoon came at the Palladium. It was a day for hanging around quite a lot, as none of the artists were told at what time the judges would break the news to us. By 6.00pm all of the 80 artists were put into various groups and numbered. My group was group six and consisted of a Belgian dance act called Baba Yega who had won *Belgium's Got Talent* in 2016 and actually came second in the German *Das Supertalent*. (Oh! I said I'd never mention that show again!) Also in my group was Olena from Russia who could make horse noises. Then there was Sarah, a flexible cake-eating opera singer from USA, and finally myself. There was certainly an international flavour to our group. As the judges passed through our waiting room, Alesha spotted me and gave me a big smile and a thumbs up. I felt good. At about 6.45pm our group walked out on stage.

Amanda had the microphone, "Only on *Britain's Got Talent* could this line-up be possible, and we have come to a decision." She looked directly at me and spoke, "You better thank Him upstairs sir because you are all through to the next round!" Baba Yega let off a streamer; Amanda screamed; Baba Yega then grabbed Sarah's cake and smashed it into her face; her dress fell off and the rest of the cake went flying all over the stage. I was covered in cake.

All of us came down to shake hands with the judges and thank them. David shook my hand and congratulated me. He said, "You have big decisions now to make in your life you know". I didn't really know what was behind that statement or what he was thinking. Maybe he saw me as a potential winner - I don't know. I gave Alesha a big hug and thanked her and the same with Amanda. Finally Simon gave me his two hands in a handshake and said, "Well done, see you in the semi-finals." I walked through the theatre and out the double doors at the back where the cameras were waiting for me along with Ant and Dec. All I could say was, "Ah my two Irish boys," and gave each of them a hug. I felt it was like the "Hallelujah" story all over again. I was on cloud nine. Out of the 182 acts that got three or four Yesses, only 80 were invited back that day for recording the revealing show. Out of the 80 only 40 got through to the semi-finals and I was one of them.

CHAPTER 19

....

Preparing for the
Semi-Finals

After the recording of the show, there were constant emails between the *BGT* production team and myself. Ben Clynes was the senior researcher on the *BGT* team. I had to think long and hard about the song I would sing in the semi-final, what I might wear, what I would like the stage setting and décor to be and so on. One thought that came to me was would I sing "Hallelujah" and as the Royal Wedding of Harry and Megan would be just a week or two before, I could incorporate the names of Harry and Megan in the song like I did for Chris and Leah O'Kane a few years before. I thought it might go down well with the British public and the *BGT* audience. I even considered re-recording it for such. Another idea was possibly to sing "Danny Boy" and as the recording I have on my *Where I Belong* album incorporates a little bit of Riverdance music maybe we could have some dancers perform a piece of Riverdance during the song.

The Sunday after the reveal recording show I was expected in London again. This time to meet all the legal team with whom we would sign contracts. I could not possibly get over again for that, but my agent in the UK went there and met with Talya Shalson who would be the solicitor representing me. However, the following week I was able to get over to

London to meet Talya who went through the entire contract I was signing up to with Syco, Simon Cowell's company. The contract would only come into play if I got to the final of *Britain's Got Talent*. Professor Jonathan Shalit OBE was also anxious to sign me up. Jonathan has signed up many of the top artists in the UK and the world and was very anxious to take me on too. My God, the thought of Jonathan Shalit being my agent along with Gordon had me on cloud nine. Jonathan flew in to meet me along with Gordon on the 18th March and came to see me in Oldcastle.

Afterwards he wrote in one of his first emails to me:

It was truly wonderful to meet you Father. I am really very excited about the opportunities open to you, and feel that at your 'young' age a wonderful new career and a whole array of brilliant opportunities await you around the corner. The more preparation work that can be done the better. It would be a pleasure and honour to work with you - if you (and Gordon) felt we would be good together. Your voice is quite beautiful and I love the fact you reference such artists as Josh Groban. What will separate you from other singers is the very special empathy you will have with your audience, which so clearly comes from the heart. That, coupled with your wonderful voice makes Father Ray a WINNER. I am having dinner with Dan Wootton at the Sun tonight who is the biggest music and TV journalist in the UK and will be telling him about you.

And in another email Jonathan wrote, *"I was so taken by you Father Ray that I want to make sure that where ever you come in BGT, it becomes the platform to give you a wonderful and lucrative career which I believe it can."*

So you can imagine how I felt after receiving these emails from Jonathan. I was ecstatic. I even had a management contract signed with him based on certain conditions as a result of how I might progress on the *BGT* show.

Meanwhile, I was getting dates to be in London for routining, which is where I get together with the music production team of *BGT* for a few hours and try out various songs in preparation for picking a song for the semi-final. As I was the only contestant from Ireland to make it to the live semi-finals, the filming crew from *BGT* arranged to arrive in Ireland on 18th March, 2018. It was a bank holiday weekend, and Ireland was after beating England in the 6 Nations on St Patrick's Day to claim the 6 Nations title. The weather was very cold; a lot of snow still on the ground. The crew didn't arrive until late Sunday night, so it was too late to begin filming. However, the next morning as dawn was breaking at about 6.30am I was walking around Lough Sheelin at the Crover House Hotel - me and my two faithful companions Biddy and Buddy. I put the jackets on the dogs to keep them warm, but I was not allowed the same luxury. I strolled along the lake shore with the dogs and a drone flying over me. By 8.30am we had completed our filming there and then proceeded to Oldcastle to walk along the street waving to a few shop owners as they were cleaning the front of their premises preparing for another day. TP Fox was out at his premises waving, as was Ownie Traynor, and then a quick stop into Mc Cabes shop to buy the paper. Definitely if too many people saw me strolling along in my light jumper without a coat on a cold, frosty Monday morning they would probably suggest I should be locked up. By 11.00am we moved into the parish centre for a cup of tea with many of the local parishioners gathered for more filming and a chat. At that stage my family had arrived and we moved to the church where I put on my priestly vestments of alb and chausible. I was filmed then addressing the gathered congregation of parishioners and family:

> Every great dream begins with a dreamer. I love to dream. As a teenager growing up in Ireland, priesthood was far from my mind. I had great friends to socialise with, and I loved to sing. Those years were fantastic. It was at this time that I began to entertain the thoughts of becoming a priest. Well I was ordained in 1989 and still singing at Mass. I've watched *Britain's Got Talent* for many, many years and the prize of performing before members of the Royal Family; it's such an amazing prize for the winner. With that in mind, I thought to myself, 'You know, Ray, you could have a go at this and see how it works out'. So here I am continuing to follow my dream. We have all got a dream, each and every one of us. My dream is to spread joy through my singing, so have faith in your dreams. Don't let them go, because it's never too late to make your dreams a reality.

We finished filming the next morning in the church by about 10.00am. As I said goodbye to the *BGT* filming crew, Bishop Michael Smith was driving in to confer the the Sacrament of Confirmation on the boys and girls from Scoil

Mhuire, Moylagh, and the Gilson National school in Oldcastle. This was the ceremony that was postponed from 1st March due to the heavy snow. I was back, grounded again in parish life.

After all the videotape work, I was over and back to London for more routining coupled with some vocal coaching from Annabel Williams, or Annie as she liked to be called. Annie would journey with me through all rigorous stages of the competition. It was a real pleasure to work with Annie. She called me 'lovely', probably called all her other students the same. So all during the month of April and May I would be flown over to London for a day or two to take in my routining and vocal coaching. By Saturday morning 21st April, I was free to tell the parish and social media that I would be appearing on the auditions of *BGT* that night 21st. My family knew a few days before that and were organising their *BGT* parties. However, I was to avoid telling any of the parishioners that I got four Yeses or was through to the live show semi-finals yet. All that was to be kept for the deliberation and reveal show which would be aired in another few weeks. I also got an email from the press team requesting me to direct any interviews from media to them. I think they were afraid I would reveal more than I was supposed to. However, I've had a fair bit of experience with media from the "Hallelujah" story so I was pretty confident in that area. Josephine Meyer from the *BGT* media wanted me to be available though to take interviews as well. No problem there.

That Saturday I had a wedding and was invited to the hotel afterwards for the meal, but I had the *BGT* show set to record. I just got home about 8.10pm and quickly switched on the TV as I saw myself walking out onto the stage. My friend May Farrelly was in the house minding my dogs and we watched my audition together. I watched it intently and the first shock I got was the realization that they cut my audition to bits. I sang over a five-minute song and all I got at the audition was about two minutes, but it was enough. Tears filled my eyes as it all came back to me of what had actually happened almost three months ago. Did it really happen? Was that really me? Did Simon 'The God of Judges' really say those kind words? During the rest of the evening I must have played it over and over and over as I responded to phone calls and texts from family and friends. It was amazing. By Sunday morning the emails started coming in as well as getting standing ovations from my parishioners as I walked out onto the altar to say Mass. It was the "Hallelujah" story all over again.

Radio stations wanted me for live interviews on their breakfast shows like Sarah Ruane for *Bobby's Late Breakfast Show* on Newstalk, Rosie Wright from Premier Christian Radio, Liz from *Today with Maura and Dáithí* and *The Six O'Clock* show on TV3. Then the tabloids carried all kinds of headings: "A holy show! Crooner cleric Fr Ray to sing on *Britain's Got Talent*", "Holy Cowell BGT's singing priest is praying for the chance to perform with SuBo[Susan Boyle]", "Fr Ray's divine inspiration", "High Prays for Ray" and "R.E.M. praise priest for his 'powerful rendition'". Anyway, the tabloids went on and on. Indeed, sometimes trying to turn a positive experience into something negative. Then there was the guest appearance on the Holly and Phil show *This Morning*. Much of the focus of that interview was the fact that at one stage I was signed up with Universal Music for my two albums with Phil asking me about the present situation. However, I was no longer signed with them since 2015 so it was no longer an issue. Of course that didn't stop the tabloids from writing about that too, almost implying I should not have been in the competition even though I was no longer involved with Universal Music. Many of the other artists had at one time been signed up with record deals too. I guess when one is up there, one has to be prepared for everything and I suppose I was.

There were numerous emails too from people who found my rendition of the song powerful and positive for them. For many, besides my voice and the sentiment of the song, it was the last three words that I spoke that impacted on so many, *"You're not alone"*. I remember one such email I got from a lady and it floored me. It really did because sometimes one never gets feedback from people on how someone or something can have an impact on their lives. The email read:

> *I think you literally saved my life. Due to some serious health problems, I'm in excruciating pain every day. I'd gotten to the point where I just couldn't face going on. Had decided death was my only option and had even written a suicide note. Something made me just take a look at YouTube and your audition popped up. Listening to you sing, I literally felt the Grace of God wash over me. Although I will always have to live with the pain, I can also live with hope. God placed you on that stage for a reason, and I believe you impacted many many people. So thank you for being a blessing to me, and I'm sure others.*

I remember just reading that letter over and over. I then went into to the Blessed Sacrament in the Church and cried. Even now almost a year later, I find I get emotional thinking about that lady. I wrote back to her some months later to thank her for her openness in sharing. She wrote back to me to tell me a new drug had come on the market that has eased her pain considerably and she was now living a more full and active life living with hope.

Another lady from Honolulu in Hawaii wrote to me also sharing the impact "Everybody Hurts" had on her:

> *Rev Kelly, as we go through life sometimes we have no idea how we affect others or the impact we have. I have been very low and at the end of my rope. Ready to give up on life and last night while I couldn't sleep I was going through YouTube videos and your audition on Britain's Got Talent popped up. You sang 'Everybody Hurts' and it was absolutely beautiful! You touched my soul! I truly believe God sent you to me! I am not alone. Thank you. You have definitely made a difference and even if it's only for a day, it is time to regain my footing. I live in Honolulu, Hawaii and who would think a parish priest in Ireland could have such an affect on someone thousands of miles away.*

Quite recently and over a year after my televised audition, I received an email from a lady from as she said 'the other side of the pond':

> *Dear Father, not so sure if this is your real address or if I'm emailing a fan site or a scammer or whatnot but I*

thought I'd give it a go. I want to tell you how many times you have saved me. If it is you I'm sure you get a lot of these so my message is nothing special. I just want to say thank you. Every time I'm in a low point of depression, I watch your first audition on BGT. The last moment of that song, where you say "you're not alone", the way you said it has helped me often. I am a no one in this world and sometimes my days are ones that make me feel as if I have nothing. And so I watch your first audition again and hear you say those final words, and I have another day or two or three or weeks of being ok. The depression hits again, but it will always come back to me watching your BGT audition and those last three words, "you're not alone". Thank you for reminding in my dark moments that I am not alone, thank you always for your version of that song, I know you went on and did other things but that one moment you spent on stage oft sees me through another day. My Facebook friends know I've had a trying day when I post "and once again I end my day with Father Ray" with a link to your video. Thank you for being the Parish Priest that reminds this random lost soul that she is not alone.

Again, most of the time we never even know how what we do or say impacts people's lives negatively and positively. When I receive these emails I like to call them my "Tabor" moments; knowing that despite my faults and failings as a human being, I am on the right track. I can still bring light and hope into people's lives by allowing God's Holy Spirit to work through me.

Meanwhile, I seemed to be at Heathrow airport nearly every week over and back for more routining and vocal coaching. After a long list of suggested songs being tried and tested, I had it narrowed down to two songs, and I knew the song I wanted to sing in the semi-final. If I was lucky enough to get to the final, I had another song ready too.

CHAPTER 20

....

The Semi-Final

After the heightened emotion and feelings that rose from so many people as a result of my rendition of "Everybody Hurts", the music production team at our routining sessions wanted me to sing a song that might create similar emotions and feelings with people. A few months after Regina died I came across a beautiful song written by Vince Gill. The song gave me a lot of comfort in my grief. Gill began writing the song following the untimely death of a country music superstar, Keith Whitley. However, he didn't finish the song until a few years later following the sudden death of his brother Bob. The song is called "Go Rest High On That Mountain". I started singing the song at some of my charity concerts in remembrance of my sister Regina and dedicating it to anyone in the audience who had lost a loved on through cancer. Initially, the routining team was not sure about the song as it was not well known. Once they realised why I was going to sing the song they went along with it. As there was only one day between the last semi-final, and in the chance that I would make the final, I also had "Bridge Over Troubled Water" ready. I had worked very hard with Annie my vocal coach to have the songs just right and I was ready to go.

The dates were set for the semi-finals and the final at the London Hammersmith Apollo Theatre - a 5,000 seat theatre close to the centre of London. The semi-finals would take place from Monday 28th May to Friday 1st June. The final would be held on Sunday night 3rd June. I was scheduled to compete in the last semi-final on Friday 1st June. I flew into London on the Wednesday evening, while my two nieces Gillian and Amy would fly in the next day.

The most frequently asked question levelled at me is "how can you get time off from your parish to be travelling around so much?" My answer is always the same; I use up my four-weeks annual leave holiday time to travel. Another way the question might come is "does your parish mind you being away so much?" Well they don't because in fairness I am not away from my parish any more than any other priest or indeed taking more time away than I am entitled to. What my new found "celebrity status" has done is put Oldcastle on the map. Quite often, many people fly in from the USA or UK or Germany and they come to Oldcastle to meet the singing priest. If I am available, I am always open to welcoming them and having my photograph taken with them. In fact sometimes couples come to Oldcastle to renew their wedding vows in our church with me officiating and of course singing "Hallelujah" before they leave. This is what I love most of all; meeting people and making their trip to Oldcastle memorable.

My first appointment in London on Thursday morning was to the ITV studios for an interview on ITV's *Lorraine Show* with Christine Lampard. It was a very warm and beautiful interview. Christine was really lovely. The production team of the show had obviously done their homework on me because they delved into my past seminary life with a shot of the sleeve of the vinyl record I recorded with a few other guys from the seminary when we formed that infamous boyband called Rafiki. After my interview at the ITV studios I met up with Gillian and Amy and we had a lovely day around London together.

On Friday it was straight to the Hammersmith Apollo for a full day of rehearsals and preparation for my semi-final that evening. Once I got to the Hammersmith Apollo and signed in I was accompanied by a crew member. Then it was across the road to the pre-fab dressing rooms. My first appointment was to the costume room where I met the team who would decide if my suit was the right colour for the show. I brought my own suit, however if I didn't have it they would supply one for me along with black shoes. Obviously they were in short supply of clerical shirts and roman collars. After all there were usually very few priests taking part. They held on to my suit and blue clerical shirt for a little bit of pressing. It was back to my dressing room then for a short while until I heard one of the crew on the phone, "Has Fr Ray been to the hair stylist yet?" I was on the move again. I got to the hair stylist and I'd say they trimmed millimetres of my hair as I had it groomed at home in Justin's the week before. Then it was back to my room again for about a half hour before I was brought for a 20 minute vocal coaching session with Annie.

Annie thought I sounded a bit hoarse so she hung a sign out of me saying 'Voice Rest'. I felt like an 'idiot'. It meant of course that no one was to speak to me and vice versa. Perhaps I should have told Annie that I had a little bit of chocolate before I went for my coaching. I found out after-wards that chocolate can cause phlegm and make one's voice crack causing hoarseness. So it was plenty of water for a few hours to clear all that and no talking, definitely no talking.

Gordon and I then went for a lunch break because in the early afternoon it would be rehearsal time.

All of the eight acts gathered in the foyer of the Hammersmith Apollo. Our first rehearsal was where all of the contestants were put on the stage in particular places. We were now going to have a run through of what would happen when the results were coming in, as Dec announces the name of the act and says, "You are going home," or, "You are in the top three". If my name was called and I was going home, the spotlight would go off me and I would exit stage right. If my name was called and I was in the top three I would stay on the stage. After that each contestant was assigned a time for a rehearsal of their act. I was feeling very nervous when called for rehearsal, but I noticed Annie there so that relaxed me a little. I was going to be using my in-ear monitor which allows me to hear my track for singing and my own voice as well as the gospel choir. As I walked onto the stage I also got for the first time a full view of the set behind me. It was designed with stain-glass windows like in a church, and either side of me at the back was a gospel choir. I have to say I was really impressed and when the lights went up on the whole set it was really spectacular. I was thrilled. Certainly after two or three runs through the song I was very happy with the whole thing.

In the meantime, I got a text saying my brother Joe and his daughter Lorraine had arrived for the show and my other two nieces, Gillian and Amy, had met them and brought them to the hotel. My friend from Wexford, Brid Carroll, along with my cousin Pat Finnegan and his wife Elizabeth and their niece Claire Finnegan along with Elizabeth's sister

Doris and her husband Henry had also secured tickets for the show. I was so happy for them.

It was back to my dressing room now for about two hours to relax a little bit before the final call to get dressed and head for the makeup room. Then by 6.30pm it was straight to the lobby of the Hammersmith Apollo where I would gather with all of the other contestants as we could hear all of the audience passing through security on their way to their seats in the theatre. As we mingled with each other and took photographs of each other and selfies, it was obvious that everyone was filled with excitement as well as being tense and nervous. We were all rooting for each other. In the few hours that we had together in the Hammersmith Apollo and around the dressing-rooms area, we had become a little family. We had a small TV in our waiting area, and though the sound had been lowered we knew everything that was going on in the theatre. At the rehearsals earlier we were all very much aware that this was the first semi-final series of *Britain's Got Talent* that Dec had to carry on his own. While I knew he would be brilliant and carry off the show like the true professional, after presenting TV shows for over 30 years together it must have been a bit strange for Dec to carry this one on his own. Of course our hope was that Ant would soon be back to join his long time pal Dec.

The time was 7.30pm when I heard the voice of Dec introduce each act with a little bit of their audition. I was the second last act and the last singer of the night and could hear a little bit of "Everybody Hurts" ring out over the theatre and I'm sure across the TV screens of UK, Ireland and the world. Then the judges were all introduced, and before they appear on stage out comes Dec wrapped up in a Union Jack flag. Finally, after a little chat and banter with the judges, Dec introduced the first act Demille & Mouneke, a singing duo who love to sing jazz. Their song went down a treat - a Frank Sinatra classic "That's Life". They got a standing ovation from the judges and the audience. Next on stage were Lexi and Christopher, ten and eleven-year old dancing school children. Children on this show are always loved and adored and these were no different. Their technique and footwork was superb. Up next was the first of two comedians in this semi-final Mickey P. Kerr, A 36 year old primary school teacher who feels that being a teacher and being a comedian are quite similar jobs. He was brilliant and his jokes went down a treat. He got a standing ovation from the judges and everyone in the theatre. After Mickey, we had Sarah Llwellyn the cake-eating opera singer. Only instead of eating cake she was enjoying spaghetti and managed to get the dress off before the end of her performance too. Next up was one of my favourite acts: Bring it North, a five-piece little boy band. Five typical ten and eleven year olds who sang a perfect song for their age from *The Greatest Showman* called "A Million Dreams". I loved them, so young, so confident and as Simon said if they keep together in about 20 years they would be world class. The second comedian/magician came on next, Mandy Muden. Simon called her a witch. She used the judges as part of her act, as do many magicians and comedians on the show. She was brilliant and loved by the judges with standing ovations all around.

I was next and I was situated in one of the royal boxes in the theatre as Dec announced, "Time for a break, but we will be right back with the singing priest himself, Fr Ray Kelly".

The camera went on me as I gave the royal two-handed wave to the camera and the world. "We will see you in a few minutes," Dec said and then straight into an advertisement break to give me time to get from the side of the theatre to the back stage. I was then having my in-ear monitors fitted as Dec came back on television. "Our next act is a singing priest who says he's in the semi-final cause the almighty himself spoke to him directly; his exact words were 'Ray I didn't like it I loved it,'" he said imitating Simon, " 'you're through to the live semi-finals', it's Father Ray Kelly". I was enjoying the footage of Oldcastle behind the stage on the television monitor which was filmed six weeks before when I was ushered out onto the stage. As I walked out I quickly took one look at Regina's photo in my pocket and then set myself centre stage to sing "Go Rest High On That Mountain".

When I finished the song I got a standing ovation from the audience, the judges stayed seated. My brother Joe told me afterwards that when I changed key on the last chorus Robbie Williams stood up and raised his arms in acclamation. Imagine, I sang in front of Robbie Williams. That's on my CV forever, no one can take that from me. Afterwards Dec joined me on the stage and gave me a big hug.

He then went down the line of judges for their critiques and verdicts. Amanda started, "Well done darling tell me about the song because I didn't recognise it at all." "The song was written and recorded by a man called Vince Gill when his brother died from a drug overdose. And I got it a couple of years ago after my own sister died of oesophageal cancer," I said, "I sing it now in church and I sing it at funerals, sometimes I sing it at a concert particularly for people who have

gone through bereavement and lost loved ones from cancer."
A huge round of applause followed. Simon followed, "I had
so much positive feedback when you were on the show, when
you did the audition. And like I said at the time, genuinely, it
was one of my favourite ever auditions. Now I know the story
about the song, why you chose it, it was a hundred percent
the appropriate and right thing to do, and when you lifted
that song on the second part it was glorious. I mean it was really really powerful. I really think and I hope that you're going
to make it through to the next round. I think, this is just on
a very personal note, I think if you make it through I would
love to hear you sing something like "Everybody Hurts",
which was so unexpected, and you sang it so brilliantly, but
with a voice like yours and a personality like yours you can do
it. But tonight boy did you make an impact." David joked,
"Yeah you did brilliantly, it must have been so difficult singing it to four people who are definitely going to hell. You're a
beautiful man and you've got a beautiful soul and you made
a beautiful sound tonight. Well done."

My seven and a half minutes on television were over. I
was exhausted, emotional, happy, excited. I knew I'd given
my best shot and I got the height of praise from the judges.
A member of the crew was still sticking to me like plaster
and brought me back to the waiting area with all of the other acts. There was huge congratulations and well dones and
pats on the back.

Finally the Giang Brothers, stunt performers all the way
from Ho Chi Minh City in Vietnam, who are best known for
their balancing act with one of the brothers balancing verti-
cally atop of his brother's head, were up. Together, they hold

two Guinness World Records. They were brilliant and the judges and audience loved them.

It was voting time and a break from live TV as an episode of *Cornation Street* was on to give people plenty of time to vote. I felt confident being the only Irish act that I had the entire country behind me. We were held up in the theatre lobby for the half hour or so until just before we went on air when all the acts were located in one of the royal boxes of the theatre. I was one of the ones picked to answer Dec's question, "Fr Ray what would it mean to you to get through to the final?" I replied, "It would be amazing Dec, it would just be fantastic for me and for my family and particularly for my parish in Oldcastle as well. They're all really supporting me big time ye know." Then as Tokio Myers, the 2017 winner of *BGT*, took to the stage for a guest performance we were all ushered to the back of the stage to get ready to take our places for the result.

"Welcome back to *Britain's Got Talent* the result, where it is time to find out who is coming back for the grand final on Sunday," Dec said as he welcomed all eight acts back on stage. Three acts would be moving on from the vote, and two would be in the final. Over 1.1 million people voted and the verdict was: "Sarah Llwellyn you are going home. Lexi and Christopher you are going home. Giang Brothers you are in the top three. Bring it North you are going home. Mickey P Kerr you are in the top three. Demille & Mouneke you are going home. So we are down to two acts now Mandy Muden and Fr Ray Kelly. Only one of you can win a place in the top three," Dec paused. "The final act in the top three tonight is Mandy Muden, commiserations Fr Ray and to the rest of you. You've all been brilliant tonight, what a semi-final. Let's give it up one more time for tonight's *Britain's Got Talent* Semi-finalists." So to a huge round of applause I walked off stage with the other semi-finalists who didn't make it. Mickey P Kerr won a spot that night. The judges had to decide between Mandy and the Giang brothers. The judges tied it, a split decision, and Dec went back to the public vote where the Giang Brothers won out.

Like the rest of the contestants who didn't make it, we made our way unaccompanied back to our dressing rooms across the road. In other words, there was no crew escorting me anymore. I was now on my own. I got to my dressing room, phoned my family who were making their way out of the theatre and asked them to wait for me at the front of the building. I sat for a few minutes but not for too long. I was not going to entertain negative feelings because I didn't get through. As I found out afterwards, I came fourth on the semi-final and fourteenth over all in the competition out of 182 acts, and 40 who made the semi-finals. So I felt very proud of myself and happy. I quickly changed my clothes and packed them and went out to meet my brother Joe and my nieces and my good friend Brid. After warm and loving hugs, my cousin Pat and his wife Elizabeth, her sister Doris, husband Henry and their niece Claire came on the scene. Meanwhile there were many people coming out of the theatre who came over to me to congratulate me and to have a photo with me.

We all went back to our hotel for a beer where we mingled with many of the other contestants. Needless to say there were big discussions and post mortems on the entire show. As I found out soon after the show, many people from home were unable to vote - only those with landlines or a particular network. I kept thinking that if I got the votes from home from all the people who tried I might have made the final. But I'm not one for crying over spilled milk. For over six months my life had been consumed by *Britain's Got Talent*. The contracts I signed with Simon Cowell's recording company, Syco and with Jonathan Shalit were now null and void because I didn't make the final. That I find hard to understand, as I haven't changed, the contracts were drawn up from what they saw at my audition with "Everybody Hurts". If I got to the final, I think those contracts would have been honoured. I guess that's the way of the music business. "You're up high today and you're back down to earth tomorrow." I've experienced this before, remember? And I have no regrets.

I feel so appreciative for all the messages of support that I received on my journey through *BGT*. I can only say that for myself, the messages and emails I have received from strangers who, in their despair, have been touched by my singing and have found hope has been extraordinary. I think that indeed is the greatest positive of all about my *Britain's Got Talent* journey. To touch people's lives with my singing is indeed a privilege in my ministry. To make a difference through a talent I enjoy so much is a very special bonus. I have been truly blessed. The whole experience of *BGT* has been amazing for me and it is something I shall never regret taking part in and and a wonderful journey that I shall never forget.

A big thank you to all of the *Britain's Got Talent* team and a thank you to everyone who took the time and effort to vote for me or try and vote for me. God willing my singing journey carries on.

CHAPTER 21

....

The Cruise

It was in St Patrick's Historical Church, in Toledo, Ohio, at one of my concerts during the month of July 2017, that the initial contact was made regarding me taking part in a cruise. The concert was organised by Tracey Coryell, thanks to the invitation of Maury Collins, and was a fundraising event for one of the parish's local charities. The concert was indeed very successful with an attendance of over 600 people and it raised thousands of dollars for the charity. As I was returning in September of that year to fulfil more requests for concerts in US, I was invited back to Toledo and St Patrick's Historical Church for another concert. Initially, I was reluctant to accept because returning so soon after the first concert in July I thought it would not be supported. But I was wrong. In fact, the attendance was much bigger than the first concert. So it was another successful fundraising event for Maury and the local parish charity.

After the second show a gentleman approached me and asked me, "Have you ever been on a cruise?" I said, "No, I was never on a cruise ship in my life." His next question was, "Would you consider doing a cruise if you were offered it?" I replied, "What would I have to do?" He indicated to me that I would be a chaplain and possibly an entertainer as well. "Wow," I said, "I'd love to do that." "Well I know a lady in New York who organises holidays with totally Irish entertainment on cruise ship around the world and I think she would be very interested in getting to know about you. Can I give her your number?" he asked. I gave him my number and I guess within about an hour a lady called Gertrude Byrne phoned me and chatted for a while and invited me to be on a cruise to the Caribbean in November. I knew it was a bit short notice for me, as I knew I had some parish commitments in November and December, so I declined. Well she said, "I have another cruise coming up in May of 2019 in Alaska, could I put your name down for that one?" I said, "Definitely". And so Alaska 2019 here I come.

The cruise would be for one week from 12th May to 19th May. I would fly to Vancouver via Toronto from Dublin and pick up the ship there. Of course from September 2017 to May 2019 was a long time and plenty of notice for me. In the meantime, I was finding out more and more about this lady Gertrude Byrne, a native of Cong, Co. Mayo, and her organisation of Irish Entertainment Cruises. She started over 30 years ago sailing out of New York harbour with 80 passengers and some of New York's finest musicians. Gertrude was always a great one for promoting different Irish events, however, she admits that taking on a cruise was, as she thought, way above her league. Her very first cruise was on a small ship – simple staterooms but incredible food. She was assigned a small lounge on the top part of the ship to host her Irish entertainment. Needless to say the craic was mighty and the envy of many other passengers on the cruise ship. They were dancing the night away with Old Time Waltzes, Polkas, Jives and the Siege of Ennis. From there, numbers began to rise with hundreds of requests to Gertrude from other passengers to join the next cruise. So what began as a small cruise of 80 people has now turned into chartering an entire ship. Gertrude's policy remains steadfast, that is, providing her guests a first class experience from the moment they step on the pier for embarkment. As she says, "Upon arriving at the pier the mood is set. Each guest is personally greeted followed by a champagne reception, and of course the live Irish music is already underway." Her reputation has spread all over the world, and she now charters Holland America's vista class ships every year catering for up to 2000 passengers. I was in awe because she seemed to be able to get the cream of the Irish Entertainment Industry on board as well for her cruises. Her star attractions on this cruise were Daniel O'Donnell, Nathan Carter, Michael English, Jimmy Buckley, Dominic Kirwan and his sons Colm and Barry, Declan Nerney, Mary Darcy, Brendan Shine and his daughter Emily, Tony Kenny and many more. I knew I would be star-struck among such celebrities and array of talent.

As the months went by coming up to the cruise I spoke to many people who had been on previous cruises. My cousin Pat Finnegan and his wife Elizabeth who are regular cruisers could fill me in on life on the ship. I was warned about so much food on the ship that I would return home at least half a stone heavier. I could spend all my time on the ship or get off at the various stops the ship would make each day. And while off the ship I could take in some of the tours that were on offer as well. There would be two sittings for evening dinner each day in the main dining room, and I would be able to avail of one of these formal gatherings with live entertainment on stage in the main theatre after each dinner sitting. I could also choose to avoid the main dining room altogether and use the main restaurant on the ship and eat as much as I liked. So as the departure day came closer and closer I was really getting very excited about my new experience. But I was also full of apprehension. I knew I could fulfil part of what Gertie wanted me to do on the cruise, Mass for all the passengers; but to be in the line up with Daniel, Nathan, Michael, Dominic, Derek, Jimmy and many other big stars of Irish Country Music, the thought of that really scared me. I think those feelings began about nine days before the cruise on Friday night 3rd May when I saw all that line-up on *The Late Late Show* country music night. I rationalised to myself that none of those artists have almost 68,000,000 hits on YouTube with "Hallelujah" or over 11,000,000 hits with "Everybody Hurts" and I too had appeared on *The Late Late Show* many times.

The 11th May, the day of departure arrived and I was booked in to travel with many of the entertainers and band members. As many of us gathered queuing at the Air Canada desk in Dublin Airport Terminal 1, I noticed Michael English, Jimmy Buckley, Brendan Shine, Dominic Kirwan and Declan Nerney. I felt I was really in the company of stars. I met Tony Maher and some of his band The Conquerers. I had been in touch with Tony long before the cruise, giving him a list of songs about five in all that I would perform on my night of entertainment. Our flight to Vancouver took about 12 hours stopping over at Toronto for about two hours. As I learned afterwards Daniel O'Donnell and Nathan Carter were flying out on a different flight. However, the next morning at breakfast in the hotel I met them before we were all heading off to the ship. Prior to boarding the Holland America Westerdam Cruise we all had to queue at US emigration as we were leaving Canada and entering the USA. The queuing took almost three hours for many of us and I know I was very tired afterwards, but a lot of the tiredness was caused by the eight-hour time difference too.

Soon I was located in my stateroom. No sooner was I in my room than an announcement was made to get ready for a Mandatory Passenger Emergency Muster Drill and to assemble at area 11 assembly point. So in the event of a real emergency I knew exactly where to head for. As the Westerdam set sail the party was beginning on the Lido deck with Tommy Flynn's band. Meanwhile Gertrude had asked me if I could celebrate an Express Mass at the main stage. I was fortunate as Daniel O'Donnell was there to sing a few hymns at the Mass. Daniel would be performing two concerts on the main stage later in the evening after dinner was over. Meanwhile other entertainment was taking place at the BB King's Blues Club with Erin's Melody and later Thomas Maguire and Fhiona Ennis, while at the Crow's Nest venue The Conquerors featuring Derek Feery and later Declan Nerney's Showband were playing. Another venue, the Ocean Bar, featured Taylor's Cross. For the next two days the ship was at sea.

On the Monday morning I awoke to the ship's clock moving back one hour. The day began for me with a 9.00am Mass. Fr Ken Walsh, the other chaplain on the cruise, led the liturgy. The 9.00am Mass began the day for over one thousand people every day, and Fr Ken and I would alternate the leading of the liturgy. Later that day The Captain's Cocktail Party was formal dress. The Monday night entertainment included Mary

Darcy, Gerry Finlay, John McNicholl and Barry Kirwan. If you felt like learning a bit of Irish Set Dancing, Foot Tappers were there to show you how. Meanwhile on the big stage for two shows was Brendan Shine, George Casey a comedian and the great Michael English.

On Tuesday we began sailing through Glacier Bay. This was the first sighting of high peaks covered in snow and spectacular scenery, in a vast area of Alaska's Inside Passage, a coastal route that has regular cruise ships visiting. I didn't see any humpback whales or puffins but they are common in this area. When darkness fell we were treated to the music of the Cunningham brothers and Stephen Smyth while on the big stage Tony Kenny, Trish O'Brien, the comedian Gene Fitzpatrick, and the great Jimmy Buckley entertained.

When I woke up on Wednesday morning the ship was docked in a small town called Juneau, the capital city of Alaska. We had a full day here to get off the ship from 7.00am; we could walk around the town and shop at the various souvenir shops, or, if the credit card was able for it, shop more luxuriously for diamonds and jewellery. Once we set sail at 8.30pm the music started up on the ship at the various locations. I looked forward to the big attraction on stage – Nathan Carter himself preceded by Annette Griffin and comedian George Casey. Nathan was his usual brilliant self and once he started "Wagon Wheel" the theatre rocked.

On Thursday morning Skagway was our port of call. It is home to Gold Rush era buildings now part of the Klondike Gold Rush National Historic Park. I signed up for a three hour White Pass Summit Scenic Railroad trip, enjoying some of the most beautiful scenery I have ever seen. Thursday night on the stage was my big night. I had a 5.45pm rehearsal and sound check with The Conquerors Show Band. However my rehearsal was cut short because Gertrude's Cocktail Party ran into my rehearsal. Nevertheless, I was good to go.

Robin Averill, a Canadian/Irish singer, was on first and then it was my turn. The MC on all the shows was Tony Jackson – a self-confessed Cavan man but living in the US for many years and Gertrude's right hand man on the cruises. Tony introduced me with a little of the "Hallelujah" story and I was on. I opened my performance with "Love Shine A Light" followed by the Brendan Graham song "Isle of Hope" – a much loved song by many Irish Americans. I shared my *BGT* experience then before breaking into "Everybody Hurts" and then shared my "Hallelujah" story inviting the audience to sing along the chorus with me. I was about to announce my finale song "New York, New York" when Tony walked on to the stage to thank me for my performance. I left the stage to a huge round of applause as Tony announced the comedian Gene Fitzpatrick. I was devastated. I felt the rug had been pulled from under me as I was about to announce my final song. Tony found me in the dressing room afterwards and I said, "You pulled the rug from under me." "I'm sorry," he said "but you went way over the time allowed. We have another show later and we can't be late for starting it." Of course as the MC I understood his predicament and why he pulled me. However, as I said I was told to have five songs ready and no one put a time limit on it for me. I remember Dominic Kirwan who was the last act of the evening coming over to me. He obviously saw the disappointment on my face. He said, "Don't worry Fr Ray it happens to us all." I know

I calmed down after that as I completely understood why it happened. Yet, the old negative feelings of inadequacy and disappointment were there for a few hours. In fact, I would say that experience affected my second performance a couple of hours later. I also knew to limit my second performance to the four songs. I consoled myself at the piano bar from midnight afterwards where the maestro Michael English was tickling the ivories. He soon spotted me and – guess what – I got to perform my "New York, New York" anyway. Wow.

On Friday our stop-over for over seven hours was at Ketchikan, a popular cruise stop noted for its many Native American totem poles. Here people could avail of a two and a half hour seaplane to view fjords, waterfalls and lakes. However, two days before we got word of two of the seaplanes crashing in mid-air with two fatalities from a cruise ship. I think hearing that certainly put a stop to most of our people on the cruise ship availing that particular experience. The main stage on Friday night was the beautiful Celtic Angels along with Declan Nerney and John McNicoll.

After a few songs with Michael English on the Friday night after the midnight piano bar session, I woke up to the clocks having moved forward by one hour. The farewell Mass was scheduled for 8.00am and the ship was being tossed about in the sea. I soon discovered I didn't have sea legs because by the end of Mass I was breaking into a sweat. The Meet & Greet was scheduled for an hour after the Mass at 10.00am in the Lido area. This was the opportunity to meet people, have our photo taken with them and possibly sell some of our merchandise. I had brought about 80 CDs in my luggage and I was not prepared to carry them home again. So sickness or not, I was seeing this through. For about two hours I smiled, and autographed my CDs. I was churning inside, but I got through it and was delighted to sell all of the *Where I Belong* CDs. By the time they were all sold the ship seemed to be in calmer waters. I certainly didn't feel as bad, but then I was after being dosed with tablets and drops provided by some ladies who saw me in a sickly, sweaty mode.

The Grande Finale show was that evening on the main stage where all the performers got to do another song. I was asked to give "Love Shine A Light" another airing and I duly obliged. I guess after the Grande Finale everyone was on a high but exhausted. I know I was. I went back to my room and finished my packing. All the passengers were under instructions to leave our packed cases outside our bedroom doors to be picked-up and taken off the ship where we would collect them in a storage room before facing emigration back into Canada. Looking back on my whole cruise experience and the fears I went through prior to departure, all I can say is they were totally unfounded. I met and mingled with some of Ireland's finest artists and they were all so beautiful and such friendly people to be with.

Conclusion and Acknowledgements

In all my years on this planet, it was never my intention to write about my life, about 66 years of me. However, I always had an ambition to write about my mother Mona and her life as a midwife for nearly 40 years. And this year the one hundredth anniversary of her birthday would have been the ideal time to do it. What she went through bringing new life to so many families; the hardships, the primitive conditions she and expectant mothers had to endure to give new life. I imagine, and forgive me if I am wrong, that to expect an pregnant woman today to give birth in such conditions there would be a serious outcry. Such were the times. And thank God so much has changed.

So when I started writing about my own life over a year ago a myriad of emotions came to the surface. You will see from the 66 years of my life there was joy, drive, wonder, nervousness, excitement, even a bit of pride and maybe too a smidgen of melancholy. But above all it has been a positive journey for me. While writing about this journey, the underlying question that always surfaced was did I do enough? Did I do my best? Is there more to give? I never thought I would be a priest. I never thought I would be a singer and a recording artist. Certainly, my vocation and priesthood was ultimately my decision. I could have said no. I didn't. I'm glad. But as regards being a singer and entertainer, well I never thought that would be on my CV. But do I regret it? No, definitely not. I have enjoyed the journey since the "Hallelujah" story began on 5th April, 2014. Of course many will say and have said "you were a singer and entertainer long before Hallelujah". Sure there have been successes and failures in that part of the journey, some of my own making. But I know that whatever I have done or tried to do, my heart has been in it for the right reasons. I cannot ask anymore of myself than that.

So for now I thank God for the life he has given me. I thank my parents Mona and Joe and sister Regina who still are very much part of my life and urging me on from "resting on that high mountain". I thank my brother Joe and my sister Rosemarie, my nieces and nephews and grand-nieces and grand-nephews and all my family for the support they have shown me throughout my years. Friendship is indeed a beautiful gift and so important in every aspect of life, so I thank all those who have been a friend to me and shown me the true value of friendship. I thank all those who journeyed with me from the beginning of my priesthood in South Africa to the present time in Oldcastle and from all those places in between. Thanks also to Michael Brennan for making that initial contact and believing that I had a story to tell in the first place and to Columba Books and all their team for believing in me too. There is more to do, more to give, more to sing and above all more to make every moment count. I will continue to dream for one more major event in my life. If it does not happen, it will remain just my dream. If it does happen, you will read about it someday. So I dedicate this book, my story to my mum, Mona, for the life she has given me. May she rest in peace.